CANNABIS CAREERS

CANNABIS CAREERS
The Insider's Guide to a Budding Industry

ROB MEJIA
WITH DANIEL JOHNSON

ROWMAN & LITTLEFIELD
Lanham • Boulder • New York • London

Rowman & Littlefield
Bloomsbury Publishing Inc, 1385 Broadway, New York, NY 10018, USA
Bloomsbury Publishing Plc, 50 Bedford Square, London, WC1B 3DP, UK
Bloomsbury Publishing Ireland, 29 Earlsfort Terrace, Dublin 2, D02 AY28, Ireland
www.rowman.com

Copyright © 2025 by Rob Mejia and Daniel Johnson

All rights reserved. No part of this publication may be: i) reproduced or transmitted in any form, electronic or mechanical, including photocopying, recording or by means of any information storage or retrieval system without prior permission in writing from the publishers; or ii) used or reproduced in any way for the training, development or operation of artificial intelligence (AI) technologies, including generative AI technologies. The rights holders expressly reserve this publication from the text and data mining exception as per Article 4(3) of the Digital Single Market Directive (EU) 2019/790.

British Library Cataloguing in Publication Information Available

Library of Congress Cataloging-in-Publication Data Available

ISBN 978-1-5381-9653-3 (cloth : alk. paper)
ISBN 978-1-5381-9654-0 (ebook)

For product safety related questions contact productsafety@bloomsbury.com.

∞™ The paper used in this publication meets the minimum requirements of American National Standard for Information Sciences—Permanence of Paper for Printed Library Materials, ANSI/NISO Z39.48-1992.

To Beth Ann, who relishes a life of service performed in several acts and to my Cannabis Ospreys—it's time to go to work. *RJM*

To Mom, Dad, Kayla, and Erin—for your endless support while I tinker with words. *DJ*

Contents

Foreword		xi
Acknowledgments		xiii
Introduction		1
1	CANNABIS ESSENTIALS AND THE STATE OF THE UNION	3
	The Cannabis Essentials	3
	Cannabis Prohibition	7
	Understanding Medical and Adult-Use Cannabis	16
	Methods of Cannabis Consumption	19
2	CANNABIS SCIENCE	27
	An Evolving Discipline	27
	The Endocannabinoid System	39
3	A FEW WORDS ABOUT HEMP AND CBD	43
	The Hemp Plant	44
	CBD	48
	Looking Forward	50
4	THE CANNABIS INDUSTRY PIVOT	53
	How to Get Started: Career Analysis	53
	Advice from the Professionals	60
	Navigating Cannabis Stigma	62
5	CANNABIS HANDLING CAREERS	65
	Plant-Touching versus Ancillary Roles	65
	The Dispensary	66
	Cannabis Retail Careers	72
	Cannabis Cultivation Careers	76
	Opportunities in Cannabis Cultivation	81

Contents

	Extraction and Processing	86
	Career Opportunities in the Extraction and Processing Sector	94
	Examining the Hemp Industry	98
	Career Opportunities in Hemp	100
6	ANCILLARY CANNABIS BUSINESSES	107
	Introduction to Ancillary Roles	107
	Back-Office Operations	108
	The Supply Chain	118
	Construction	122
7	THE CANNABIS INDUSTRY'S EXPANDING HORIZONS	127
	Green Health: Cannabis and the Healthcare Industry	127
	Opportunities in the Cannabis Healthcare Field	129
	Green Education: Exploring Careers in Cannabis Ed	138
	Creating Change with Compassion: Exploring Nonprofit Careers in the Cannabis Realm	144
	Government Roles in Cannabis Regulation: Nurturing the Green Industry	149
	Opportunities in Cannabis Tourism, Hospitality, Marketing, and Communications	152
	Cannabis Tourism and Hospitality Roles	157
	Unusual Cannabis Careers	160
	Federal Legalization's Impact on Planning, Shipping, Tracking, Storage, and Distribution	168
	Research Opportunities	168
	International Opportunities	169
	Final Words	169
8	CANNABIS CAREER RESOURCES	171
	Sample Job Descriptions	171
	The Cannabis Careers Resume	177
	Sample Follow-Up Emails	190
	Interview Tips	191
	How and Why to Ask for a Letter of Reference	193
	Job Search Websites and Resources	196
	Cannabis Education Resources	197

CONTENTS

Cannabis Podcasts	198
Selected Website Resources	199
Glossary	205
Notes	211
Bibliography	221
Index	231
About the Authors	247

Foreword

When I first discovered the cannabis industry, I was struck by its incredible potential and the vast number of opportunities it presented. I launched Vangst with a clear and ambitious goal: to help build the cannabis industry by bridging the gap between talented job seekers and the businesses that need them. My journey has been driven by relentless hustle, a keen eye for emerging trends, and a strong commitment to fostering growth within the industry.

To meet the growing needs of the cannabis sector, I secured funding to ensure Vangst could provide the necessary skilled professionals. This support enabled us to develop innovative staffing solutions tailored specifically for cannabis businesses. My passion for creating employment opportunities in this field goes beyond business—it's about supporting an industry with significant economic and social benefits. Whether you're a seasoned professional or new to the workforce, the cannabis industry offers a wealth of opportunities. I am excited to share insights and guidance in this book, *Cannabis Careers: The Insider's Guide to a Budding Industry*, to help you navigate this exciting landscape.

I was introduced to cannabis professor Rob Mejia by our mutual friend Ashley Piccolo, who runs a cannabis consulting business called Point Seven Group. Rob and Ashley connected through his book, *The Essential Cannabis Book: A Field Guide for the Curious*, which featured Ashley's cannabis and business biography. Their shared dedication to cannabis education kept them in touch, and it made sense for us to connect as well, given that Vangst's success is built on the appreciation and implementation of cannabis education.

At Stockton University in New Jersey, where Rob Mejia has been teaching for five years, they offer a minor (and now a major!) in cannabis studies. One of the program's goals is to help students secure jobs in the hemp or cannabis fields. Through his courses, panels, podcasts, and interactions with cannabis businesses, Mejia has gained deep insights into the industry. His students hold positions throughout the sector, and he often jokes that he sees former students in nearly every dispensary or cultivation facility he visits. If you met him, you would describe him as an affable cannabis tour guide, and that voice and expertise shine through in this book.

You are probably asking yourself many questions about the cannabis industry. Common questions for those looking to work in the industry include:

- What do I need to know to enter and succeed in the cannabis industry?
- Why is cannabis still federally illegal?
- How does cannabis work in the body?
- Can I apply skills that I have learned in other industries to cannabis?
- What kinds of cannabis jobs are available?
- Which resources should I refer to as I'm learning about cannabis?

Thankfully, this book addresses those questions and more.

By reading this book, you will gain the essential knowledge needed to start in the cannabis business. You'll learn how to evaluate your relevant skills, helping you determine where you can best succeed. From there, you will discover the myriad of jobs available, including many roles you may not have considered. Finally, this book offers useful resources such as books, videos, websites, and podcasts that cater to different learning styles.

So, if you are ready to join one of the fastest-growing, opportunity-rich industries in the world, let's get started. It's time to go to work!

Proud to work in cannabis,
Karson Humiston, CEO and Founder,
Vangst Cannabis Staffing

Acknowledgments

Rob Mejia

I did not choose to write this book; it chose me. After many conversations about my students and others who were interested in joining the wild, wonderful world of the cannabis business—one friend calls it "joining the circus"—those closest to me challenged me to write this book. So, here we are. But without their love, support, and patience it would not have been possible.

Of special note is the role that writer Daniel Johnson played. He was a sounding board, deft editor, and friendly voice on the phone. When you read this book and come across a "damn fine sentence," it is probably Daniel's handiwork.

Big thanks are due to the hemp and cannabis experts who generously shared their insights. Their words breathe life into these pages, radiating passion and sage advice. They inspire me every day, and I am confident they'll do the same for you.

Finally, I owe you, the reader, a heartfelt thank-you. You're taking the plunge to see if you belong in the cannabis world, and spoiler alert: you do. And we need you. So, here's to your journey in the cannabis world—may it be as rewarding and transformative as the plant itself.

Daniel Johnson

I'm very grateful to Rob Mejia. For years, I've watched as he's become an expert and influential figure in the cannabis space. He possesses a thirst for knowledge, a determination to learn, and the grit to persevere in his passion. His expertise and cannabis community connections are wide-ranging, and none of it is accidental or circumstantial. The knowledge

Acknowledgments

he's shared on these pages is happily won, though not without patience and dedicated work. He's truly a self-made man in cannabis.

One million thanks to Mom, Dad, and Michaela, who have, from the very beginning, been unwavering in their support of my efforts to put ink on paper. And to Erin for her endless encouragement of my words, sentences, paragraphs, poems. None of it happens, at least not contentedly or confidently, without the love you all bless me with each day.

Finally, I hope that this book might contribute to the ongoing efforts happening all over the world for a more commonsense, equitable approach to cannabis. This plant, and the issues of the cannabis industry, are highly intersectional. To be educated about cannabis is to see clearly so many other problems within contemporary life: systemic racism, a broken criminal justice system, the inherent inequality that permeates modern American economic life. If the sentences in this book equip even one person to adequately combat these issues and more, that is enough for me.

Both authors would like to give special thanks to Jacqueline Flynn, Victoria Shi, and the Rowman & Littlefield team for their help with, and belief in, this project. We're so grateful to work with you!

Introduction

Curious about cannabis and the cannabis industry? You're not alone. As the legalization and social acceptance of medical and adult-use cannabis rapidly increase, the opportunity to become part of one of the fastest-growing industries in the United States (and the world) is an exciting prospect.

Currently thirty-eight states have legalized medical cannabis, and twenty-four states have an adult-use cannabis program. This means that in over half of the United States, cannabis is legal. According to a recent Gallup poll, US support for cannabis legalization is at an all-time high, polling favorably at 70 percent.[1] Too, the US government is in the process of rescheduling cannabis, which will open markets and spur investment, with national legalization not far behind.

Already the cannabis industry has created more than four hundred thousand full-time jobs in the United States.[2] *Forbes* estimates that the cannabis industry will be worth $72 billion by 2030.[3] Additional opportunities to support the industry exist in professional ancillary positions as diverse as website designer, consultant, real estate professional, attorneys of all stripes, and more. Surprisingly, these positions actually outnumber the full-time positions! Yet so many feel lost when it comes to getting involved in the cannabis space, wondering: How can I be part of what looks to be a once-in-a-lifetime opportunity?

This book will give an insider's perspective on how to get into, and thrive in, the exploding cannabis industry. Above all, *Cannabis Careers: The Insider's Guide to a Budding Industry* is designed to distill and demystify cannabis basics, such as history, cultures, and terminology, and then to introduce the reader to the myriads of cannabis career opportunities. Most importantly, readers will learn how to use their current skills and knowledge to seamlessly pivot into the industry.

Introduction

The five vital touchpoints of *Cannabis Careers* are (1) Essential terms and definitions and essential cannabis history, which will equip any would-be cannabis industry employee with the tools they need to understand and interact with the cannabis space. (2) A Cannabis State of the Union, including coverage of the hemp industry, the legalization movement, where cannabis is now, and, importantly, where cannabis is headed next. (3) How to pivot towards the cannabis industry. This section provides guidance on how to analyze one's current career position to best understand where and how they might fit into the space, touching on how to research and find cannabis careers and opportunities. (4) Exploration of the multitude of employment opportunities and careers in the cannabis industry, covering both "plant-touching" and ancillary positions. This section will be interspersed with comments from successful business owners and leaders currently working in the cannabis and hemp industries. (5) Specific guidance and resources covering sample job descriptions, job search websites and cannabis education resources, a sample resume, cover letter, email follow-up note, and interview tips.

The cannabis industry is a completely new economic space that promises so much opportunity yet is still surrounded by challenges such as barriers to essential knowledge, legal red tape, and lingering stigma. It's no wonder that it might be intimidating or even logistically challenging to enter! However, by acquiring a baseline of cannabis knowledge bolstered by one's own unique qualifications and expertise readers will be well on their way. *Cannabis Careers: The Insider's Guide to a Budding Industry* is a culmination and organization of industry how-to which is the perfect first step for readers beginning their own cannabis career journey!

CHAPTER 1

Cannabis Essentials and the State of the Union

THE CANNABIS ESSENTIALS
No matter the form of cannabis one sees in dispensaries today, it's the same type of plant species: *Cannabis sativa*.[1] This plant, which has grown naturally all around the world, has been here for as long or longer than humans have. Early mentions of cannabis appear in historical texts as far back as 2737 BCE when Chinese Emperor Shen Nung espoused cannabis's promise as medicine for gout, rheumatism, constipation, and more.[2] Ramses II and the ancient Egyptians are also on record for utilizing cannabis for recreation and medicine.[3] And in *Cannabis: A History*, Martin Booth calls hemp an essential medicinal tool.[4]

Sativa and indica are the two main subtypes of *Cannabis sativa*. There are other cousins, like *Cannabis ruderalis*, but indica and sativa are what predominate the medicinal and recreational cannabis markets. Strain is the term that refers to a genetic variant of plant species. For the most part, any strain available in a dispensary will be one or the other, or a hybrid. Sativa (not referring here to the broader species, *Cannabis sativa*) and indica are the two types commonly seen, produced, and consumed in both cannabis culture and the marketplace. Sativa and indica are both psychoactive, meaning that the tetrahydrocannabinol (THC) levels in both plant types are potent enough to give the consumer a "high." Sativa is a taller, skinnier plant with long, thin leaves. In terms of effects, sativa is known for producing an energetic, euphoric psychoactive experience.

Indica, however, is a short, fat plant with broader leaves, and it's known for its more relaxed, sleep-inducing effects. Some experienced users also claim that sativa gives the consumer more of a head high, while indica produces more of a body high.

It is important to note that most cannabis strains in the marketplace are hybrids, which means they are a cross between a sativa, an indica, and maybe even a ruderalis strain. Some breeders claim that "pure" strains of indica or sativa no longer exist, and that every cannabis strain is technically a hybrid. Cannabis strains vary in ratios of THC and cannabidiol (CBD), as well as size, shape, smell, taste, color, potency, and more. Cannabis growers work hard to breed strains that yield specific results when consumed. Cannabis products, whether it's flower, pre-rolled joints, edibles, or infused drinks, are labeled and marketed as sativa or indica dominant, which gives the consumer some certainty in terms of what experiences to expect when consuming.

Hemp is the final, must-know type of *Cannabis sativa*. Hemp is distinct from indica and sativa in both usages and legal status due to its negligible THC levels—less than 0.3 percent THC.[5] This low THC level means hemp cannot produce the psychoactive effects of the "high." And while hemp hasn't been utilized in the same way as its cousins, it has found its way into shops, from dispensaries to local pharmacies and chain grocery stores, due to its high CBD levels. The CBD ointments, oils, tinctures, and more that consumers see on shelves across the United States are commonly derived from the hemp plant.

Hemp has also been a staple crop for farmers and industrialists for hundreds, even thousands, of years. Hemp's uses are nearly endless. Hemp can produce rope, clothing, paper, biodiesel fuel, building materials, health and beauty aids, car panel doors, animal bedding, food, and more. Hemp has also been shown to be a powerful agricultural tool as a rotation crop that cleans and revitalizes soil.

Cannabis Chemistry
Of course, there are hundreds of chemical compounds within cannabis, but the two most essential are THC and CBD. THC is the component in cannabis that produces the euphoric high feelings that many cannabis

consumers enjoy in the same way that alcohol consumers enjoy the feeling of a beer. While each person's body chemistry will influence how one experiences cannabis consumption, the percentage of THC within the product and the quantity of product consumed are general determining factors for potency of experience. Cannabis products sold today are usually between a mild experience of 5 percent and medium to high experience at 15–25 percent THC, though some products push to 30 percent and beyond, which would be very potent, especially to an inexperienced consumer.

Legal at the federal level, CBD is the component in cannabis that does not produce a psychoactive effect. However, CBD can provide health benefits such as analgesic, anti-inflammatory, and antianxiety effects. The Farm Bill of 2018 legally separated hemp from other cannabis types, and so CBD products, like infused foods, soap and bath products, tinctures, and ointments, have popularized and hit consumer shelves in local grocery stores and pharmacies. Companies are even producing veterinarian-endorsed CBD-infused dog treats!

Terpenes and flavonoids are two compounds that are important to understand when it comes to cannabis. Neither are cannabinoids, and neither are unique to cannabis. You'll find both in vegetables, coffee, tea, wine and more. Both affect cannabis color, shape, smell, and taste and have health and therapeutic benefits. For example, flavonoids have antioxidant properties. Terpenes are also involved in "steering" the experience of consuming cannabis. That is, cannabis strains with high amounts of certain terpenes can be energizing, sedative, or pain relieving, depending on how the terpenes interact with other elements of the cannabis plant.

And while THC and CBD are two of the most prominently known biological compounds in cannabis, there are hundreds of others, known as cannabinoids. Cannabinoids are found naturally in the cannabis plant, as well as in the human body. In humans, cannabinoids make up and interact with the endocannabinoid system (ECS). The ECS is a neuromodulatory body system that helps the body reach and maintain homeostasis. It's made up of endogenous cannabinoids, which are cannabinoids created within the body, cannabinoid receptors, and enzymes that create and break down cannabinoids. Interestingly, again, it was only discovered in the 1990s!

Cannabis in the United States
Cannabis has grown in North America for as long as you want to go back. For example, it's widely documented that many Native American cultures used and cherished the cannabis plant far before the colonial period. Mary Jane Oatman of the Nez Perce tribe, activist and executive director of the Indigenous Cannabis Industry Association, said in a December 2023 interview with the *Cannabis Business Times*, "at some point in many tribal histories, prehistories, [they] had a relationship with many sacred plants including, for some communities, cannabis."[6] Cannabis is often part of the wealth of traditional plant knowledge that many indigenous nations possess.

Cannabis was present in the colonial era as well. Hemp was a required crop in colonial Jamestown. The British government required each landowner to grow one hundred hemp plants for export back to England in the form of a tax. Similar requirements were imposed in the Massachusetts and Connecticut colonies some years later.[7]

Throughout the nineteenth century, Cannabis was legal and sold widely in pharmacies. Cannabis was listed in the *U.S. Pharmacopeia* from 1850 to 1942. Founded in 1820 and still continuing today, the *U.S. Pharmacopeia*'s goal has been to acknowledge and set standards for medicines and to improve public health. According to Richard Glen Boire, JD, and Kevin Feeney, JD, in *Medical Marijuana Law*, "By 1850, marijuana had made its way into the U.S. Pharmacopeia [an official public standards-setting authority for all prescription and over-the-counter medicines], which listed marijuana as treatment for numerous afflictions, including: neuralgia, tetanus, typhus, cholera, rabies, dysentery, alcoholism, opiate addiction, anthrax, leprosy, incontinence, gout, convulsive disorders, tonsillitis, insanity, excessive menstrual bleeding, and uterine bleeding, among others."[8] Indeed, cannabis was common in the pharmaceutical marketplace, especially in the form of tinctures produced by the likes of Eli Lilly and Tilden's.

CANNABIS PROHIBITION

The Marijuana Tax Act of 1937 and the Controlled Substances Act (1970) were the major legislative steps to cannabis prohibition. However, the cultural origins of cannabis prohibition are variable, and it is difficult to point to a single event as responsible for cannabis illegalization. A combination of factors, such as racism, xenophobia, economic competition, and political expediency all contributed to the outcome. However, at least one thing is certain: cannabis prohibition has been a disaster, especially for some of the most vulnerable communities in the United States and around the world.

Racism, Propaganda, and Harry Anslinger

Harry Anslinger (1892–1975) was a key figure in the origins of cannabis prohibition. Anslinger headed the Federal Bureau of Narcotics, the organization that preceded the Drug Enforcement Administration (DEA), for more than thirty years.[9] Anslinger guided the pivot of the organization to target cannabis after alcohol prohibition was repealed in 1933 by the ratification of the Twenty-First Amendment. Over his career, Anslinger would wage an anti-immigration, antidemocratic culture war that would stoke and leverage public fears toward minorities, from Mexican immigrants to black jazz musicians, using cannabis prohibition as a weapon.

During the first few decades of the twentieth century, there was an influx of Mexican immigrants fleeing conflict during the Mexican Revolution. Among the cultural norms these immigrants brought with them was cannabis consumption by smoking. In the wake of racial tensions that arose during the immigration influx, proponents of cannabis prohibition made a calculated choice, pushing to replace the term "cannabis" with "marihuana," or "marijuana" in the social consciousness. They wanted to conflate cannabis with racism and xenophobia, to shift mainstream white American society to viewing cannabis as something foreign and dangerous.

Anslinger was an early proponent of many of the stereotypes and myths about cannabis, such as the Stepping Stone Theory, what we now know as the Gateway Drug concept. He also propagated the myth that consuming cannabis made consumers crazed and violent. Anslinger set the kind of propagandistic and misinformation cultural tone that the infamous film *Reefer Madness* struck in 1936. Anslinger went before Congress many times to fight against cannabis and to push for prohibition. He's quoted as saying such heinous and abhorrent statements like, "Reefer makes darkies think they're as good as white men. There are 100,000 total marijuana smokers in the U.S., and most are Negroes, Hispanics, Filipinos and entertainers. Their Satanic music, jazz and swing result from marijuana use."[10]

Legislation, Political Expediency, and Mass Incarceration
The Marijuana Tax Act of 1937 and the Controlled Substances Act (signed into law in 1970 and put into effect in 1971), which was part of the Comprehensive Drug Abuse Prevention and Control Act, are two landmark pieces of legislation that established cannabis prohibition in the United States. Harry Anslinger helped draft the Marijuana Tax Act of 1937. Although it didn't technically make cannabis illegal, the act made it so financially burdensome to produce that most would-be consumers couldn't purchase cannabis in a store. Though in 1969 the bill would be struck down as unconstitutional, it succeeded in striking a major blow to cannabis accessibility and cannabis's cultural image.

Too, Richard Nixon almost immediately replaced the Marijuana Tax Act with the Controlled Substances Act (CSA). The Controlled Substances Act (1970) is a piece of legislation that is still in effect today. The CSA groups various substances on a range of "schedules." Currently, the CSA lists cannabis on Schedule 1, alongside the likes of heroin and LSD. Substances on Schedule 1 are defined as "having no currently accepted medical use and a high potential for abuse. They are the most dangerous drugs of all the drug schedules with potentially severe psychological or physical dependence."[11] This classification, which has been repeatedly shown to be not only an unfair characterization of cannabis but also one blatantly without basis, is the reason that it's nearly impossible to do research on or with cannabis as the federal government is bound to abide by the definitions laid down by the CSA, namely that cannabis has "no currently accepted medical use and a high potential for abuse."

And so, while cannabis has been shown to have numerous therapeutic effects and health benefits from seizure treatment and prevention to glaucoma treatment and beyond, research into cannabis's potential as a medicine has been badly hampered by its federal classification via the CSA.[12] In terms of the cannabis industry, although twenty-four states and the District of Columbia have legalized recreational cannabis, it remains federally illegal, and this federal status still casts an uncertain shadow across the cannabis industry, whether it is market uncertainty or lack of banking access for businesses. Note, though, that President Biden recently ordered a review of cannabis's status as a Schedule 1 substance, and it is likely that it will be moved to Schedule 3. This would help cannabis business owners because they could take normal business deductions and may open the doors for more research, but federal and state laws would still conflict and other changes are up for debate.

Controlled Substances Act[13]

Perhaps Anslinger's most destructive legacy was his thought leadership in terms of utilizing cannabis prohibition as a cudgel to target and disrupt minority and opposition communities. This legacy has lasted through the twentieth century and remains today. For example, through a series of interviews with John Erlichman, a top Nixon advisor and Watergate coconspirator, it's become widely known that Nixon, whose administration coined the term "war on drugs," cast drugs as "public enemy number-one,"[14] and created the DEA, which strategically used cannabis prohibition to disrupt opposition communities, such as the black community and the antiwar left. Erlichman is quoted as saying, "We knew we couldn't make it illegal to be either against the war or black, but by getting the public to associate the hippies with marijuana and blacks with heroin. And then criminalizing both heavily, we could disrupt those communities."[15]

The crisis now commonly known as mass incarceration has its roots in the leveraging of drug prohibition to arrest and incarcerate millions of people, especially Black and brown folks. Mass incarceration refers to the

Table 1.1 CSA Schedule Chart: Understanding the Five Classes of Controlled Substances

Schedule	Description
Schedule I	Drugs with no currently accepted medical use and a high potential for abuse. They are the most dangerous drugs of all the drug schedules with potentially severe psychological or physical dependence. Examples of schedule 1 substances are cannabis, heroin, and LSD.
Schedule II	Drugs with a high potential for abuse, with use potentially leading to severe psychological or physical dependence. These drugs are also considered dangerous. Examples of schedule 2 substances are cocaine, methamphetamine, and oxycodone.
Schedule III	Drugs with a moderate to low potential for physical and psychological dependence. Schedule III drugs' abuse potential is less than Schedule I and Schedule II drugs, but more than Schedule IV. Examples of schedule 3 substances are ketamine (the most popular anesthetic in the world), anabolic steroids, and codeine. NB: This is the schedule where cannabis is likely to end up.
Schedule IV	Drugs with a low potential for abuse and low risk of dependence. Examples of schedule 4 substances are alprazolam (Xanax), clonazepam (Klonopin), and diazepam (Valium).
Schedule V	Drugs with lower potential for abuse than Schedule IV and consist of preparations containing limited quantities of certain narcotics. Schedule V drugs are generally used for antidiarrheal, antitussive, and analgesic purposes. Examples of schedule 5 substances include Robitussin, Lomotil, and Motofen.

fact that the United States incarcerates more of its population than any other country in the world. Despite having just 5 percent of the world's people, US prisons hold 25 percent of the world's prison population.[16] Essentially, each administration, to one degree or another, from Nixon to Reagan, from Bush to Clinton, and beyond, took increasingly strong and conservative stances on crime. Incentivized programs for police departments and the advent of mandatory minimum sentences, which forced judges' hands to disregard the contexts of individual cases, made it disturbingly commonplace to incarcerate people for very long sentences, even for life, for nonviolent drug offenses. Proponents of mandatory minimum sentencing, which began with the Boggs Act of 1951, claim that longer, more severe sentences deter crime, but this assertion has been proven false over many decades.[17]

The war on drugs themes of the Nixon administration continued with subsequent administrations. When Reagan took office in 1981, the prison population was 329,000,[18] but by the time he left office, the numbers had essentially doubled to 627,000. Then, George H. W. Bush crafted his "tough on crime" presidential campaign, running the famous, fear-mongering Willie Horton ad which created a symbol of crime as Black and violent. Bush also passed the 1990 Crime Control Act,[19] which found bipartisan support from the likes of Joe Biden. And Clinton doubled down, both in theme and action. The Clinton campaign and administration were responsible for bringing the term "superpredator"[20] into the public domain, as well as the 1994 Crime Bill, which saw yet more lengthy prison sentences, further extension of police powers, and the continuation of millions of dollars misspent on punishment, rather than pragmatic prevention or education.

These politically expedient stances capitalized on artificially inflated public fear and satisfied voters with increasingly inflammatory language and more prisoners, bricks, and barbed wire. Overall, American leadership of the second half of the twentieth century was widely guilty of increasing their commitment to cynical, harmful methods of crime control. Rather than focus on the underlying social problems that create and exacerbate drug problems, or the poverty that validates crime, or look into the legalization and commonsense regulation of cannabis, government leadership merely poured more fuel onto the "tough on crime" fire of mass incarceration and criminalization.

Economic Competition and Political Pressure

One of the most head-scratching developments of cannabis prohibition is how hemp was dragged into the illegalization picture. Hemp is a type of cannabis with negligible THC levels and has been farmed as an industrial crop. The answer to why hemp was also targeted for prohibition has never been quite clear. Most cannabis historians agree that there is a certain likelihood that lawmakers at the time were simply uneducated in the difference between the two kinds of cannabis and that hemp's resultant legal status was the product of lazy bureaucracy. However, one theory that has proliferated the cannabis space was that there was economic motivation for some of America's most powerful business moguls, who had the ears of the era's lawmakers, to lobby for hemp to be included in the cannabis prohibition framework. The hemp industry was a direct competitor of the paper industry, and the likes of major American companies like DuPont and figures like J. D. Rockefeller, William Randolph Hearst, and Andrew Mellon, who was related to Harry Anslinger by marriage, would benefit from removing hemp from the marketplace.[21] These tycoons had heavily vested interests in the paper and petrochemical industries, so it's not unreasonable to believe that economic opportunism was a serious factor in the prohibition decision.

Tauhid Chappell is an adjunct professor at Thomas Jefferson University who teaches a graduate-level course, Cannabis Social Justice and Equity Policies: Evaluating Impact and Outcome, which emphasizes the importance of understanding the history of prohibition for cannabis industry participants, "Understanding cannabis history, and more broadly history of injustice in general, provides a deeper level of nuance, perspective, empathy, and consciousness that can enable a person to push for a better industry that aims to help, and heal, people no matter what title or role they find themselves in; to dream up and create an industry where cannabis businesses and services providers, locally owned and operated by those directly impacted by cannabis prohibition, can collectively work together to provide pathways, initiatives and programs that address these historical injustices and achieve a positive future that's grounded in centering people, not profits."

Chappell goes on to explain the lasting impact of the war on drugs by describing the pernicious effects. "Lives lost, communities ruined, relationships and families broken up, an increase in poverty and incarceration, towns and cities divested from, towns and cities directly razed to the ground, ongoing stigmatization, stereotyping, racism and xenophobia, ignorance and lack of consciousness, the rise in right-wing fascist rhetoric aimed at suppressing and oppressing all non-white communities and people."

So, you can see that understanding the intricate history of cannabis prohibition in the United States sheds light on broader injustices and enables individuals to advocate for an industry centered on healing and equity. The history of cannabis prohibition as summarized by Chappell's insights emphasizes the urgent need to address historical injustices and build a future where cannabis businesses prioritize people over profits, fostering pathways to positive change for all.

Cannabis Legal Status Today

As of January 2024, thirty-eight states and the District of Columbia have legalized medical cannabis.[22] California was the first state to legalize medical cannabis, heavily influenced by the efforts of the LGBTQ+ community and AIDS patients' advocates. In 2012, Colorado and Washington became the first states to legalize recreational cannabis, and now there are twenty-four, plus the District of Columbia, which have legalized recreational cannabis. Recreational and medicinal cannabis are both legal in Canada. Canada made the shift in 2018, and Mexico is expected to make the transition soon.

The cultural climate has drastically shifted, and many feel as though it's inevitable that cannabis will be federally legalized. After all, cannabis is one of the only bipartisan issues in the United States,[23] with voices from nearly all demographics of American politics speaking favorably of the economic and medicinal opportunities that cannabis presents,[24] as well as the simple, commonsense facts of what cannabis legalization would mean for so many individuals and communities harmed by the war on drugs and the crisis of mass incarceration.

US Cannabis History and Prohibition Timeline
Precolonial Era

- The Indigenous relationship to cannabis: Cannabis was used and cherished by many Native American cultures far before the colonial period. Mary Jane Oatman of the Nez Perce tribe noted that many tribes had a relationship with cannabis.

Chapter 1

Colonial Era

- 1600s: Hemp was a required crop in colonial Jamestown. The British government mandated each landowner to grow one hundred hemp plants for export to England. Similar requirements were established in the Massachusetts and Connecticut colonies.

Nineteenth Century

- Cannabis in Medicine: Cannabis was legal and widely sold in pharmacies. Listed in the *U.S. Pharmacopeia* from 1850 to 1942, cannabis was recognized for treating numerous ailments, including neuralgia, tetanus, cholera, and more.

1930s

- 1936: The film *Reefer Madness* propagates myths about cannabis, portraying it as a cause of insanity and violence.
- 1937: The Marijuana Tax Act is passed, making cannabis so financially burdensome that it becomes effectively illegal.

1970

- Controlled Substances Act: Cannabis is classified as a Schedule 1 drug, deemed to have no accepted medical use and a high potential for abuse, alongside drugs like heroin and LSD.

Late Twentieth Century

- 1980s–1990s: The war on drugs intensifies under the Reagan, Bush, and Clinton administrations, leading to mass incarceration, especially of minority communities. The prison population rose dramatically due to tough-on-crime policies and mandatory minimum sentencing.

Twenty-First Century

- 2000s–2010s: Increasing state-level legalization of medical and recreational cannabis. California legalized medical cannabis in 1996, and Colorado and Washington legalized recreational cannabis in 2012.

2020s

- 2024: As of January, thirty-eight states and the District of Columbia have legalized medical cannabis, and twenty-four states plus the District of Columbia have legalized recreational cannabis. President Biden orders a review of cannabis's status as a Schedule 1 substance, potentially reclassifying it to Schedule 3.

Figure 1.1 is a map of the United States which is a visual reference indicating which states have decriminalized cannabis, those that allow for medical cannabis use, and those that allow for both medical and adult-use cannabis. As mentioned, twenty-four states allow for the adult use of cannabis and thirty-eight states have a medical cannabis program (see Figure 1.2).

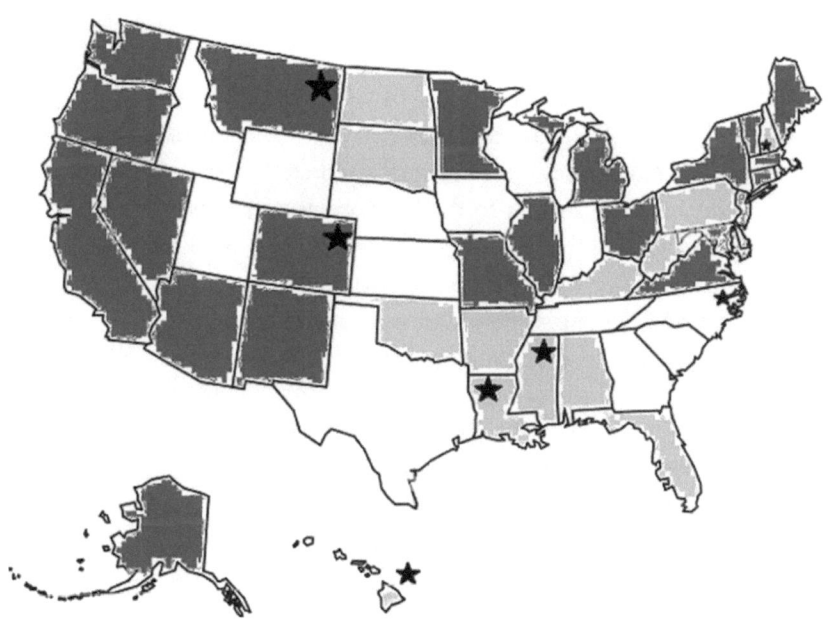

Figure 1.1 Cannabis Legalization Map of the United States. Rob Mejia

Figure 1.2. Key to Legalization Map of the United States. Rob Mejia

UNDERSTANDING MEDICAL AND ADULT-USE CANNABIS

Legal cannabis has been divided into two categories: medical and adult use. Adult use refers to the recreational market, or the cannabis market which might be more similar to the beer or wine industry. Medical cannabis refers to the legal availability of cannabis as a medicine or drug as recommended by doctors. (Because cannabis is federally illegal, doctors cannot prescribe cannabis; they can only recommend it.) The medical uses of cannabis are rapidly evolving, and each state is developing its list of qualifying medical conditions.

Distinctions between Medical and Adult-Use Cannabis

Medical and adult-use cannabis often share the same products. For instance, one person might smoke a certain strain recreationally, while someone else might use the same strain and consumption method but for medical reasons. So medical cannabis and recreational cannabis can be the same end product, but the purpose and way they are each used is what differs. Medical patients go to a doctor for relief from a particular medical condition. They may discuss strains, potency, and dosing for their particular condition, or their physician will simply give them a recommendation to use cannabis and leave it to the dispensaries to provide guidance about what product to use and at what dose.

Recreational users, on the other hand, often seek out cannabis for relaxation or euphoric effects. Both THC-dominant and CBD-dominant strains are used for medical treatment. Depending on the condition one is trying to treat, different products, different THC or CBD potencies, different consumption methods, and particular doses are employed. Medical patients, in consultation with their physicians, consider the rate of absorption, how much medicine will be delivered to their body, and if patients are limited to particular ingestion methods. For example, a patient may have trouble swallowing pills, so they may look to smoking, vaping, topicals, or suppositories. Each of these methods provides some benefits and challenges, but the good news is that more and more options are available and the creativity in this market shows no evidence of slowing.

Patients must see, or connect via telemedicine, with a qualified doctor to acquire their medical cannabis cards. They need to present their card for purchase and to carry their card for legal protection. Some states offer reciprocity when it comes to medical cannabis, which means if a patient travels to another state, they still have access to their medicine.

In practical terms, medical patients may have access to products that are not available to recreational users. Medical cannabis products are often less expensive than recreational products and are often not taxed. Medical patients can usually buy more products in a single purchase as well. And things continue to change. For example, until recently, medical patients in Oregon had access to one part of a dispensary, and recreational users were led to another part of the dispensary. Now they shop in the same aisles for the same products. In New York, medical patients initially could not buy flower at dispensaries because of a long-lasting no-smoking campaign led by the state but that changed quickly. In Washington State, where adult use is legal, many of the medical dispensaries have merged with the recreational ones, making for a one-stop shop for any cannabis user.

What Conditions Is Medical Cannabis Used to Treat?

In the United States, roughly two-thirds of the states allow for legal medical marijuana—something unthought of not too long ago. Each state has its list of qualifying medical conditions, but the most common conditions include epilepsy, multiple sclerosis (and other related muscle spasticity conditions), cancer, chronic pain, wasting syndrome,

Table 1.2 Medical Table

Most Common Qualifying Conditions for Medical Cannabis	Description
Chronic Pain	Persistent pain not responsive to other treatments.
Cancer	Disease and treatment for symptoms like pain, nausea, and loss of appetite.
HIV/AIDS	Severe pain, nausea, and loss of appetite.
Epilepsy and Seizures	Reduces seizure frequency and severity.
Multiple Sclerosis (MS)	Manages muscle spasms, pain, and tremors.
PTSD (Post-Traumatic Stress Disorder)	Alleviates PTSD symptoms.
Crohn's Disease and other Gastrointestinal Disorders	Conditions like IBS and inflammatory bowel diseases.
Glaucoma	Reduces intraocular pressure.
Amyotrophic Lateral Sclerosis (ALS); also known as Lou Gehrig's Disease	Manages muscle spasticity and pain.
Parkinson's Disease	Alleviates tremors, rigidity, and pain.
Severe Muscle Spasms	Severe and persistent muscle spasms.
Autism Spectrum Disorders	Manages symptoms related to autism.
Fibromyalgia	Manages chronic pain and fatigue.
Migraine	Manages chronic migraine symptoms.
Cachexia or Wasting Syndrome	Severe weight loss and muscle atrophy.
Alzheimer's Disease	Manages agitation and insomnia.
Spinal Cord Injury with Spasticity	Manages severe muscle spasms and pain.
Severe Anxiety	Recognized in some states for severe anxiety.

glaucoma, HIV/AIDS, ALS (i.e., Lou Gehrig's disease), Crohn's disease, and posttraumatic stress disorder (PTSD). Interestingly, one of the conditions that is being added to some states' list of qualifying conditions is opioid replacement.

For your reference, Table 1.2 is a chart listing the most commonly accepted medical conditions for a medical cannabis card across the United States. Note that each state has its own rules and regulations, and you should consult your state for specific information and guidelines.

Methods of Cannabis Consumption

Some of us remember starting our relationship with cannabis by smoking a joint, a pipe, or a bong with friends. But cannabis can be consumed in many ways and the market for creating new and innovative ways to consume cannabis is growing every day. Each method of consumption can deliver different amounts of THC and CDB (dosing) to obtain certain effects over a certain amount of time. Today you can get CBD-infused teas, coffees, and pet treats. There are gummies and chocolate bars and cookies. There are tinctures and cartridges. Not all products are available in all states and different dispensaries, whether medical or adult use, carry different products.

Inhalation: Smoking and Vaping

Smoking is the most common form of cannabis consumption. The smoke is inhaled, passes into the lungs, and then is absorbed into the bloodstream. It's the method that produces effects most quickly, within a minute or two.

Vaping is an alternative inhalation method. Vaping has become hugely popular because it is discreet, portable, and probably healthier than smoking a joint. It is reportedly healthier than smoking because it does not release the toxins that smoking does. Vaping is done with a vape pen, which is a small, battery-operated handheld inhaler. It works with cannabis buds or a concentrate, which are liquid drops that come in a cartridge.

Tinctures
A tincture is a liquid that is infused with active cannabis ingredients. It is often made with high-proof alcohol that evaporates, leaving potent drops that work well by putting a dropperful under the tongue or between the cheek and gums. The effects are felt relatively quickly in about twenty minutes. They are discreet, quick acting, and easy to use and dose.

Topicals
Topical products include lotions, salves, pain sprays, and transdermal patches. They are applied directly to affected areas such as sore hands. The topical then goes to work fighting inflammation where it is applied. Cannabis topicals are a relatively new area of cannabis consumption that is mostly composed of CBD rather than THC.

Suppositories
A suppository is a medicine that is inserted into the body via the rectum, vagina, or urethra, to dissolve and administer medication. Cannabis suppositories are almost exclusively used medicinally. They benefit users who need quick relief, or those who may have nausea or other issues that limit the ingestion of edibles and who don't want to smoke or vape. Suppositories deliver an efficient amount of medicine to the body, working in about fifteen minutes or less. For people with inflammatory bowel syndrome (IBS) or Crohn's, or women suffering from symptoms associated with menstruation, suppositories can be an effective method of consumption.

Edibles
The fastest-growing mode of consumption is via edibles. In simplest terms, an edible is a food or beverage that has been infused with cannabis. "Pot brownies" are the classic edible example. The ingestion experience and effects are different from smoking. The amount of time for users to feel effects varies from thirty minutes to two hours, and for many, it is more of a body high. Edibles must travel through the stomach, liver, and intestines, which is why the effects take a while to kick in.

As well, everyone's body is different, and so several biological factors influence the psychoactive experience. It is very easy to overconsume edibles because their effects can take so long to kick in. Consuming edibles should be a mindful, deliberate experience. The best advice is to start with a low dose and to resist the urge to have more. For example, you may not feel any effects with a small dose such as 2.5 milligrams but that is fine because you will know that you can tolerate a higher dose next time, such as five milligrams. The user should increase their dose at these small increments to find the smallest dose that is effective for them.

Cannabis Concentrates

Cannabis concentrates are potent forms of cannabis that contain high levels of cannabinoids like THC and CBD. They come in various forms such as oils, waxes, and shatter, and are typically consumed through dabbing or vaporizing. Concentrates are popular among users seeking quick and powerful effects. Because of their potency, it's important to start with a small amount to avoid overconsumption. For those new to concentrates, starting with a tiny dab and gradually increasing the amount can help find the right dose without overwhelming effects. Young users of concentrates should also be careful as there is evidence that concentrates may affect brain function.[25] For your reference, Table 1.3 summarizes the most common cannabis methods of consumption.

Cannabis Methods of Consumption and Efficiency: Synthetic Cannabis

Not surprisingly, several pharmaceutical companies have developed synthetic versions of cannabis. The reason for this is simple: Doctors can prescribe these synthetic drugs and insurance companies will pay for them. Two of the most popular synthetics that you may have heard of are Marinol and Sativex. Marinol is similar to cannabis in that it is high in THC. It is a gel capsule used for medical conditions like HIV/AIDS and cancer. Weirdly, it is listed as a Schedule 3 substance. Sativex, on the other hand, is a minty spray that consists of a 1:1 CBD to THC formula and is taken orally. Multiple

Table 1.3 Consumption Table

Method	Time for Effect	Efficiency	Advantages/Drawbacks
Smoking (including joints, pipes, and bongs)	Approximately 5 minutes	Good	Simple, quick-acting / Loss of potency
Blunts	5 minutes	Good	Simple, quick-acting / Tobacco ingestion, loss of potency
Vapes	15 minutes	Good	Discreet, portable, quick-acting / Loss of potency
Tincture/Drops	20 minutes	Good	Easy to use and dose, quick-acting / Some may have difficulty swallowing
Edibles/Medibles	30 minutes to 2 hours	Average	Many choices / Hard to dose correctly, loses a lot of potency; long lasting
Topicals	Difficult to calculate	Average	Direct application, many products / Loses most potency
Suppositories	15 minutes	Excellent	Quick-acting, retains most potency / Rectal or vaginal insertion
Nasal Spray	15 minutes	Good	Easy to use and dose / Uncomfortable for some; not widely available
Transdermal Patches	15 minutes	Good	Enters body efficiently / Sensitive skin may limit use
Cannabis Concentrates	Immediate	Good	Quick acting, highly potent / Easy to overconsume, requires special equipment

*Efficiency refers to the length of time required for the product to take effect, how much "medicine" is delivered, and how easily the body absorbs and uses it.

sclerosis is the most common condition that Sativex is prescribed to treat. But the maker of Sativex, GW Pharmaceuticals, a British subsidiary of Jazz Pharmaceuticals, is hoping that it will eventually be approved for diabetes, schizophrenia, epilepsy, and cancer as well. Though it's legal in thirty countries, Sativex is not yet legal in the United States.

For your reference, here is a form that you can use if you are a medical cannabis patient or simply want to better track how effectively you are using cannabis.[26]

TEXTBOX 1.1. CANNABIS USE JOURNAL

The following information should help you keep track of your consumption to help you become a more effective consumer. Below are prompts and reminders that will lead to reflective journaling. Note that you can use a simple notebook to record your responses.

Journal Entry Date:
Record the date of your entry to keep track of your cannabis journey.

Product Details:

- **Strain or Product Name:**
  Record the specific strain or product you are using. Write its name and any notable characteristics.
- **Quantity:**
  Note how much you consumed. Consider the portion size in relation to your experience.
- **Cost:**
  What was the cost of the product? Does it seem reasonable given the effects and experience?
- **Purchase Location:**
  Recall where you obtained the product. Was it a dispensary, somewhere else, or at an event?

Potency and Composition:

- **THC Potency:**
  What is the potency of THC in the product? How does it compare to the potency in products you usually consume?
- **Terpenes:**
  Record which terpenes are present. Which ones are the most prominent, and what are their potential effects?

- **CBD Potency:**
  What is the potency of CBD in the product? How does it compare to the potency in products you usually consume?
- **Other Cannabinoids (CBG/CBN, etc.):**
  Make a list of other cannabinoids that are present. Do you know how they contribute to overall effects? If not, this may be an interesting area of research for you.

Method of Consumption:
How did you consume the product? Was it through smoking, vaping, using a tincture, consuming edibles, or another method?

Effects Observed:
Reflect on the effects you experienced. Did you notice any of the following? Consider the impact on your body and mind.

- Euphoria
- Increased Creativity
- Extra Energy
- Lack of Energy
- Increased Focus
- Lack of Focus
- Relaxation (Body)
- Relaxation (Mind)
- Pain Relief
- Hunger
- Dry Mouth
- Reduced Anxiety
- Increased Anxiety
- Sleepiness
- Other Observations

Summary of Feelings:
Reflect on how you felt after consuming the product. Consider different time intervals to see how the effects changed over time.

- **One Hour After Consumption:**
  Reflect on the immediate effects and how you felt after an hour.
- **Two Hours After Consumption:**
  Consider how the experience evolved after two hours. Did the effects intensify or diminish?

- **Next Day:**
  Reflect on any lingering effects or overall impressions the following day.

Favorite Strains/Products:
Keep a list of your top strains or products. Reflect on what made them your favorites.

Miscellaneous Notes:
Jot down any additional thoughts, tips, or reflections on your experience.

Usage Tips:
Start with a low dose and increase gradually until the desired effect is achieved. Remember, cannabis has become more potent in recent years, so proceed slowly. Begin with low-potency strains (0-10 percent THC) or even just CBD if you're new to cannabis.

Reminder: This journal is for personal use only and should not be shared with others. Keep it in a safe and private place. And pat yourself on the back for taking the time and initiative to find out how cannabis uniquely interacts with your one-of-a-kind body!

Chapter 2

Cannabis Science

An Evolving Discipline

Recently I gathered forty cannabis professors from around the country at an event called a Cannabis Curriculum Convening to talk about what we teach and how we teach our cannabis courses. One of the panels focused on teaching the Science of Cannabis course and immediately got bogged down in a discussion about cannabis terms, definitions, and the functions of the plant.

This happened because there is a major disconnect between cannabis science and botany and the consumer market. That is, when you read most cannabis articles, listen to a podcast, or go into a dispensary, most of the time you will be asked what type of cannabis you want while being presented with a list of sativa, indica, and hybrid strains. But what exactly are you being offered?

In the case of the budtender discussing a product, there are some generalizations about the effect of the cannabis plant based on a few main factors: how much THC the product contains, how much CBD the product contains, and, if the budtender is knowledgeable, which terpenes are present. Common recommendations of sativa-dominant products assume that they will energize, spur creativity, and be best for daytime use. On the other hand, it is assumed that indica-dominant products will help with relaxation, tamp down anxiety, and even aid with sleep. A hybrid strain might combine some of these factors. And all strains may be effective for pain relief, which continues to be the number one reason why consumers use cannabis.

It's clear that there's a lot to understand, from the parts of the cannabis plant to what effects cannabis can have on the body, when it comes to being a cannabis consumer. As you become more familiar with the effects of THC, CBD, other minor cannabinoids, terpenes, and flavonoids, and track your consumption in a journal, you will become a more educated consumer. An educated cannabis consumer understands what methods of responsible consumption work best for them, what proportions of THC and CBD are most effective, and how they respond to terpenes and flavonoids.

Chemovars and Chemotypes

One classification system that is gaining some traction is using the terms chemovar and chemotype to help steer and define user experience. Chemotypes or chemovars use the breakdown of a plant species according to its chemical composition. This classification system is essential for breeders, cultivators, and consumers. Chemical characteristics can determine, for example, what a cannabis sativa plant's ratio of THC to CBD is, which terpenes it contains, and in what quantities.

To go beyond the "strain" definition system discussed at the beginning of the chapter, New Jersey is using the following classification system on cannabis flower packaging in dispensaries along with traditional strain names.[1] We'll see if other states follow suit.

Chemotypes shall be displayed as:[2]

a. "High THC, Low CBD" where the THC to CBD ratio is greater than 5:1 and the total THC percentage is 15 percent or greater;

b. "Moderate THC, Moderate CBD" where the THC to CBD ratio is between 5:1 and 1:5 and the total THC percentage is between 5 and 15 percent;

c. *"Low THC, High CBD" where the THC to CBD ratio is less than 1:5 and the total THC percentage is less than or equal to 5 percent;*

or d. "Where usable cannabis does not conform to one of the three chemotypes, it shall be listed as the closest chemotype determined by mathematical analysis of the ratio of THC to CBD."

One criticism of the traditional method of classifying cannabis by strain or cultivar neglects the chemical composition of the plant (ratios of THC to CBD) and especially the role of terpenes. So, this system of classification was implemented to help consumers determine which type of product(s) can be most effective for their health and wellness.

A Look at "New" Cannabinoids

Chapter 1 covered THC and CBD, the two most commonly known cannabinoids. However, there are hundreds of cannabinoids being researched in the contemporary cannabis space, and several are proving to be noteworthy for their potential uses. We will now examine the seven following minor cannabinoids: CBN (cannabinol), CBG (cannabigerol), CBDV (cannabidivarin), CBC (cannabichromene), THCA (tetrahydrocannabinolic acid), Delta-8 THC, and THCV (tetrahydrocannabivarin).

CBN

After THC and CBD, cannabinol (CBN) is the most prominent cannabinoid in the cannabis plant. When THC degrades over time, it oxidizes creating CBN as a byproduct. Many cannabis consumers report that "old THC" makes them sleepy. Remember that bud you left in your dresser drawer? When used, it will often leave the user feeling relaxed and even sleepy. Now CBN is being marketed as a sleep aid. Further, CBN is mildly psychoactive, and a 2020 study shows promise in using CBN to help with attention-deficit hyperactivity disorder (ADHD).[3] Clearly, CBN is worthy of further study, and you are likely to hear more about this cannabinoid soon.

CBG

Cannabigerolic acid (CBGa) is the precursor to all other cannabinoids. This means that when a plant is young, it develops CBG that will then turn into THC, CBD, CBC, and many other cannabinoids. Some are wondering if CBG is the new CBD.[4] Like CBD, it is nonintoxicating and can be used to alleviate anxiety, to control inflammation, nausea, and pain relief. Some studies claim that it can help fight cancer,[5] including one study that showed it reduced growth rates of cancer cells in rats.[6]

One of the biggest challenges facing CBG researchers and cannabis companies that want to create CBG products is the minor amount of CBG present in the plant. While some cultivators have been able to develop high-potency CBD strains that may contain 20 percent CBD, CBG strains in the past have normally only had 1 to 2 percent CBG. To maximize the amount of CBG extracted from a given plant, it's best to harvest early in the plant's life. Still, however, it requires an immense amount of plant material to create CBG-focused products. Another option is to create CBG in a lab (often using a yeast base).

CBDV

Cannabidivarin (CBDV) is a nonintoxicating cannabinoid that is being studied for the treatment of "early life" seizures.[7] It has been found that when a cannabis strain is high in CBD it also tends to be high in CBDV. First isolated in 1969 by German researcher L. Vollner, it seems to appear in higher concentrations in cannabis strains native to Asia and in several indica strains.[8]

CBC

Cannabichromene (CBC) may have a similar effect to CBD,[9] which means it reduces inflammation, and at the right dose, it leaves the user feeling relaxed. CBC has been studied for its anti-inflammatory, anticancer, antidepressant, and neuroprotective effects. Years ago, before cannabis cultivators began to grow primarily for THC and CBD, it appeared as the second most plentiful phytocannabinoid.[10]

THC-A

THC-A is nonintoxicating, and it is found in both "raw" and "live" cannabis, mostly in the trichomes. Essentially, THC-A is the chemical precursor to THC. When the plant dries, THC-A slowly converts to THC.[11] If you heat THC-A, it quickly converts to THC, which is what happens when you smoke or vaporize cannabis flowers. However, the usual consumption method for THC-A is to eat the raw leaves or to juice raw cannabis with ingredients like celery, cucumber, green apple, parsley, chia seeds, strawberries, or blueberries.

THC-A works to fight inflammation and pain, is a neuroprotectant, and may help stimulate appetite for those suffering from anorexia nervosa or cachexia, a wasting syndrome often associated with HIV/AIDS patients. There is even promising research showing that THC-A may help slow the growth of cancerous cells. For a condition like pancreatic cancer, which is now a very common, and quickly fatal, type of cancer, THC-A could be a game changer.[12]

D8 THC or Delta-8 Tetrahydrocannabinol

Today, Delta-8 has to be created in a lab to produce any meaningful quantities. It does exist in trace quantities in cannabis and in slightly greater quantities in hemp. This is where it gets tricky. Because hemp is nationally legal, some enterprising hemp farmers found that they could produce Delta-8 and sell it as an alternative to Delta-9 (another name for THC).

Delta-8 does have a psychoactive effect. Users describe the high as milder, and many report that they're less likely to experience feelings of paranoia. One recent study also touts its use to prevent vomiting during chemotherapy for cancer patients.[13]

But the biggest issue is that Delta-8 is not regulated or tested, which means the user does not know if it is safe. Hemp expert Brett Goldman warns against using Delta-8, saying, "You do not know how it was produced, and the product likely has not been tested. So don't buy it. And definitely don't buy it from a gas station!"

THCV

Tetrahydrocannabivarin (THCV) is a minor cannabinoid present in cannabis mostly in high sativa strains like African Durban Poison. Using a low or moderate dose will not cause a high, though higher doses may result in a mildly euphoric state of mind. It also offers some unique benefits including appetite suppression that could lead to weight loss. THCV may also speed metabolism to burn more calories.

But what has researchers excited is that THCV appears to control insulin levels and modulate other hormones associated with diabetes.[14] Given that roughly 11 percent of the population in the United States has diabetes, this could truly be life-altering.[15]

Other medical benefits of THCV may include stress reduction and control of or even relief from panic attacks. Researchers who focus on PTSD see promise in THCV as do researchers who are concentrating their efforts on Alzheimer's disease and Parkinson's disease, as well as multiple sclerosis.

Chemical Synergy: Terpenes and Flavonoids

One area of great recent interest and research is the study of another common compound found in cannabis called terpenes. Terpenes are the oils in cannabis that give it a distinct smell, such as mint, lemon, pine, or mushrooms. This can be important in cooking with cannabis, as some cannacooks and cannachefs like to pair particular cannabis strains with certain dishes. Although over two hundred cannabis terpenes have been identified, some are far more common than others. Some researchers believe that terpenes help to direct a user's experience. That is, if you start with an energizing strain or cultivar and it also contains an increased amount of limonene-d, the energizing effect will likely be magnified. Conversely, if you started with an energizing strain but it contained a good amount of linalool you are likely to be more relaxed.

This is why it is so important to track your consumption and to pay attention to which terpenes are present in your cannabis. If your state does not require dispensaries to provide terpene information on a label, be sure to ask your dispensary attendant to provide this data. Right now, most dispensaries are reporting that consumers are asking for the highest THC product because they think it will have the most profound effects. But this is not true. It's important to look at percentages of THC, CBD, and the combination of terpenes present to figure out how to get the results you want. Part of being an educated consumer is keeping track of the balance of terpenes, CBD, and THC that your body best responds to.

Cannabis researcher and terpene expert Russ Hudson is the author of the landmark publication *The Big Book of Terps: Understanding Terpenes and Synergy in Cannabis*, which contains more than 1,300 citations and covers the top thirty-five terpenes along with a discussion of flavonoids and the notion of synergy in cannabis. Hudson has a talent for explaining the world of terpenes. He writes in his introduction,[16] "Terps, terps, everywhere; in the stain on wooded stair, in the shampoo in your hair, in the magic of your bong, in the trichomes thick and strong. Smell them here and taste them there; terps, terps, everywhere."

He points out that, "Terpenes are everywhere."[17] Chances are high that you have experienced, consumed, or otherwise ingested multiple terpenes at some point in the last twenty-four hours. Despite the pervasiveness of terpenes, most people have never heard of a "terp." Those who have likely learned about these compounds because of their experience with cannabis, but they're essential chemical components of the world around us.

For your reference Table 2.1 contains common cannabis terpenes listing their aromas, effects, other plants they are found in, potential medical benefits, common cannabis strains that feature these terpenes, and their boiling points. Note that boiling points are included primarily because this information is useful when cooking with cannabis. But it also shows the reader which terpenes are "lost" when one vapes or smokes at high temperatures.

Flavonoids are another common element in cannabis and many everyday foods and beverages. Flavonoids contribute to the color of cannabis, as well to a lesser degree to the flavor and smell. One way to remember the function of flavonoids is to know that the word comes from the Latin word *flavus* which means yellow. Like terpenes, you

CHAPTER 2

Table 2.1. Terpenes Table

TERPENE	AROMA	EFFECTS	ALSO FOUND IN	POSSIBLE MEDICAL BENEFITS	STRAINS/ CULTIVARS	BOILING POINT
LIMONENE (Note that there is limonene-d and limonene-l; this information applies to limonene-d)	Citrus, Lemon, Orange	Elevated Mood, Stress Relief	Lemon Rinds, Orange Peels, Peppermint	Antidepression, Antianxiety, Gastric Reflux, Antifungal	OG Kush, Sour Diesel, Super Lemon Haze, Bubba Kush	349°F 176°C
HUMULENE	Woody, Earthy	May Suppress Appetite	Hops, Coriander	Anti-Inflammatory, Antibacterial, Pain	GS Cookies, White Widow, OG Kush, Sour Diesel	388°F 198°C
PINENE	Sharp, Slightly Sweet, Pine	Memory Retention, Alertness	Pine Needles, Conifers, Sage	Inflammation, Asthma (Bronchodilator)	Jack Herer, Dutch Treat, Blue Dream, Romulan	311°F 155°C
LINALOOL	Floral, Citrus, Spice	Sedating, Calming	Lavender, Laurel, Birch, Rosewood	Insomnia, Stress, Depression, Anxiety, Pain, Convulsions	Lavender, Skywalker OG, Headband	388°F 198°C
CARYOPHYLLENE	Pepper, Wood, Spice	Relaxing and Soothing	Pepper, Cloves, Hops, Basil, Oregano	Antioxidant, Inflammation, Muscle Spasms, Pain, Insomnia	GS Cookies, White Widow, OG Kush, Bubba Kush, Chemdawg	320°F 160°C
MYRCENE	Musk, Cloves, Herbal, Citrus	Sedating, Relaxing, May Enhance THC's Psychoactivity	Mango, Thyme, Lemongrass, Bay Leaves	Antiseptic, Antibacterial, Antifungal, Inflammation	Green Crack, Alien OG, Granddaddy Purple, Blue Dream	334°F 168°C

consume flavonoids every day. Examples of some foods and beverages where flavonoids are present include berries, wine, dark chocolate, apples, cabbage, and soy milk. Scientists have discovered more than five thousand different flavonoids. When the cannabis plant grows, flavonoids also help filter ultraviolet (UV) rays, repel pests, and inhibit the growth of fungus.[18]

Your Nose Knows Terps

As previously mentioned, terpene expert Russ Hudson contributed to this section of the book and he goes on to explain,

> *Did you smell roses, begonias, geraniums, or other flowers today? Did you walk by a lawn filled with dandelions, clover, goldenrod, or buttercups? Perhaps you encountered the sweet smell of lilacs, lupine, or lilies? Flowering thistle or burdocks? Orange, cherry, or apple blossoms? Those fragrances are all caused by terpenes—thousands of different carbon-chain compounds that are found widely in the plant kingdom.*
>
> *But terpenes impact more than just smell. These dynamic molecules interact with the human body in ways that affect our mood, our health, and even our decisions. Think about if there are pine, spruce, aspen, or fir trees near where you live or work. Terpenes cause that fresh, minty evergreen scent that pervades these trees, and your olfactory senses are actively registering these aromatic molecules.*
>
> *On the Tongue*
> *In the last twenty-four hours: Did you eat an orange, or take lemon in your water or tea? The smell and taste of both oranges and lemons are due to terpenes, while the vibrant colors of these fruits can often be attributed to flavonoids.*
>
> *Did you choose between one variety or another of pears, apples, berries, or other fruits? You made that decision based partly on which terpenes and flavonoids your senses detected.*

Did you drink beer? The hops in your brew contain terpenes that impart potent sedative and relaxant effects to the beverage. These include myrcene, beta-caryophyllene, and to a lesser degree, humulene.

Did you use tobacco? Terpenes are present in these products as well, especially if you smoke menthols, which get that minty flavor from terpenes.

Are you the type of person who prefers to snack on candy, or do you prefer salad? Either way, you are consuming terpenes. In candy these compounds are often used as flavoring agents, and most salad items are rich in natural terpenes and flavonoids.

Did it rain near you? The fresh, earthy aroma that is present after a rain is caused by terpenes.

Although terpenes are naturally occurring compounds, this doesn't mean that you will only find them in natural or minimally processed foods. Terpenes are used in a wide variety of food products, especially sweets like ice cream, puddings and gelatins, baked goods, candies, and even chewing gum. Terpenes are also used in enriched food products and beverages, often to improve the taste of less palatable ingredients.

In addition, you'd even find terpenes in toiletries, used for industrial lubricants, and as important components of the fragrance and perfume industry.

Synergy and the Entourage Effect

Since we have discussed both major and some minor cannabinoids along with terpenes and flavonoids, it is useful to know that all of these elements, plus lipids, omega fatty acids, and chlorophyll, interact with each other in the cannabis plant to produce different effects. You can imagine that if one examined all of the elements in cannabis you would be looking at hundreds, even thousands, of variables.

Given that each person's body is different, it is quite possible that not all sativa, indica, or hybrid strains follow the expected patterns regarding effects. Because there are so many parts of the cannabis plant—estimates cite that each plant contains well over one hundred different cannabinoids, along with hundreds of non-cannabinoid chemicals—it can be difficult to predict how all of these components will work together. This notion has traditionally been called the entourage effect.

The entourage effect was posited by Israeli scientist Raphael Mechoulam. He states that all parts of the cannabis plant work more effectively together. The implications here are that stripping the plant of terpenes or minor percentages of THC or altering it in any way makes the plant less effective.

More recently, cannabis scientists have been proposing the idea that the parts of a cannabis plant work synergistically. In other words, each cannabinoid, terpene, and flavonoid has an impact on each component, but the impacts are not always complementary. Rather, these components might be "antagonists." An antagonist is a compound that opposes the physiological effects of another compound. Still, it is equally likely that they do sometimes magnify the positive effects as well by working together. Research is still ongoing into the complexities of these chemical dynamics, and both the entourage effect and synergistic effects of cannabis are active areas of study.

What Is a "Strain"?
A strain is a variety of cannabis that has been selectively bred and selected for certain traits. Cultivar is another term used in this arena which refers specifically to a strain propagated by humans, like a genetic variation of cannabis bred by a professional grower. Cultivar is a portmanteau of "cultivation variety." Would you believe that there are easily over five hundred different strains and new strains are being developed every day?

One cannabis substrain, Ruderalis originated in Eastern Europe and Russia. It is much smaller than the other plants but can contain high amounts of CBD, which makes it an inviting source of hemp oil. Ruderalis also "autoflowers," meaning it blooms predictably, with age rather than because of light cycles. For this reason, ruderalis strains are often combined with sativa or indica substrains.

The story of how cannabis was originally classified goes back to scientist Carl Linnaeus, who you may remember from your high school biology class as the Father of Taxonomy. Over his lifetime, Linnaeus named more than ten thousand life-forms, including *Cannabis sativa* L in 1753. The letter L stands for Linnaeus since he was the first person to name it. And when he did name it, he thought it was a single species. But roughly thirty years later, another scientific luminary, Jean-Baptiste Lamarck, identified a second cannabis species: *Cannabis indica* Lam (for Lamarck). Then, in the twentieth century, a group of Russian scientists identified a third species: *Cannabis ruderalis*. These terms are the same naming conventions that we mostly continue to use today.[19]

Today, a large percentage of cannabis strains are hybrids. Hybrids are constantly being created as growers attempt to magnify the best effects of the many strains available. Hybrids are also produced via cuttings and grafting, which accelerates the growth process. According to some growers, nearly every cannabis plant exhibits some evidence that it is at least part hybrid, to the point that now a more useful designation between plants may be thin leaf versus broad leaf.

A handful of heirloom or landrace cannabis strains have also been found. These are the "original" strains, such as an indica strain like Afghani or a sativa strain like Durban Poison, and they are often used to create hybrids. For example, the Afghani strain's profile appears in most hybrids that are indica dominant. As with plants like heirloom tomatoes, some growers are trying to preserve landrace plants and seeds.

Among some growers, there is an emphasis on creating the most powerful THC strains to meet market demand. On the other hand, as noted, there is also interest in preserving landrace strains or in creating high CBD strains. CBD strains are especially beneficial for consumers who have medical issues but do not want to experience any high or heightened anxiety. Be aware that these strains do contain some THC. High CBD/low THC strains are great for beginners, and strains with 1:1 CBD/THC ratio are also great options.

For your reference, Table 2.2 is a chart listing some of the most popular strains in 2024. As new strains are being developed—and enjoyed—you may want to annotate this list and add some new strains as they become available; space has intentionally been placed on this chart for that purpose.

Table 2.2 Strains Table

Sativa Dominant Strains	Indica Dominant Strains	Hybrid Strains
Sour Tangie	Ocean Beach	Gello
93 Cough	Chem Pie	Bazookies
Ya Hemi	Fruity P. OG	Cheetah Piss
Amnesia Lemon	Member Berry	White Runtz
AK-47	Garlicane	Gary Payton

THE ENDOCANNABINOID SYSTEM

When it comes to how the body works, we were taught about systems such as our digestive, immune, and nervous system. But did you know your ECS is as important as your other systems? All mammals, including your companion cats and dogs, have an ECS, and its key function is to maintain homeostasis or to keep your body in balance.[20]

Some researchers think of the ECS as the body's supercomputer. In 1964, both THC and CBD were identified as the active components in cannabis, and then in 1988, the vast ECS was discovered. This receptor system, which is the "master regulator" of the body, allows cannabinoids to interact with CB1 and CB2 receptors. When this happens, balance or homeostasis is maintained, and an impressive number of illnesses are treated.[21]

The ECS is like a network that exists throughout the body. This "net" is made up of three parts: receptors, namely the CB1 and CB2 receptors, endocannabinoids (which are cannabinoids that are naturally produced in the body), and enzymes that break down both endocannabinoids and cannabinoids. Most CB1 receptors are found in the brain but also occur throughout the body. CB2 receptors also exist throughout the body but the majority of CB2 receptors are found below the neck. The CB2 receptors follow the digestive, immune, and nervous systems. These receptors play a key role in neuromodulation.[22]

Israeli scientist Raphael Mechoulam was a trailblazer in studying the ECS. In 1964, Mechoulam and Yehiel Gaoni, PhD, isolated the plant's two most common compounds, CBD, and THC. This discovery was fortunate because it also led them to endogenous cannabinoids (cannabinoids that exist in our bodies whether or not we use cannabis). The endogenous cannabinoids they discovered and focused on were anandamide and 2-AG (2-Arachidonoylglycerol), which also interact with the CB1 and CB2 receptors.[23]

But as you can imagine, there were still plenty of questions to answer. One important discovery was made in 1988 by chemist Dr. Allyn Howlett. He found a large collection of receptors in the brain's cortex, cerebellum, hippocampus, and basal ganglia. These areas control and coordinate movement, emotions, pain, pleasure, and memory. There are no receptors in the cardiac or respiratory regions in the brainstem, the areas that control the heart and lungs. This is why no one has ever died from a cannabis overdose!

Some overenthusiastic cannabists would tout the ECS as proof of a reciprocal relationship between humans and cannabis. But Mechoulam, a natural sciences chemist, knew that the human body wouldn't create receptors to respond to plant substances and this led his team to search for a substance like THC that the body naturally creates. Fortunately, in 1992 graduate student William DeVane and researcher Dr. Lumir Hanus, who were working in Mechoulam's lab, found a chemical in the brain that mimicked the effects of THC. They named this chemical anandamide after the Sanskrit word *ananda*, which means bliss or pure joy. Mechoulam drolly quipped that he, "couldn't think of a single happy word in Hebrew," which is why this chemical is not named after a Hebrew word.[24]

Similar to THC, anandamide magnifies sensory experiences, stimulates appetite, affects short-term memory, and triggers feelings of pleasure. The same lab mentioned earlier found another chemical that functions like CBD. It is called 2-AG or 2-Arachidonoylglycerol. When needed, both anandamide and 2-AG are produced from acids in your cell membranes. These discoveries led to the important finding that endocannabinoid receptors extend into every organ, gland, immune cell, and connective tissue.

As discussed briefly, receptors in the brain are known as CB1 receptors and those in the periphery are called CB2 receptors. Many tissues contain both CB1 and CB2 receptors and each is responsible for a different action.[25] The chemical structure of anandamide is like that of THC.

Similarity in structure allows both compounds to be recognized by the body and to alter neural communication.

In simple terms, neurotransmitter systems are like cell phone networks. The brain sends chemicals and electric impulses that direct cells to communicate with each other. Other neurotransmitter systems, the dopamine, serotonin, and histamine systems, may be better known because they were discovered earlier, but the ECS is the largest and most pervasive system. In addition, it communicates with cells in two directions! Not only do commands originate from the brain, but when an organ is in trouble, endocannabinoids transmit signals back to the brain in a cry for help.

Dave Gordon, MD, owner of 4Pillars Health & Wellness, elegantly summarizes the function of the ECS, "The endocannabinoid system (ECS) is the cornerstone of our well-being and survival, quietly orchestrating balance among all bodily systems. With the ECS spanning over 600 million years of animal evolution, understanding and optimizing its function is crucial for our overall health and vitality."

Further, as a regulator, the ECS steadies body temperature. It also regulates blood sugar, immune function, muscle and fat tissues, hormones, pain centers, reward centers, and metabolic functions. It maintains the heart's steady beat, the stomach's digestion, the lungs' bellows, and the speed at which bones heal. It enables us to forget pain and rewards us for exercising, consuming healthy food, meditating, and having sex. Cannabinoids are also found at the intersection of the body's various systems, which allow different cell types to communicate. When an injury occurs, cannabinoids decrease the release of activators and sensitizers from the injured tissue, stabilize nerve cells by opening potassium channels to prevent excessive firing, and calm immune cells to slow the release of inflammatory substances.

Since 2003, the US government has owned patent #6,630,507, titled "Cannabinoids as Antioxidants and Neuroprotectants."[26] One of the three patent signatories is Julius Axelrod, the Nobel Prize–winning biochemist who discovered dopamine pathways in the brain. Cannabinoids were so intriguing that, according to the National Institutes of Health, "This patent describes the therapeutic potential for cannabinoid chemical compounds that are structurally similar to THC, but without its psychoactive properties, thereby treating specific conditions without the adverse side effects associated with smoked marijuana." Despite the proven biochemistry and therapeutic benefits, the US government still classifies cannabis as a Schedule 1 drug that has "no currently accepted medical use and a high potential for abuse."

But as this book is going to press, efforts are underway to reclassify cannabis as a Schedule 3 substance, which means that the US government is finally admitting that cannabis has medical applicability and is relatively safe. Given that, thousands of studies have been conducted regarding cannabis—just go to PubMed's website to research. Search the word cannabis, and nearly thirty-five thousand results will immediately appear covering hundreds of medical conditions.

If you examine several articles, you will soon see that there is a bias in the funding of cannabis research. For every neutral or potentially positive study about the effects of cannabis, dozens show the harmful or negative effects. By examining who is funding these efforts you will see that stigma exists even in cannabis research. But we are making progress; by placing cannabis on Schedule 3, research opportunities will become more commonplace and that benefits everyone.

CHAPTER 3

A Few Words about Hemp and CBD

Economic opportunities in cannabis aren't limited to the new arena of legalized THC. The possibilities surrounding the hemp plant and CBD are seriously underestimated. While the legalization of THC-active cannabis sales has grabbed much of the limelight, the advent of CBD products and the renewed interest in hemp as an industrial material, agricultural tool, biofuel, and even foodstuff also warrant serious attention.

Ashley Walsh, president and founder of Pocono Organics in Pennsylvania, explains how she got started in the hemp business. She says, "Plant-based CBD wellness products were a huge part of my health journey and helped save my life. Hemp is an incredible plant for both human and planetary health. I wanted to grow the cleanest hemp for both CBD and industrial uses and am proud that Pocono Organics became the grower of the World's 1st Regenerative Organic Certified Hemp, ROC Silver level! We developed a unique partnership with Rodale Institute starting in 2019 and marked our sixth year of hemp research with them in 2024."

Walsh continues, "In 2020, we started making USDA Certified Organic CBD wellness products in our on-site Formulation Lab which has expanded from tinctures, salve sticks, lip balms, and creams to our Food Innovation Lab run by a Chopped Champion Chef, Lindsay McClain. We have developed an innovative USDA Certified Organic water-soluble CBD emulsion for delicious and healthy gourmet infusions." Walsh goes on to talk about some of the most important products that can be created with hemp. She enthuses, "Hemp is just an incredibly versatile and necessary crop, with more than 50,000 uses and it's been kept out of our supply chain for more than 70 years. My current priorities for hemp centers on three products and uses—(1) Plant-based wellness through innovative USDA Certified Organic CBD products. (2) Hemp Microgreens: (raw and powdered) as a nutrient dense superfood boost to our nutrient depleted diets. (3) Utilizing hemp for bioplastics. Replacing plastics with an eco-friendly plant based compostable alternative that provides jobs for American farmers and manufacturing. This innovation that was developed in collaboration with Jefferson University will also keep hazardous plastics out of our oceans and the environment."

THE HEMP PLANT

Hemp comes from the same *Cannabis sativa* parent as the commonly known psychoactive cannabis indica and cannabis sativa and consuming it will not get the user "high." Hemp is legally defined as cannabis which contains 0.3 percent THC or less. If a hemp crop surpasses the 0.3 percent THC, known as "going hot," it becomes legally classified alongside THC-active, high-producing cannabis and often has to be destroyed or remediated.[1]

Physically, the hemp plant is a more sturdy and fibrous plant than its cannabis cousins. More similar to flax or jute, tough, woody "hurds" surround parts of the hemp stalk.[2] Hemp is perhaps best known for its application as a fiber material. As far back as ancient China, people manufactured clothing, canvas, rope, and more with hemp. Hemp cordage is tough and durable, so it is an ideal material for long-lasting products. However, that's just a start when it comes to the product possibilities for hemp.

Hemp History

Hemp was a significant part of economic and domestic life for many Native American nations long before the arrival of European colonists. Hemp was used for clothing, shoes, rope, paper, fishing nets, and as a foodstuff. Mary Jane Oatman, of the Nez Perce Tribe and

A Few Words about Hemp and CBD

executive director of the Indigenous Cannabis Industry Association, spoke about native legacies with hemp in an interview with Oregon Public Broadcasting:[3]

> *For us in particular, the hemp rope is a part of our creation story, and has played an integral part in our fishing economy since time immemorial. Our people have utilized the gifts of the creator for our preservation and way of life, and in perpetuating that for over 16,000 years, documented on our homelands here . . . and our creation story, having that presence of the hemp rope, in this epic battle between Coyote and the Swallowing Monster. And the lessons that come from that story, the creation story of the Nez Perce people, I think is really important for us to embrace, that we're not only reclaiming an economy for our people, but this agricultural value of the fiber, the textile, and specifically, the rope.*[4]

As well, hemp was a necessity in colonial America. For example, the early Jamestown colonists were required to grow one hundred stalks of hemp each to send to England in the form of a tax.[5] This practice also spread quickly to Connecticut and Massachusetts. Later, hemp was a common crop at George Washington's Mount Vernon.

However, the hemp industry began to decline in the nineteenth century as technology advanced. For example, the advent of steamships replaced the need for hemp sailing materials, and the United States began importing cheaper fibers. Essentially, by the Civil War's end, only a few states, such as Kentucky, still had substantial hemp industries. Hemp had a very short resurgence during and just after World War II, as the government asked farmers to grow hemp for wartime materials,[6] such as rope, canvas, and uniforms in a campaign called Hemp for Victory.[7] But overall, the Marijuana Tax Act of 1937 levied taxes so financially prohibitive that farming hemp became unfeasible. And when the government enacted the Controlled Substances Act of 1971, the law officially grouped hemp with the other types of cannabis, making all cannabis illegal.

For years hemp was legally categorized alongside THC-dominant cannabis which people consumed for recreational purposes. As mentioned in chapter 1, some speculate that this legal classification came about in part because American business tycoons like Hearst, Mellon, and Du Pont wanted to eliminate economic competition.[8] Hearst, for example, was in the paper business, and hemp was a material competitor to his logging and pulping interests. These figures had a direct lobbying line to Harry Anslinger and others in government and were certainly capable of influencing the series of lawmaking decisions that culminated with the Controlled Substances Act. However, it's also true to say that many people simply were unaware of the differences between the various cannabis types. To an extent, this is still true today, and cannabis education and stigma-breaking across the various cannabis spaces are important ongoing movements.

From an international standpoint, America's legal stance on hemp has been anomalous. No other country prohibited industrial hemp in the same way. In a contradiction representative of the legal history of cannabis, the United States simultaneously outlawed the agricultural and industrial opportunities in hemp while importing plenty of hemp and hemp-derived products from the likes of China, Canada, France, and several Latin American countries.[9]

However, President Obama signed the Farm Bill of 2014, which legally separated hemp from "delta-9 tetrahydrocannabinol (THC)." The bill also allowed state-run pilot programs for researching industrial hemp potential.[10] It wasn't until the Farm Bill of 2018 that hemp was legalized for general industrial farming. Further proof that cannabis is a truly bipartisan issue, even Kentucky Senator Mitch McConnell touted hemp's importance as a replacement crop for Kentucky tobacco farmers.[11] Now hemp is federally legal, and there are at least forty-seven states with some variation of legalized hemp or state-run agricultural hemp programs.[12]

The Possibilities of Industrial Hemp
Environmentalists are excited about the agricultural possibilities of hemp due to two main factors. First, hemp needs less water to grow than other

commercial crops. It's also useful in crop rotation,[13] and it's a natural weed-deterrent because the hemp stalks can grow very close together.[14] Second, hemp is a carbon-negative crop, which means that it captures more carbon than it creates, pulling carbon dioxide from the air to convert it into its fibrous stalks and leaves. Hemp absorbs four times as much carbon dioxide out of the atmosphere as trees.[15] Plus, hemp has the potential to make big public health impacts. It is a powerful tool for soil remediation, as hemp can "soak up" unwanted substances from the soil. For example, hemp was planted near the Chernobyl nuclear site to extract heavy metals from the ground.[16]

Hemp can also be used to remediate soil contaminated with PFAs,[17] which are per- and polyfluoroalkyl substances that are cancer-causing compounds. These compounds are so resistant to being broken down that they are called "forever chemicals." PFAs bind to proteins and bioaccumulate in soil, water, and even the human body! In typical environmental conditions, they can stick around for hundreds and even thousands of years. PFAs were popular for years because of their nonstick properties and were used in carpeting, cookware, and firefighting foam. In simplest terms, PFAs are drawn from the soil into the stem and leaf tissue, and the hemp plant is then taken to a designated waste site. This means that contaminated soil may once again be useful and safe. Because of the extent of contaminated soil in the United States and around the world, hemp has the potential to be a world healer.

Hemp has also been used to create building materials since Roman times.[18] Hempcrete is a biocomposite building material made of the fibrous, woody core of the hemp plant, called hurd or shives, which is bound together using a lime mixture.[19] It's been more popular in Europe in the last few decades, especially in France. And it's been recommended for construction in earthquake zones because it has some flexibility and resists cracking. Much lighter than concrete, it's a highly durable natural insulator. Plus, due to its carbon-negative crop origins, hempcrete yields better-embodied energy, a term for the assessment of the total energy expended to create a structure. Another promising development is that hempcrete recently received certification in the US Residential Building

Codes document. This certification allows hemp-lime/hempcrete to be used as a standard material in residential construction starting in 2024.

Hemp material has also been used in creating biodegradable plastic.[20] Bioplastics are cheaper and environmentally friendly. Hydrocarbon polymer plastics, which are fossil fuel-based and never degrade, have been the norm, and if we went back in time to replace polymer plastics with hemp plastic, we'd be taking millions of tons of permanent waste off the earth!

Bioplastic water bottles are just the start: Henry Ford, interested in alternative energy and materials, was working toward creating a hemp plastic car.[21] Ford said, "Why use up the forests which were centuries in the making and the mines which required ages to lay down, if we can get the equivalent of forest and mineral products in the annual growth of the hemp fields?"[22] Indeed, hemp has shown potential as a candidate for producing biofuel. Processors have figured out how to make hemp into both biodiesel fuel and ethanol. Biodiesel can be used in any diesel-powered vehicle, and it can be stored and transported just like diesel fuel, so no new supply systems have to be created. The smell of the fuel is like hemp rather than traditional diesel as well. Ethanol, on the other hand, is usually made from corn or barley, and it is added to fuel. However, unlike corn or barley, hemp can be grown in more challenging conditions, can still be added to fuel, and can, again, be transported just like diesel fuel. While it looks like hemp won't be the complete answer to sustainable fuel, it looks to be a strong step in the right direction.

Now, hemp and hemp seeds are being recognized and popularized as an important foodstuff,[23] and even a burgeoning superfood, like kale, acai, flax, and chia seeds, which are commonly recognized as exceptionally healthy,[24] rich in vitamins, minerals, and antioxidants. Throughout history, hemp and hemp seeds have been baked into foods like pies. Hemp seeds contain 75 percent more protein than flax and chia seeds, and hemp seeds, which are high in fiber, contain all twenty amino acids.[25]

CBD

CBD (cannabidiol) is the major nonpsychoactive component in cannabis. It's found in the flowers, stalks, and leaves of the cannabis plant. The compound has been popularized in the last decade or more as it's been shown to work with the ECS to have analgesic, anti-inflammatory, and antianxiety properties. Alongside hemp, CBD was legalized via the 2014 Farm Bill. Now hemp farmers can grow hemp specifically for CBD extraction. CBD products have proliferated across retail sectors. *Forbes* reports that from 2014 to 2022, CBD sales jumped from $108 million to $1.9 billion.[26] Other reports valued the global CBD trade at just under $8 billion.[27] You'll find CBD-dominant products in dispensaries, chain grocery stores, pharmacies, and even local shops. CBD tinctures, lotions, soaps, teas, coffees, and even dog treats are becoming regular consumer purchases.

CBD is a desirable product because it shares the properties of common synthetic drugs like Tylenol, Ibuprofen, and Motrin, but CBD has been shown to work without any of the potentially harmful side effects of these medications. Also, in the cannabis world, CBD products are attractive to demographics who want to access the benefits of consuming cannabis without the psychoactive or recreational aspects of THC. So, CBD often appeals to older demographics who've grown up in the stigma-laden cannabis prohibition era and who are more likely to need the medical and therapeutic aid that CBD could provide. Of course, there have been headline-worthy stories of families with children suffering from severe epilepsy[28] finding medical CBD products to be highly effective, even life-changing.[29]

CBD products are made in several ways. One method is pressing hemp plants, obtaining the oil from hemp plant stalks, stems, flowers, seeds, and resin. Another method uses liquid solvents or carbon dioxide to extract the compounds. The three main kinds of CBD products are full spectrum, broad spectrum, and CBD isolates. The main ways to consume CBD are topicals like ointments or salves, orally in the form of edibles, gummies, or beverages, sublingually in tinctures dropped under the tongue, and via vaping or smoking. Naturally, CBD products come in all these forms.

Full-Spectrum CBD
Commonly known as the most effective kind of CBD product, full-spectrum CBD products include CBD but also minor amounts of THC,

other cannabinoids, terpenes, flavonoids, and essential oils that are naturally found in the hemp plant. The products undergo no additional extraction processes which aim to isolate or remove any cannabis compounds that are present naturally in the hemp plant. The idea is that the entourage effect of all these compounds working together is stronger, or more therapeutic or healthful than CBD on its own.[30]

Broad-Spectrum CBD
Very similar to full-spectrum CBD, broad-spectrum undergoes one additional extraction process to remove all (or nearly all) THC from the product. Sometimes there are still trace amounts of THC in broad-spectrum CBD products, but comparatively less than full-spectrum CBD products.[31]

CBD Isolate
CBD isolate products only contain CBD in terms of cannabis-extracted substances. Consuming this kind of product means that one won't get the potential benefits from the entourage effect of the various components of cannabis working in conjunction.[32]

One important reason to pay attention to whether a CBD product is full spectrum, broad spectrum, or isolate is in case you are likely to be drug tested. Drug tests only test for THC. This means if you take full-spectrum or even a broad-spectrum CBD product you may show positive results on a drug test. Isolate is your best bet, but you are not getting the best medicine possible.

LOOKING FORWARD
Several key issues that we will have to address in the near future concerning hemp include an upcoming 2025 Farm Bill, a push from individual states to regulate or even ban synthetic cannabinoids that are being created from hemp, such as Delta-8 products, and further national and even international economic opportunities.

As more hemp processing facilities are built, the seed and fiber portion of the hemp business should grow quickly. Products such as apparel, bioplastics, hempcrete, and health and beauty aids could be produced in greater quantities and could begin to compete with cheaper, traditional goods.

In terms of CBD products, the market is begging for the Food and Drug Administration (FDA) to step in to issue regulations. These regulations and standardization would help separate legitimate, compliant companies from the hucksters. The CBD market is full of untested and even possibly tainted tinctures, beverages, oils, lotions, and edibles. However some companies grow their organic hemp, process it responsibly, test their products, and do not make bogus health claims. Until this happens, consumers should know who grows their hemp, look for test results, and read all labels carefully.

The new Farm Bill should expand opportunities in hemp cultivation as interstate commerce and research initiatives are expected to be funded and promoted. Many farmers would welcome adjusting the allowable percentage of THC in a hemp plant from 0.3 to 1 percent. This would alleviate some pressure on farmers in terms of keeping their crops from "going hot" and having to be destroyed or repurposed. One percent is still a negligible level of THC, and losing entire crops due to this percentage margin makes an unnecessary negative economic impact. The new Farm Bill may also address cannabinoid extraction, which would lead to the regulation or even outright ban of synthetic cannabinoids such as Delta-8, Delta-10, THC-O and many more synthetic forms of cannabis derived from hemp. Finally, the bill may also update packaging and labeling standards.

It's simply common sense that hemp should be a resource that various industries invest in and utilize. When our processing abilities catch up to our hemp crop production capabilities, many new products and careers will be created, and in time the CBD market will stabilize and flourish under reasonable regulations. Indeed, the hemp industry, in its multifaceted nature, has the potential to outgrow the recreational cannabis market in time.

If your area of interest in the cannabis industry is working in hemp, stay tuned as future chapters will examine career opportunities here. But now, let's look at how you can analyze your career options and pivot (or start) your career.

Chapter 4

The Cannabis Industry Pivot

How to Get Started: Career Analysis

You might be asking the all-important question: "Do I have a place in the booming hemp or cannabis industry?" An encouraging note: I have seen many, many people successfully pivot their careers into the cannabis industry. They may be attracted to the industry because of its massive growth and new opportunities or perhaps they have a passion for cultivation, holistic health, or social change. What's more is that you have the potential not just to get involved in this new industry, but also to shape its future for yourself and others!

Whatever brought potential job seekers to this point, rest assured that they have chosen a market ripe with opportunity. A recent Vangst jobs report revealed that there are over 440,445 full-time cannabis jobs right now.[1] And this does not include support or ancillary jobs which outnumber "plant touching" jobs.

Another important note is that because the cannabis industry is still evolving, many of the rules and regulations are in flux. While this sea change may present challenges it also represents a major opportunity. For example, if you have food or restaurant industry experience you may be able to use your skills to create cannabis edibles. In most cannabis markets new edibles are being created every day and now include gummies, chocolates, baked goods, infused oils, savory snacks, popcorn, and even ice cream. With a superior product, strong branding, and distribution, a new product can become an established product.

CHAPTER 4

The first step in pivoting one's career is to focus on cannabis education, which can take many forms. Note that chapter 8 includes cannabis job resources which you should consult once you have developed a baseline of cannabis knowledge. I like to call this being cannabis fluent. One can become cannabis fluent in many ways; it's about seeking information! As we all learn in different ways it is important to embrace the way that you best learn which may be by:

- Reading books like the author's *The Essential Cannabis Book: A Field Guide for the Curious* or any of Jorge Cervantes's books including *The Cannabis Encyclopedia* or any number of his top-notch cultivation books (and there are many others!).
- Listening to cannabis podcasts.
- Watching YouTube videos.
- Taking in-person or online cannabis courses (some of which are even available through colleges and universities).
- Participating in networking and in-person events.
- Reaching out to cannabis experts in your area of interest.
- Tuning in to state cannabis regulatory board meetings.

While cannabis is currently federally illegal, thirty-eight states plus the District of Columbia have a regulated medical cannabis market. Twenty-four states plus the District of Columbia also have a regulated adult-use market. Because of this gap between federal and state regulations, each state has its own unique rules and regulations. You must know the rules and requirements in your state; you may even have to get special certification to qualify for a particular position.

Section 280E of the federal tax code provides another wrinkle when it comes to owning a cannabis business. The Vermont legislature describes 280E this way, "Section 280E of the Internal Revenue Code forbids businesses from deducting otherwise ordinary business expenses from gross income associated with the 'trafficking' of Schedule I or II substances, as defined by the Controlled Substances Act."[2] For example, this means that cannabis businesses cannot deduct rent, overhead, employee, and shipping expenses. This makes a cannabis business much more expensive to run and cuts significantly into profits. But as you learned in an earlier chapter, there is serious consideration on the federal level that cannabis will be rescheduled from Schedule 1 to Schedule 3. If this happens, 280E will no longer apply to cannabis businesses, which would be a welcome development for existing operators. It may also spur investment into this sector, which would further help the cannabis market.

Yet another consideration when opening a cannabis business is that it is difficult and expensive to secure banking services. Banks have to comply with Federal Deposit Insurance Corporation requirements and as long as cannabis is federally illegal, major national banks such as Wells Fargo, Capital One, Chase, TD Bank, and HSBC won't work with cannabis businesses. However, some businesses have had success working with state-based banks or credit unions. It seems that this hurdle will persist until cannabis becomes federally legal or Congress passes special banking legislation.

Where Do You Fit?

One of the most enjoyable and challenging activities one can undertake is to spend time evaluating what you like to do. When we were locked down during the COVID-19 pandemic, many students and workers did just that. The result was a major shift in employment, with many people starting their own businesses, switching jobs to mission-based organizations, pursuing higher education, negotiating to work in a home office on a part- or full-time basis, or taking up new hobbies as side hustles.

It became a time to consider what kind of lifestyle fits who you are. And because the hemp and cannabis industries intersect with so many different parts of our world, options abound. As you will see in the following chapters, you may find roles in cultivation, processing, customer service, management, inventory, compliance, logistics, sales, product development, branding, marketing, social media, health services, consulting, and more. I would challenge readers to think of an industry they are currently involved in where their skills do not translate in some way to a cannabis business.

CHAPTER 4

Think of it this way: "____ and cannabis." How do you fill in the blank with your passions, desires, knowledge, and expertise? A useful first step is to research the cannabis industry, initially on a macro and then micro basis. Earlier chapters in this book looked at cannabis on a macro level, covering such topics as:

- Learning essential terms and definitions.
- Examining cannabis history, including cannabis in indigenous America and the story and effects of prohibition in the United States.
- Understanding cannabis scientific and botanical facts.
- Understanding the differences between hemp and cannabis.
- Learning about cannabis's utility as medicine and how it works in the body.

Then, dissecting the cannabis industry on a micro level means finding and reviewing your state's cannabis rules and regulations. Since cannabis is still federally illegal, this means that each state creates, issues, and enforces its particular cannabis rules and regulations. Be warned that your state's rules may be contained in a document that is well over one hundred pages long! But it's important to do the difficult work to become best able to navigate the cannabis space. These regulation documents will enumerate what kinds of licenses are available, which is an important consideration as this dictates what type of businesses can be created in your state. For example, if you live in New York State a cannabis operator can run a greenhouse-type cannabis operation where they can sell seeds, clones, fertilizers, pots, and other gardening equipment to individual home cultivators. This license is generally not available in other states. This is important because if you have greenhouse experience and live in New York state you can see that this would be a logical and relatively easy career pivot to start or work in this business.

Once you are familiar with your state's cannabis rules and regulations, take a deeper dive into the kind of cannabis business you may want to work in. Think about tapping into any existing connections you have to network, have informative conversations, and maybe even get a facility tour. As well, keep reading books, listening to podcasts, taking courses, attending events, reaching out to experts, and watching cannabis regulatory board meetings.

Skill Evaluation
Skills and capabilities you should examine include an evaluation of your current career, specific industry and technical skills you possess, soft skills you feel you have, and goals that motivate you. An evaluation of your current industry and job includes looking to see if there is a similar existing role in cannabis. For example, if you are an accountant, there are cannabis industry-specific accountants. But what makes them valuable? They take traditional accounting skills and best practices and also learn what specific guidelines cannabis businesses have to follow. Remember, right now cannabis businesses are subject to section 280E of the Internal Revenue Code. You will recall that this forbids businesses from deducting ordinary business expenses from gross income stemming from working with Schedule 1 substances. Knowledgeable cannabis accountants advise businesses on how to work with this requirement.

Sales and retail positions are good examples of roles that are highly transferable. Like all industries, cannabis needs salespeople to sell all kinds of goods and services, and retail skills translate well into dispensary operations. Most industries and jobs have some sort of transferable connection to the cannabis industry.

After examining your current job and industry, look at any technical or special skills you have. This may include social media expertise, experience with specific software programs, graphic design know-how, and more. If you have spent years developing and honing your expertise in a particular area, this will likely also translate into the cannabis industry.

Combining Expertise with Passion
Then, think about what interests and motivates you. Does horticulture speak to you? Do you like getting your hands dirty, and do you feel pride when it is harvesttime? If so, cultivation could be for you. Or perhaps you're an entrepreneur at heart. No industry space rewards innovation

more than cannabis right now. Because the rules are continuously being written and rewritten, forward-looking individuals can see opportunities on the horizon. For example, there is no question that national legalization of cannabis will present new opportunities. What will they be and how can you make a living by embracing these opportunities? That is what the bright entrepreneur will figure out.

To illustrate this point, one notable cannabis entrepreneur, Brian Dowling, founder and president of Sussex Cultivation, pointed out that to be a successful cannabis entrepreneur, you have to "pinpoint a promising market with potential for growth, strategically distribute your assets to key sectors, and establish your foundation with a team of experienced professionals." Further, "there is a high level of complexity that goes into building a successful vertically integrated cannabis company. The important elements include securing funding, acquiring property, obtaining necessary resolutions and permits, crafting design, mastering engineering, managing day-to-day activities, and creating positive organizational culture."

Because human interests are limitless, this can be both a fruitful and trying exercise. But remember that most people change jobs often, so you don't have to get it right the first time. Your path in the cannabis industry will become clear as you learn more and experience different parts of the business. Trust the process, trust your instincts, and lean into the kind of life you want to live.

Finally, if you are someone who likes to take personality or skills assessment tests, and finds them to be useful, there are plenty of resources available to you. One of the best is the CliftonStrengths Assessment,[3] formerly known as the StrengthsFinder Test. Millions of business professionals have found that this tool has been instrumental in their career journey. Whether they're recent graduates or transitioning from another industry, this assessment offers a tailored approach to understanding personal strengths and applying them effectively in a new professional context. With approximately 177 questions designed to uncover innate talents, the CliftonStrengths Assessment delves into various aspects of work experience and interaction styles, providing comprehensive insights beyond traditional skill assessments.

In the cannabis industry's dynamic landscape, where roles can vary widely and innovation is paramount, the CliftonStrengths Assessment equips individuals with a profound understanding of their unique strengths. By identifying top talents from a pool of thirty-four themes, individuals gain clarity on their capabilities and potential career paths within the industry. Moreover, as teamwork and adaptability are crucial in cannabis ventures, the assessment's emphasis on team building and leveraging individual strengths for collective success aligns seamlessly with industry demands. For those who utilize it, tapping into the strengths revealed by CliftonStrengths can empower aspiring cannabis professionals to confidently navigate challenges, boost productivity, and reach their full potential in this ever-changing industry. Note that there is a charge associated with the use of this assessment.

Researching and Networking

Chapter 8 is packed with resources to guide you in exploring cannabis business opportunities. Here, you'll learn how to research job openings, understand cannabis job descriptions, find useful websites and educational materials, and get tips on crafting resumes, cover letters, and emails and acing interviews.

But one of the best ways to accelerate your career aspirations in cannabis is to become an effective networker. As you begin to research the cannabis industry you will find many events that you should consider attending. The events can range from topic-specific meetings, such as how to find banking services for your business, to networking and educational events, to, frankly, a cannabis party! Evaluate why you may want to attend each event, or not, and be intentional and strategic with your efforts. If you are not used to networking, here are some useful tips that will maximize your presence at various cannabis events:

- Research and Prepare: Before attending, research the event, its speakers, and attendees. Identify key players and topics of interest. Prepare questions and talking points to engage with others effectively.

- Be Genuine and Approachable: Approach conversations with authenticity and openness. Show genuine interest in others and their experiences. Smile, make eye contact, and be approachable to encourage interactions.
- Listen and Learn: Actively listen to others' stories and insights. Be curious and ask thoughtful questions to learn more about the industry and the different roles within it. Take notes to remember important details and follow up later.
- Share Your Story: Be prepared to share your background, skills, and what you hope to learn or achieve in the cannabis industry. Highlight your unique perspective and how it can contribute to the industry's growth.
- Exchange Contact Information: Collect business cards or exchange contact information with individuals you meet. Follow up with personalized emails or LinkedIn messages to strengthen connections made during the event.
- Attend Workshops and Panels: Participate in workshops, panels, and discussions to deepen your understanding of industry trends, challenges, and opportunities. Engage with panelists and speakers during Q&A sessions to build rapport.
- Explore Exhibition Booths: Visit exhibition booths to learn about different companies, products, and services in the cannabis space. Engage with exhibitors, ask questions, and explore potential job opportunities or partnerships.
- Follow Up: After the event, follow up with individuals you connected with to reinforce your relationship. Send thank-you emails, call when appropriate, share relevant articles or resources, and express your interest in staying connected.

Advice from the Professionals

In chapter 8, we go into some depth regarding your career search. We offer:

- Job research guidelines
- Sample job descriptions

- Job search websites and cannabis education resources
- Sample resumes
- Sample cover letter
- Sample email follow-up guidelines and sample
- Interview tips

If you have read the preceding chapters, you should start to feel like you are becoming fluent in the cannabis industry. Much like learning a new language, you will find that you are beginning to recognize terms and definitions. You are also developing a basic understanding of how this intriguing industry works. Note that as the cannabis and hemp industries evolve, we will keep up with new opportunities and important changes that affect the job market via our website: www.OurCommunityHarvest.com. We will also post resources and other useful tidbits there.

Here, we conclude the chapter by hearing from highly respected cannabis professor, Michael Zaytsev. Zaytsev, who is the academic director of the Business of Cannabis at LIM College and founder of High NY, is the author of *The Cannabis Business Book* and *Cannabis Business Coach*. He has advised many would-be cannabis business participants, and I posed the following questions to him:

What advice would you give someone who wants to get into the cannabis business?

> "Do your research and understand what you're getting yourself into. This industry is complex, volatile, and can be extremely challenging. Have a strong sense of purpose for pivoting into this industry. If you're doing it just because you think it will be fast or easy money, think again."

What are the most important skills to develop to enter the cannabis industry?

> "You need deep knowledge of cannabis, business acumen, patience, compassion, grit, flexibility, and perhaps above all else, ethics and integrity. Beyond that, you need to remain curious, humble, and learn continuously as the science and policy around cannabis is constantly evolving."

CHAPTER 4

Why would someone want to change careers to work in the cannabis industry?

"The cannabis industry represents an unprecedented opportunity to do well and do good at the same time. Cannabis is an incredibly powerful and versatile natural resource that has the potential to uplift humanity in a multitude of ways. Most of the people in this industry are seriously passionate about the plant and are mission-driven. It's exciting, fun, challenging and rewarding."

NAVIGATING CANNABIS STIGMA

Often, individuals who work in cannabis, or even those who are considering cannabis opportunities, run into unpleasant or awkward moments because of lingering cannabis stigma. To a degree, it's understandable, as the public has been fed a steady diet of misinformation about cannabis for decades. Even current headlines largely focus on the perceived dangers of cannabis while glossing over its medicinal and even business applications. There is a massive deficit of commonsense cannabis education, and on the other hand, there's plenty of cynical misinformation available.

Against this backdrop you will have to learn how to navigate these sometimes difficult conversations. Not surprisingly, it takes knowledge and practice to fight ignorance. You may find that it is best to practice with family and friends first to hone your message. It will also help you to find reputable sources to back up your assertions. Over time, you will become more comfortable having these conversations, and sometimes you may even start to change hearts and minds. It can also be tiring, but your passion will help you find the drive to persist. Here then, are strategies we've learned in terms of addressing cannabis misinformation and stigma.

Begin with active listening. Start by showing genuine interest in the other person's perspective. You might say, "That's an interesting perspective. Tell me a bit more about what you know about cannabis." This not only shows respect for their viewpoint but also gives you insight into their knowledge and concerns. Understanding their perspective allows you to address specific misconceptions and provide relevant information.

Then, share informative insights. Once you've listened, gently introduce some of your thoughts and knowledge. For example, you might explain that hemp, a type of cannabis, is our oldest-grown domestic crop. You may continue this strand of conversation by pointing out that hemp is just a crop, like corn. And how many people have a "beef" with a crop? Whatever you find exciting and enjoyable to talk about, there are plenty of these kinds of eye-opening factoids and reference points in this book!

Sharing personal stories can be powerful, or, if not personal stories, then there are plenty of well-known stories of the positive impacts of cannabis. Talk about individuals like Charlotte Figi, a young girl whose severe seizures were significantly reduced by a special strain of CBD-forward cannabis known as "Charlotte's Web."[4] Recall, too, that CBD does not get the user high, and no parent wants to see their child suffer. From here, you may want to ask if the person you are talking to knows anyone who has had cancer. Unfortunately, the answer is almost always yes. Explain that cannabis helps treat cancer symptoms by providing pain and nausea relief, as well as stimulating a patient's appetite. This is a strong message that will make an impact. Overall, highlighting the medical benefits of cannabis, such as its positive effects on epilepsy, cancer treatments, seizures, anxiety, migraines, and other conditions, can help illustrate its potential beyond recreational use.

Another angle to take is to provide historical context explaining why and how cannabis has been stigmatized. Chapter 1 covers many of these themes. Mention that cannabis was listed in the *U.S. Pharmacopeia* until the 1940s recognized for its medicinal properties, including reducing opioid addiction. Explain how the cannabis stigma, and prohibition, was the result of systematic campaigns to link it to racist feelings toward minority groups and how it was also used as a cudgel to disproportionately target people of color for arrest, incarceration, and general community disruption. This historical perspective can help others understand that the stigma is rooted in artificial social and political factors rather than scientific evidence.

Conclude the conversation by reinforcing the idea that discussing cannabis openly and factually helps reduce stigma and fosters a more informed and accepting society. Encourage them to continue learning and share what they've learned with others. And, finally, you should consider graciously exiting any conversation when there's nowhere left to go. Some folks simply choose to never hear reason! Be confident in your knowledge, and know that your positive, professional, and accepting behavior is actively counteracting any negative stigma that certain parts of society still hold.

Key Takeaways
- Listen Actively: Show respect and understanding for their perspective.
- Share Informative Insights: Use historical and practical examples to inform.
- Use Personal Stories: Illustrate the benefits of cannabis through real-life examples.
- Provide Historical Context: Explain the roots of cannabis stigma.
- Address Social Justice: Highlight racial disparities and the need for change.

By following these steps, you can help shift perceptions and foster a more informed discussion about cannabis.

CHAPTER 5

Cannabis Handling Careers

PLANT-TOUCHING VERSUS ANCILLARY ROLES
The cannabis industry is divided into two general categories that are defined by their proximity to the cannabis plant or product: the plant-touching sector and the ancillary sector. This chapter will delve into the plant-touching side of the cannabis industry, which ancillary businesses either support or depend on. Plant-touching roles are perhaps the first kind of roles that one thinks of when one considers pivoting to the cannabis industry, and there are seemingly countless opportunities to work in a position that allows you to work directly with the cannabis plant. The plant-touching sector of the cannabis industry includes:

- Dispensaries and retail operations, which include budtenders and management positions, community relations officer, diversity officer, and farmgate operations
- Cultivation, which revolves around growing the cannabis plant, including roles like trimmers, processors, growers, and master cultivators
- Laboratory work, which includes testing and quality control, and packaging roles, as well as culinary work with edibles, concentrates, oils, tinctures, topicals, suppositories, nasal sprays, and transdermals
- Distribution, wholesaling, and delivery

Because cannabis is not yet legal at the federal level, all "legal" cannabis is now regulated by individual states, which means there is little uniformity in terms of industry regulations state by state. These regulations are intricate and still evolving, so it's important that as you push into the industry, whether you're opening your own plant-touching business like a dispensary or simply beginning as a budtender or trimmer, you do the work to educate yourself about your own state's rules and regulations.

The Dispensary

Beginning at the "finish line" of the cannabis production chain, the dispensary is the sales point of the cannabis industry. A dispensary is a retail building where adult customers (twenty-one or older) can purchase products such as cannabis flower, vape pens, edibles and infused beverages, concentrates, topicals, and more. All products sold in a dispensary must be tested, labeled for potency, and packaged according to state regulations. In addition, not all products are approved for sale in all states. The goal of a dispensary is to educate its customers about proper, responsible cannabis use, to offer a variety of cannabis products, to be a good community partner, and to run a compliant business. The national dispensary landscape is highly variable. Some states only have dispensaries for qualified medical patients, while other states have dispensaries designated for adult users. Then, some states accommodate both medical patients and adult users, and a handful of states, while cannabis has been legalized, still do not have any sort of cannabis dispensary program yet.

Some states allow "vertical" dispensaries. A "vertically integrated" dispensary means that the company may cultivate their cannabis, perform extraction and processing, create their products, and sell their products, as well as others' products if they choose. In other words, they handle each part of the cannabis grow, product production, and sales process from seed to sale in their dispensary. Not all dispensaries are vertically integrated. Others will only sell other companies' products. The vertical distinction has major implications on hiring needs, capabilities, and scale of operations. Notably, to diversify the industry and make it more accessible to more would-be participants, most states are moving toward the nonvertical model to maximize space for higher numbers of participants. The cost and scope of a vertical operation make it prohibitively expensive and complicated for would-be small-business owners, or hopeful participants who don't possess the same financial capital as other larger corporate operators.

Due to difficulties accessing banking services, some dispensaries are only able to accept cash payments. Too, dispensaries are mandated to have a certain number of security cameras installed at specific intervals. Operators must observe restrictions regarding where and when a dispensary can advertise. Hours of operation are regulated as well. Paperwork and records must be kept meticulously; a dispensary must account for its inventory, its cash receipts, incoming and outgoing deliveries, and employee background checks, and must have certain state certificates.

The Customer Experience

The customer experience in a dispensary is more choreographed due to mandatory ID checks and other regulations. Dispensary employees must check customer IDs as soon as the customer enters the premises. Usually, this is done in a staging area separate from the dispensary sales floor. Some dispensaries will have chairs or couches to sit on because only a certain number of people are allowed in a dispensary at one time; this is both for security and to give customers an individualized experience with a salesperson, often called a budtender. Cannabis products in dispensaries aren't laid out for customers to handle like in a clothing or home goods store, or even a liquor outlet. Instead, customers must be served by a budtender who can handle and present products individually. The ID check room often has a "menu" of popular products and prices that customers can look at before entering the room with cannabis products.

The most popular and best-selling products are loose, smokable cannabis flower, pre-rolled joints (referred to as pre-rolls), vape pens, edibles, and concentrates. Dispensaries often carry many other products such as topicals, lozenges, or gel caps. Dispensaries often sell cannabis accessories such as pipes, trays, bongs, apparel, and cannabis books. Some dispensaries may advertise educational events and festivals too. Overall, the goal of the dispensary is to provide a comfortable, safe customer experience with a broad variety of products sold by knowledgeable, compassionate staff.

CHAPTER 5

The COVID-19 era has had lingering effects on dispensary operations, placing an even higher emphasis on an operation's online presence and menu. Preordering via websites, curbside pickup, home delivery, and even drive-through shopping were all measures that were implemented during COVID-19, when dispensaries were deemed essential operations. These new procedures and operating maneuvers ensured customer safety, and some dispensaries actually increased their sales because of them. For example, preordering from online menus has become commonplace.

Opening a Dispensary

If you are considering opening a dispensary, be prepared for sticker shock, the complexity of details, and an extremely competitive licensing procurement process. Often, dispensary owners must reside in the state they operate in, unless they are involved with a major, deep-pocketed multistate organization that can leverage their interstate connections. It has become more common for dispensary licenses to be granted to individuals from other states, but many states are trying to carve out a part of the cannabis business for their state residents.

Your first step would be to read the regulations and state legislation regarding dispensaries. Be prepared to spend some time with this document as it can be dense and may run over one hundred pages. This, or a separate document, will also outline how to apply for a license, will list application costs, deadlines, how licenses will be judged, and which state entity will evaluate them. Most often, a separate commission appointed by the state will be responsible for reviewing, evaluating, and granting licenses.

Realistically, the process is highly onerous, time-consuming, and financially demanding. Some states require at least $150,000 in capitalization to even begin the process, an inexpensive number and barrier for many. This is one of the major reasons that dispensary licenses are largely going to large organizations and wealthy individuals.

The Dispensary Licensing Process

The licensing process will be state-specific, but five requirements apply in nearly all states:

1. Your financing, at a specified minimum amount, must be in place.
2. You must have a team in place with relevant experience preferably from highly regulated industries such as pharma, casinos, and the alcohol industry.
3. A thoughtful, thorough business plan must accompany your application.
4. You must have access to a facility that is compliant with regulations (such as being far enough away from schools, churches, and daycare centers) and that you own or lease.
5. Your facility location and operation must be approved by local and state officials; that is, your application must spell out how you will follow all state and local regulations and you must have local permission and applicable permits to operate (a federally illegal business).

License applications are often assessed via point systems. It's important to note that several states have intentionally carved out numbers or percentages of licenses specifically for operators and businesses from communities harmed by the war on drugs and prohibition. These states are beginning to pay attention to social justice issues and the needs of neighborhoods that were unfairly penalized by cannabis arrests so extra "points" on applications are often given if the management team includes a person of color, a woman, or a veteran and if the facility will operate in specific neighborhoods. A few states also give extra "points" for employee training programs and for working with unions. Above all, pay attention to your specific state regulations and research other successful dispensary applications to maximize the appeal of your application. As with any retail operation, many items need to be put in place before opening day. The cost of opening a dispensary generally ranges from $150,000 to $2 million.[1]

Chapter 5

Opening and operating a dispensary consists of at least:

- licenses and permits, rent or mortgage payments, legal fees, insurance
- security surveillance and alarms, safe and storage system
- employees, point of sale system, advertising strategy, web page, social media strategy, logos, and signs
- furniture, display cases, phone, internet, computer and printer, refrigerator, scales, standard office equipment (paper, scissors, pens, etc.), and inventory

Advice from the Experts

According to Ashley Picillo, founder and CEO of cannabis industry consultancy Point Seven Group, the three main mistakes that dispensaries make when they first open are:

1. Not having enough product or variety of products
2. Failing to adequately staff the operation
3. Limited hours of business

For a dispensary that operates in a new market, initial consumer response will likely be robust. We've all seen lines out the door when a new market opens. But retaining these customers in the face of new competition will be an ongoing challenge. As with other retailers, digital loyalty programs go a long way, as does personal advertising to a target market. Events, educational opportunities, and special sales are all good ways to keep a dispensary's clientele engaged. Business owners should gather and analyze data to reveal customer trends. This will reveal insights to help the dispensary owner create effective sales campaigns, and it will help target particular products or experiences to individual customers.

As the market matures, competition for customers will increase. Offering educational tours, seminars, and exhibiting at non-cannabis-specific events like health and wellness fairs can be good ways to market one's business. Curating your business's online presence is essential.

Businesses need a web page and a social media presence. Your website should attract customers by telling your business's story, separating you from local competition, presenting a menu and the sales or deals that you're running, and providing educational resources. Above all, the goal for every person who interacts with your business online or visits your dispensary is to become a regular customer. If they feel welcome, have ample product choices, get their questions answered, and feel connected to the dispensary, they are likely to be regular customers.

Seasoned dispensary operator Jason Kabbes, founder and CEO of Bridge City Collective, gave these insights about running a dispensary, "Setting up a dispensary is an immense amount of work because it is a multifaceted undertaking, employing skill sets from construction management to branding and (e)marketing to retail management." He goes on to explain that a well-run dispensary is all about a "Happy team. If your team is happy, that means all other parts of the dispensary are functioning well (economically, logistically, communally, etc.)." Finally, Kabbes notes unique jobs in a dispensary, "Compliance Director first comes to mind, marketing and sales directors soon follow. Head of visual merchandising is becoming ubiquitous among large companies. Some medically focused dispensaries staff a medical advisor type role, but you tend to find those jobs far and few between in mature markets."

Ulysses Youngblood, president of Worcester, Massachusetts, dispensary Major Bloom offers a different perspective as his dispensary operation also includes a manufacturing and delivery license. This means his company can create and sell products in a brick-and-mortar store and also via delivery. He notes, "Setting up a dispensary has been a lot of work. For a while, people would impose the 'build, and they will come' mentality; however, acquiring and retaining customers is a lot of work. Our focus has been identifying our target audience and not only offering products for them from a retail point of view but also producing products for our target market. And because we are in a black and brown community, our purpose is to contribute to our community's economic growth, which requires us to listen to our customers and our entire community."

Further, Youngblood describes his dispensary as "Agile and Authentic. As an equity business and one of the few Black integrated owners, we built our retail around two significant factors: 1. Setting up shop in a disenfranchised community, and 2. Being able to produce products for our retail shelves. You have to have a diverse team. Over 95 percent of my team is a minority, woman, veteran, disabled, or in the queer community. The team is proficient in adapting to new systems and technology, including POS, security, CRM, socials, etc."

Some unique jobs that his dispensary has include "delivery driver, greeter in the vestibule, production specialist, graphic designer, business development lead, production innovation, inventory manager—these are all jobs specific to delivery and manufacturing which is different as most dispensaries only staff 'budtenders.'"

Ulysses concludes his comments about running a cannabis dispensary by noting that the best part about running a dispensary is "Creating and selling a product which is a much different experience than just selling a product. These products are created by people who love weed and not only do they love weed but they love the community which we serve. I feel like we are outcast and so are our customers, so we connect with them in that regard."

Cannabis Retail Careers
Owner or General Manager
At the helm of the dispensary is the general manager or owner who oversees all day-to-day operations personally and through their trusted employees. They are involved in every facet of the business from calculating expenses and revenue, reviewing design plans, helping with inventory, dealing with vendors, submitting numerous required local and state reports, hiring and training employees, getting insurance, reviewing compliance procedures, and interacting with employees at all levels. This position takes broad business knowledge, and most dispensary owners have run other successful businesses often in similar businesses such as casinos, alcohol, biotechnology, pharmacy, and general consumer retail.

In addition to regulatory compliance and business management, successful managers in the cannabis industry must have strong leadership and communication skills. Building and maintaining relationships with key stakeholders, including employees, suppliers, and customers, is vital for long-term success. A visionary mindset is beneficial, as the cannabis industry is dynamic and requires adaptability to capitalize on emerging trends and innovations.

General managers face many challenges in the cannabis industry. Ever-shifting regulations mean that general managers must be up to date on political, legal, and economic developments. Furthermore, the lack of easy access to banking and financial services makes financial management more complex. Additionally, the stigma associated with cannabis may pose marketing and public relations challenges. Striking a balance between profitability and social responsibility, especially in the context of evolving public attitudes toward cannabis, is another challenge that leaders in the industry must navigate. All of these factors are influenced then by the culture that the owner or general manager creates and fosters. In terms of compensation, it is often tied to the success of the business so salary may start at a modest level but over time can be impressive, especially if there are multiple dispensary locations. Salary ranges start around $60,000 and can run above $200,000.

The Budtender

Not everyone is going to be a dispensary owner or manager though. The budtender is one of the most common starting places for someone in the cannabis industry. A budtender is at the forefront of customer interaction, guiding individuals through their cannabis journey. This entry-level position offers a unique opportunity to learn about different strains, consumption methods, and the ever-evolving world of cannabis products. Your main responsibilities will include assisting customers in selecting the right products based on their preferences and needs, providing information about the best way to consume cannabis, and ensuring a positive and educational experience for each visitor.

This role is not just a job; it's a gateway to a promising career in the cannabis industry. With upward mobility opportunities, dedicated individuals can progress into supervisory or management roles as they gain experience and expertise. Depending on the dispensary, they may offer extensive training with the expectation that workers will embrace roles in the future with more responsibility. Budtenders who excel at their jobs work well with customers and are adept at adhering to both complex regulatory procedures and a business's standard operating procedures (SOPs), including validating IDs, accurately handling cash, and opening and closing the premises.

The ideal candidate for this role is someone who possesses excellent customer service skills, has a genuine interest in and knowledge of how cannabis works in the body, and enjoys staying informed about the latest industry trends. Many successful budtenders come from diverse retail backgrounds, bringing their experience in customer interaction, product knowledge, and a passion for helping people make informed choices. If you are friendly, adaptable, and enthusiastic about the cannabis industry, this could be the perfect starting point for you.

A budtender's pay is usually minimum wage or barely higher. Some dispensaries do allow their customers to tip, and these tips are split among all of the budtenders. Union-run shops typically pay a bit more, have better benefits, and offer worker protection. So, if other factors are equal, you may want to seek out a union-run dispensary. Overall, like other entry-level retail positions across industries, this hands-on, point-of-sale position is a great role to invest in if you're seeking both customer service experience and nuanced knowledge of the cannabis industry in all of its facets, from seed to sale.

Compliance Agent
As a compliance agent in the cannabis industry, your primary responsibility is to ensure that the company operates within the bounds of all applicable laws and regulations. This involves conducting thorough audits and assessments to verify compliance with local, state, and federal cannabis regulations. You'll collaborate closely with various departments to implement and enforce compliance measures, evaluate SOPs, and keep a watchful eye on licensing requirements, product labeling, and overall operational practices. In this pivotal role, attention to detail is paramount as you navigate the complex and evolving regulatory landscape of the cannabis industry.

To thrive as a compliance agent, you'll need a strong understanding of cannabis regulations, a meticulous mindset, and excellent organizational skills. Effective communication is crucial, as you'll be working across teams to implement and communicate compliance protocols. Adaptability and a proactive approach to staying informed about regulatory changes are key attributes. Successful compliance agents in the cannabis industry are individuals who can balance meticulous attention to detail with a strategic understanding of the broader regulatory environment. If you're someone who values precision, enjoys navigating complex compliance frameworks, and is passionate about upholding industry standards, this role offers a dynamic opportunity to contribute to the compliant and ethical growth of the cannabis sector. Many times, these roles are filled by successful budtenders—especially if the company focuses on "promoting from within."

Government and Community Liaison

In the dynamic landscape of the cannabis industry, a government and community liaison serves as a vital bridge between the cannabis company and local authorities, regulatory bodies, and the surrounding community. This role requires a unique blend of interpersonal, communication, and advocacy skills, and the ability to implement company projects. A government and community liaison acts as the primary point of contact for regulatory agencies, ensuring the company's operations adhere to evolving legal requirements. Simultaneously, they foster positive relationships with local community stakeholders, addressing concerns, and promoting a harmonious coexistence.

On a day-to-day basis, the liaison engages in ongoing communication with government officials to stay abreast of regulatory changes and advocate for the company's goals. They also play a crucial role in community outreach, organizing events, and implementing initiatives to educate and involve the public in positive aspects of the cannabis industry. Effective communication and diplomacy are key, as this professional must navigate the intricacies of local politics, regulatory frameworks, and public perception.

In an industry often subject to varying degrees of public scrutiny, the government and community liaison is indispensable. Their ability to build trust, navigate complex regulations, and contribute to positive community relations ensures the company operates ethically, sustainably, and with the support of both regulators and the community. Sometimes these duties are relegated to someone in the marketing department or to someone in management if a separate position has not been established.

Salesperson or Business Development Expert
As a salesperson or business development expert in the cannabis industry, your role is to drive revenue growth and expand market share. Your responsibilities will include identifying and pursuing new business opportunities, building and maintaining strong client relationships, and meeting or exceeding sales targets. This dynamic role involves staying abreast of industry trends, understanding customer needs, and effectively communicating the value propositions of cannabis products to potential clients. Additionally, you will collaborate with marketing and product development teams to align sales strategies with overall business objectives.

Candidates for this position should possess strong sales and negotiation skills, coupled with a deep understanding of the cannabis market and its regulatory landscape. Excellent communication and interpersonal skills are crucial for building and maintaining client relationships. A proven track record in business development, meeting sales targets, and cultivating strategic partnerships is highly desirable. Adaptability, resilience, and a proactive approach to identifying and capitalizing on market opportunities are key attributes of successful salespersons and business development experts. If you are a results-driven individual with a passion for sales and a keen interest in the cannabis market, this role could be for you.

CANNABIS CULTIVATION CAREERS
Besides dispensary work, cultivation is one of the most common things that comes to mind when one thinks about the cannabis industry. After all, without the plant, there's nothing to sell! Creating a successful growing operation doesn't just mean understanding horticulture; it means understanding business. Like any industry, there are highly variable sizes and styles when it comes to cultivating commercial cannabis. Today's

largest US growing operation farms over two hundred acres of cannabis.[2] That is substantially different from a patch of personal homegrow!

The Cannabis Cultivation Process

The backbone of the cannabis business is, of course, the cannabis plant. Step one is to grow healthy, genetically identifiable, environmentally friendly cannabis. Like all plants, cannabis requires the right environment. Fertilization, water, and light are just as crucial to cannabis as every other crop.

It starts with a seed, of course. What strain, and thus seed, one chooses to grow is dependent on growing conditions like soil quality, weather, season, and topography. In addition, seed availability and the suppliers the grower works with are factors. Commercial growers often turn to seed banks or breeders; there are whole businesses involved in seed banking and sales. Seed breeders are knowledgeable about strains and what kind of potential combinations might yield quality products. When a cultivation facility opens, they usually get seeds or clones from a source in their home state. But there are plenty of stories about cultivation facilities discreetly getting seeds or clones from another state.

Only the unpollinated female plant produces the THC- and CBD-rich trichomes which gives users the use benefits they seek. These cannabinoids are produced in the female cannabis plant's buds and to a lesser degree in its leaves which are close to the flower. If you use a magnifying glass to look at a cannabis plant when it is near harvest you will see little white (or amber if it is more mature) structures that look like golf balls on a tee. As mentioned, it is imperative to identify male plants as soon as possible. When male plants are identified (little white balls appear near the stems and branches), they are immediately discarded so they cannot pollinate the female. Conversely, the female plants will have small "hairs" near the stems and branches. Early in the life cycle of the plant it does take experience and practice to tell the difference between males and females but over time it becomes second nature.

Light is essential to the growth of cannabis. In the germination stage (when seeds sprout), seedling stage (when leaves develop) and the vegetative stage (when roots and foliage develop), seeds need to be exposed to eighteen hours of light. During the flowering stage, the plant is exposed to twelve hours of light and twelve hours of darkness. This proportion of light exposure triggers the growth of buds. Of course, this does not apply to autoflower cannabis strains which have a set growing cycle that is generally shorter than cannabis plants that are triggered to bloom by twelve hours of light and darkness.

As with light, watering and giving the plants proper proportions of key nutrients (NPK = nitrogen, phosphorus, and potassium respectively) at the right time is an instrumental part of any grow operation. Water conservation should be the goal of any agricultural operation, and the cannabis industry is no different. While overwatering can kill a plant, even a little excess moisture can introduce disease or mold. Indoor growing gives cultivators the ability to carefully modulate water use for conservation. Growers are looking for ways to reclaim and reuse water and humidity because water conservation is not only good for the environment but also reduces costs. Commercial cannabis is cultivated in one of four ways:

- Indoors in soil or other growing material with artificial, electric lights, exposing plants to light at calculated intervals
- In a greenhouse, using the sun or with artificial lights or lights on timers
- Hydroponically, which means growing with nutrient-rich water and without soil
- Outdoors using natural sunlight

There are other cultivation methods such as aeroponics and aquaponics, but they are far less common, so we'll focus on these methods. Indoor growing is the most common method for dispensaries and larger grow operations. The biggest advantage of growing indoors is that the controlled environment allows for the cultivation of (cannabis) flower that is more potent, denser, and free of pests and pesticides. Indoor cultivation operations can also grow year-round. However, it tends to be more expensive than other methods. Two of the biggest challenges that add to the overall cost are electricity (one grow operation in Colorado spends $40,000 a month on electricity!) and waste disposal.

Greenhouse grow operations are a middle ground between indoor and outdoor grows. Similar to indoor grows, greenhouse grows are more able to control the cultivation environment in terms of weather, temperature, water, light, pests, and more. Greenhouse grows use a combination of natural and supplementary artificial lighting and usually require less water.

Then, hydroponic grows cultivate without soil, and the plants get nutrition through nutrient-rich water. Most often, hydroponic grow operations are located indoors, but it is possible to use hydroponic techniques outdoors. These grows require a grow medium other than soil, and that can include oxygenated water, rock wool (which is like cotton candy spun from basalt and was used for insulation), or even sawdust. Hydroponic growing results in smaller roots but bigger plants/yields when compared to soil-grown plants. The biggest drawback is that it requires daily monitoring and care as you have to adjust nutrient intake carefully. In addition, the system of water pipes, pumps, electrical outlets, and lights requires installation and maintenance.

Finally, cannabis can be grown outdoors. This method is less expensive because it uses sunlight rather than electricity. The resulting buds are also generally fluffier, and some growers claim that the flower takes on characteristics from the local soil, a phenomenon that wine producers call "terroir." However, this method is subject to natural seasons, pests, and temperatures which means growers are limited to one growing season, or possibly two with some good, advanced planning.

Regardless of the way cannabis is grown, a given state will have a method of tracking the plant from "seed to sale." The procedure is sometimes also referred to as "track and trace." This may take the form of a tag that is adhered to each plant or each pot with a unique code that can be scanned. When the tag is scanned it will yield information, such as when the seed was planted (or reached twelve inches in height), what kind of strain it is, and when it was harvested, cured, and put on sale. In this way, cultivators account for each plant. In a rare case, something will go wrong with the growing process, or a grower may be suspected of "product diversion." Product diversion occurs when an authorized seller sells a product outside of authorized distribution channels; this means that this product will end up in the underground market. This behavior threatens an operator's license. Plus, the grower may be ordered to destroy a row or even the entire crop of cannabis. But by far the biggest impact is that an operator's license may be revoked, and they will not be able to regain their license for years (or ever).

Harvesting

Cannabis is ready to be harvested when it is at its most resiny. The resin is what houses most of the THC or CBD. If you were to take a magnifying glass to a cannabis bud ready to harvest, you would see a bunch of sticky, white, miniature balls that look like Christmas lights covering the bud and leaves. When the cannabis plants are on an equal parts light and dark cycle, twelve hours of each, each day, growers need to monitor them closely. When it looks like most of the bud and surrounding leaves are covered in "Christmas lights," the plant is ready to harvest. This is usually about two to three weeks after the twelve and twelve light pattern begins.

When ready, harvesters cut the plant either right above the roots or in individual stocks. They leave enough stock to hang the plants upside down in a well-ventilated room for about seven to ten days to give the plants time to dry. Once the hanging buds or entire plant are partially dried (they should still feel spongy), they are ready to be trimmed. Trimming is the act of removing the surrounding "sugar" leaves—the surrounding leaves gently touching the bud when the plant is hung upside down. Much of the trimming of cannabis is done by hand, but some larger operations use a combination of humans and machines. Trimmed buds are placed in a sealed glass jar or another type of airtight vessel and stored in a cool, dark place. The rest of the trimmings, commonly known as "shake," are saved as well, as they can be used to create cannabis products through extraction processes. Sometimes shake is sold at dispensaries as a cheap product often used when cooking with cannabis.

Opportunities in Cannabis Cultivation

While most people think about agriculture and horticulture when it comes to growing operations, there are many other employment opportunities in the growing industry. Remember that growing operations require all of the same skills and jobs needed to run and maintain an efficient and profitable business. That means all of the following are required: operations and inventory personnel, accounting and human resources capabilities, distribution and supply chain management, construction, heating/ventilation/air-conditioning, and maintenance personnel, as well as security. In addition, electricians and plumbers who specialize in cannabis growing, seed breeders who craft unique strains, seed bank owners who provide seeds for growers and private usage, as well as different levels of cultivators—from entry-level growers to master growers—will be needed. Let's look at a few of these opportunities in more depth.

Trimmer

A trimmer is an entry-level position in the cultivation sector. When the cannabis flower is harvested and cured, the leaves around the potent buds need to be removed. Some cultivators use automatic trimmers which look like the inside of a dryer that spins the buds to remove the extraneous leaf matter. Buds trimmed by machine look very uniform and are often trimmed tightly so they look like "nuggets."

But other cultivators hire trimmers to work by hand. In this process, trimmers deposit trimmed buds in bags, using sharp scissors (bonsai scissors or shears are my favorite trimming tools). Shifts often last seven to eight hours and an hourly wage or wage based on how much plant material is trimmed determines pay. This can be a year-round occupation, or trimmers are hired during harvest season. If you do a good job as a trimmer, promotions to cultivation or to the dispensary are common. In other words, it's a good way to get your foot in the door.

Growers

One can be a grower with various responsibilities on the cultivation team within the growing process. After starting with an entry-level cultivation position, a possible career trajectory is to take a specialized position like pest management lead or manager of the clone room. From here, promotions can lead to shift leader, assistant, and even head grower. But this trajectory may take a while as it simply takes time and practice to hone your craft.

An entry-level cannabis cultivator worker plays an important role in the cultivation process, handling tasks such as planting, watering, and pruning cannabis plants. They monitor the plants for health and growth, ensuring they receive the right amount of light and nutrients. Additionally, they help with pest control and maintain cleanliness in the grow area to promote a healthy growing environment. It's a hands-on job that offers a great introduction to the cannabis industry, perfect for anyone passionate about horticulture and eager to learn the ins and outs of cannabis cultivation.

On the other hand, assistant growers follow instructions relayed to them by their direct supervisor or the master grower. These tasks depend on the time of the year and the stage that the plants are in. Largely, assistant growers help propagate (from seeds or clones which are cuttings from a "mother" plant), feed, water, prune, and generally take care of the cannabis plant. Often, they have to look for and manage pests and test the soil for proper pH and nutrient levels. They also have to keep the grow room and other work areas clean and enter necessary data as directed.

Individuals who thrive as assistant growers are curious about the plant, don't mind hard work or getting their hands dirty, often carry heavy objects, and take pride in seeing one's work result in a healthy, beautiful crop. Daily tasks change so flexibility is a sought-after quality in an assistant grower. Because the term assistant grower can be used to describe any cultivation job from an entry-level position to the position just beneath a master grower, compensation varies greatly. It can range from just above minimum wage to nearly six figures. It is important to determine what the expectations are for this position and to match your skills and experience accordingly.

Seed Breeders or Genetic Developers

Often overlooked, cultivators who know how to develop special strains, sell seeds, or work with plant tissue culture have a niche opportunity. A cannabis seed breeder or genetic developer is like a botanical artist, carefully selecting and cross-breeding cannabis plants to create new and improved strains. They study plant genetics to develop seeds that produce plants with desired traits such as higher potency, unique flavors, or increased resistance to pests and diseases. Their work involves a mix of science and creativity, often experimenting and observing over multiple generations of plants to achieve the perfect blend. It's an exciting and innovative role that shapes the future of cannabis varieties, making it perfect for those who love both gardening and genetics.

Although seed breeders' largest clients are commercial cannabis horticulture operations, sometimes they cater to a committed market of home growers. In nearly every state that has a regulated adult-use market, adults are allowed to grow a certain number of cannabis plants (from two to twelve plants with most states allowing for the growth of six plants). Some states that only have a regulated medical cannabis market allow for homegrow as well. If this interests you, be sure to check and follow your state's regulations. For this market segment, seed breeders often provide education about cultivation and may even provide access to seeds, clones, lights, fertilizers, and soil. Of course, their operations are dictated by their state's rules and regulations.

In the case of tissue culture operations, these sterile lab environments produce disease-free, replicable plants that can be stored in a small space. This means that quality is guaranteed, and genetics are replicated perfectly. For a commercial operator, it may be a good option to work with a tissue culture operation. Often those with a science and cultivation background are attracted to opportunities in tissue culture labs. That is, jobs in this sector involve both cultivators and those knowledgeable in safe lab practices.

Director of Cultivation or Master Grower

The director of cultivation or the master grower is responsible for managing all aspects of cannabis crop cultivation at the production facility.

CHAPTER 5

They can usually expect to be in charge of hundreds, even thousands of plants. A successful candidate is passionate about horticulture, has excellent interpersonal skills, has years of relevant experience, and has a drive to continually learn more about the subject.

Primary duties and responsibilities include planning, organizing, and adhering to a production schedule with the help of a motivated team. Master growers also provide input regarding facility design, and the construction of necessary systems for specific types of cultivation which may include outdoor cultivation, hydroponics, aeroponics, aquaponics, and greenhouse production. Further, they develop SOPs, train and manage employees, interface with vendors, follow all state regulations (including filing reports and maintaining all required paperwork), address cultivation issues (such as implementing pest issue control protocol), and handle anything else that might arise.

Often this candidate will have a background and degree in botany, horticulture, hydroponics, agriculture, biology, or chemistry along with relevant work experience. It is not uncommon for new cultivators to attract master growers from other established cannabis-producing states such as California, Oregon, or Colorado. This role also requires a strong math and science background. This role commands a six-figure salary as it is essential to the success of a cannabis cultivation operation. Most cultivation directors work their way up by starting as entry-level cultivators, trimmers, or assistant growers.

Valentina Fiero is a professional cultivator who has taken on increased responsibility over time. She is a cannabis cultivator and an adjunct cannabis professor at Stockton University. Fiero started in an entry-level position at a large cultivator which was purchased by a multistate operator (MSO; a cannabis business with multiple locations in two or more states). From her entry-level position, she began to manage the clone room and got involved with training new employees. Then, she was promoted to shift supervisor and hiring manager for her cultivation team. Her next step is likely to be assistant master grower and then master grower where she can use all her accumulated cannabis cultivation knowledge.

Fiero speaks about her journey in cannabis cultivation, "Cannabis cultivation has taught me patience, and how to be comfortable with being uncomfortable. A passionate and persistent cultivator makes not only the best cultivator, but the strongest leader and teacher."

Nursery Owner or Employee
The cannabis nursery business is an interesting niche in the cannabis industry. They are similar to traditional nurseries or gardening centers where consumers can buy pots, seeds, clones, soil, fertilizers (also called soil amendments), and pest management materials. Both individual cannabis consumers or home growers and commercial growers can buy from these cannabis nurseries. Often, nurseries will give classes on growing and plant care. Passionate home gardeners and cultivation educators gravitate toward this opportunity, and experience in a nursery, home garden, or gardening center is all pluses.

Farmgate Operations
Imagine that you are driving down a country road. Up ahead, a sign near a farmer's driveway says, "Eggs $5, Local Honey $10." A few miles down the road you see a sign that really catches your attention, "Farm Grown Cannabis for Sale." These two farm-based businesses are not so different!

A farmgate operation is one in which a cannabis farmer can sell their harvested cannabis directly to consumers. This model might include allowing customers to visit the farm to enjoy a tour of the cultivation process in addition to purchasing cannabis products on-site. It's similar to a winery or a farmer's market experience, providing a more personal and educational retail experience for consumers. This direct-to-consumer approach can be beneficial for both growers and buyers, as it cuts out the middleman, potentially lowering prices and fostering a stronger connection between the producer and the consumer.

Currently, farmgate operations are only permitted in a few provinces in Canada, but several states in the United States are exploring farmgate operations too. These states, including New York and California, will have to implement specific regulations and licensing requirements to ensure that these operations meet safety and compliance standards, such as only allowing adults twenty-one or older to enter the farm or purchase products.

Susan Dupej, a postdoctoral fellow at the University of Guelph in Canada who specializes in cannabis hospitality and tourism research, said that farmgate operations are important because "Farmgate allows for a licensed cannabis producer to operate a provincially regulated retail store at the facility/farm site and sell cannabis directly to the consumer. The opportunity to purchase cannabis at the production facility is a consumptive experience characteristic of agritourism attractions, as are facility/farm tours and sampling tasting rooms."

Dupej goes on to explain how farmgate operations work, "Cannabis production regulations are federally managed by Health Canada. Farmgate requires both a cannabis processing license as well as a product sales amendment in order to sell cannabis products into a provincially managed retail system. It is then up to the provinces to manage retail as they see fit and regulate where and how cannabis can be sold to the public. Currently Ontario, British Columbia and New Brunswick are the only provinces with cannabis farmgate."

For those passionate about cannabis cultivation and eager to engage directly with consumers, a career in farmgate operations can be incredibly rewarding. It offers a unique blend of agricultural, retail, and educational roles, allowing individuals to share their knowledge and products in a hands-on, interactive setting. This career path is perfect for those who enjoy working outdoors, have a knack for customer service, and want to participate in an emerging cannabis industry practice.

Extraction and Processing

All of the cannabis products you see available in dispensaries that are not cannabis flower (which is smokable cannabis) are created via extraction and processing. Extraction is the operation by which cannabinoids and terpenes are taken from the cannabis plant matter to be infused into cannabis products. Processing is the step by which those substances are turned into consumer products. New science is being applied to these procedures on an ongoing basis, so it's another dynamic sector of the industry.

One of the challenges of running a cannabis processing facility is figuring out which product or products to specialize in and to focus on quality control. The following are common examples of dispensary products created via these operations:

- gummies
- chocolates
- baked goods
- infused beverages
- vape oil
- lotions
- salves
- health and beauty aids like CBD shampoo and conditioner
- suppositories

The Extraction Process

Essentially, extraction is the process of taking substances like cannabinoids and terpenes out of parts of the cannabis plant via chemical processes. The extraction process can be performed in several ways, and they can be simple or complex. Depending on the end product the extractor is looking to create, the goals of extraction are usually threefold: to isolate compounds like THC or CBD, to produce whole-plant extracts, or to concentrate certain chemicals. There are four common methods of extraction:

1. alcohol/ethanol extraction
2. CO_2 extraction
3. butane, propane, or hexane extraction
4. solventless extraction (using heat, pressure, water, or a combination of these elements)

Chapter 5

The alcohol extraction process uses alcohol as a reagent. A reagent is a substance or mixture for use in chemical analysis or other reactions. Ethanol is the most common alcohol used in this type of extraction process. Here, cannabis is soaked in alcohol and the resulting liquid is filtered. Then, the alcohol is allowed to evaporate. Several challenges exist when extracting with alcohol: chlorophyll has to be removed or the extract will taste bitter, temperature must be closely monitored because alcohol is highly flammable, and the process takes time. One benefit of alcohol extraction is that cannabinoids and terpenes can be extracted at the same time and used in additional products.

Extracting with CO_2 eliminates the need to use a reagent, which helps cut costs and cleaning expenses. The CO_2 process uses heat and pressure to turn CO_2 into a supercritical fluid.[3] A supercritical fluid is a substance that has reached its critical point, the temperature and pressure at which the distinction between liquid and gas can no longer be made.[4] This creates a useful solvent, a substance that facilitates chemical reactions, for the removal of specific cannabis compounds. Not surprisingly, the equipment cost for CO_2 machines is very expensive, but the process provides better yields and minimizes wasted material. This sophisticated equipment can be used to extract specific compounds when the pressure, temperature, and processing time are changed, or a combination thereof. Also, after the extraction, the CO_2 can be filtered and reused, which lessens the amount of waste produced. The process is clean, as any remaining CO_2 solvent will simply evaporate, leaving the extractor with a clean product.

Extracting using butane, propane, or hexane (hydrocarbons) is a low-cost process. Usually, this process creates hash oil or shatter and usually contains THC, CBD, and some terpenes. The process starts by combining liquid butane (the most popular hydrocarbon used for cannabis extraction) and cannabis in a pressurized, heated system. Evaporation is used under a vacuum which removes the butane solvent, and the vacuum turns the butane into an easily removable vapor. Using propane is similar to the butane process but extraction can occur at a lower temperature which may be useful in preserving terpenes that "burn off" at high temperatures. There are some notes of caution surrounding hydrocarbon extraction. One is that these substances are highly flammable, so care must be used in all steps of the process. Then, these substances are toxic; extractors must be mindful to remove all butane, propane, and any other hydrocarbons from any product.

Solventless cannabis extraction is a natural method that avoids the use of chemicals like alcohol or butane, instead relying on physical processes such as heat, pressure, or water to extract cannabinoids and terpenes from the cannabis plant. This method includes techniques like rosin pressing, where heat and pressure are applied to the plant material to release its essential oils. Another technique becoming more and more popular because it is inexpensive and preserves the flavor of the plant is ice water extraction. Ice water extraction uses cold water and agitation to separate trichomes from the plant. Essentially, the cannabis plant's trichomes are flash-frozen for future use. Solventless extraction is prized for producing pure, flavorful extracts without the risk of residual solvents, making it a popular choice for those seeking a clean and natural product. While the process can be labor-intensive and yield less than solvent-based methods, it results in high-quality extracts that capture the full spectrum of the plant's compounds.

There are even a few solventless trichome extraction methods that are mainly designed for personal consumption rather than commercial sale, which create kief, hash, and rosin. Kief is the resulting "dust" in a grinder or at the bottom of a jar of cannabis buds; they are the trichomes that fall off during handling. Consumers often save their kief in a separate jar and add it to smokeable cannabis to increase its potency. Hash, which is just concentrated cannabis, is created using ice water to freeze the trichomes, which fall off the bud, and then they are pressed into a brick or ball and again, it is smoked. Finally, rosin is created with a commercial press or a hair straightener, parchment paper, and heavy heat-proof gloves. Cannabis flower is placed between pieces of parchment paper, the hair straightener is heated, and then extreme pressure is used to squeeze the bud. The result is a small stream of potent honey-like liquid. This liquid is often brushed on a joint to add potency.

Chapter 5

Edibles Production
Edibles are currently one of the fastest-growing parts of the cannabis market. To date, smoking cannabis and vaping are the number one and two methods of consumption. However, the edibles market is growing quickly. Edibles are created using CBD- or THC-infused oil or butter. Cannabis molecules just need fat molecules to adhere to, so various foodstuffs can be infused. Some of the most popular infused oils are olive oil, coconut oil, butter, and ghee. But vegetable oil, avocado oil, honey, and even maple syrup can all be infused too.

Cannabis edibles are popular because they offer a smoke-free alternative to traditional consumption methods. These tasty treats are made by infusing oils or butter with cannabinoids like CBD and THC. The process begins by decarboxylating, or slow roasting, the cannabis to activate the cannabinoids, which are then mixed with a fat-based ingredient such as olive oil, coconut oil, butter, or ghee. This infused base can be incorporated into a variety of recipes, from baked goods like brownies and cookies to savory dishes and even beverages. The versatility of the infusion process allows for a wide range of edibles, including chocolates, gummies, sauces, and more, each delivering a consistent and controlled dose of cannabinoids. This method not only provides a discreet and convenient way to enjoy cannabis but also offers a longer-lasting and often more intense experience compared to smoking or vaping. One new segment of the edibles market to keep an eye on are fast-acting or fast-delivery edibles. Fast-acting cannabis edibles are specially formulated to deliver the effects of cannabinoids more quickly than traditional edibles, often within fifteen to thirty minutes. This rapid onset is achieved through advanced nanotechnology that enhances the absorption of cannabinoids, providing a quicker and more predictable experience.

When it comes to cannabis beverages, the science of cannabis infusion is fascinating. Cannabinoids are lipids, which means they are insoluble in water. Their insolubility has posed a conundrum for those dreaming of a cannabis drink: oil is immiscible with water. Any mixture of cannabinoids and water would separate, and no one wants to buy or drink an unmixed beverage! However, cannabis scientists have found a way to emulsify cannabis molecules. Emulsion is the process by which two or more liquids that are normally unmixable—in this case, hydrophobic cannabinoids and water—can be diffused evenly throughout a mixture. In the cannabis beverage market, it is typical that the drinks are fast-acting/fast-delivery products as manufacturers are trying to mimic the experience of drinking alcohol.

One important consideration when viewing the consumption and marketability of cannabis edibles and infused beverages is dosage. Most states that allow for the sale of edibles require an individual serving portion to be ten milligrams. Sometimes each serving must be wrapped separately, or it must be plainly intuitive what a ten-milligram serving size is. For example, if a chocolate bar contains one hundred milligrams of THC and has ten squares, it is easy to figure out that an individual square of chocolate has ten milligrams of THC.

The edibles sector faces the challenge of consumer education. Traditional edibles such as brownies or cookies take a relatively long time to interact with a consumer's system, from thirty minutes to two hours, and then the high, if it is THC infused, may last up to eight hours. Conversely, fast-acting edibles or beverages produce effects in about twenty to thirty minutes. This short time frame makes for a more predictable edible experience.

Two major mistakes that edible consumers make are (1) starting with a dose that is too high (and you only know your dose after trial and error) and (2) consuming more edibles before the effect kicks in. Either of these conditions can make for an uncomfortable high, so we advise consumers to "go low and slow." In addition, there is little correlation between one's fitness, weight, or gender and when edibles will interact; it's a very personal experience learned over time. To start, a consumer may only want to take a 2.5 milligram dose and then increase the dose each time by 2.5 milligrams until the desired effect is reached.

Tanmoy "TJ" Jadhav, founder and CEO of MoJo Botanica, shares some insights on what it's like to work in a processing facility, "This enterprise sits at the intersection of a pharmaceutical grade scientific lab, a food service establishment, and a consumer packaged goods company. Our processes involve both solventless and solvent-based extraction techniques, demanding an advanced grasp of scientific principles along with meticulous attention to detail. Further, given that our products are created for human consumption, we rigorously adhere to the highest food safety standards while ensuring the creation of a consistently replicable product, safely and responsibly. We are committed to implementing good manufacturing practices to uphold superior quality standards consistently and at scale. Then, our responsibilities extend beyond production; and just like a CPG company, our products rely on the strength of our brands—the brand identity, its mission, values, narrative, and packaging. Of course, for the products to become a reality and subsequently, to get them into the hands of the end customers, the supply chain is of critical importance here, both for the business inputs as well as the outputs."

When talking about working in the cannabis industry, Jadhav goes on to say, "For me, I'm literally living the dream. In business literature, you will often read about product-market fit. Which basically says that you need to create products that the market wants. I like to add one more dimension to it: product-market-person fit. Having the right person in the role of making those products makes those products even better and makes the person working on those products happy and satisfied in their job." As mentioned in chapter 4, this is a key consideration when deciding how and where to pivot your career into the cannabis industry.

The Role of Testing in the Extraction Process

A key component of the extraction and processing of cannabis is regular testing throughout the production process. Products must be tested several times before they're finished, let alone before they're packaged and hit shelves. For example, a processor will want to know the composition of the cannabis flower they are starting with. Lab technicians use a procedure called chromatography, a laboratory technique for the separation of a mixture into its components. Liquid chromatography determines which cannabinoids are present and gas chromatography reveals terpene content. At this point, testing for impurities such as the presence of pesticides, heavy metals, microbial contamination, and mold is conducted as well. After the extraction process takes place, additional testing will show the potency of the oil and which cannabinoids and terpenes are present. Another impurity test may be conducted to ensure that there is no remaining butane, propane, or CO_2, and before a product goes to market, sometimes stability tests are required (to make sure the product doesn't change or degrade over time). A final test will document the potency and percentages of terpenes. All these tests, but especially the final test, are conducted by independent third parties who have no connection to the grower or processor. This ensures impartial, accurate results, and it is often used to market the safety of a product to consumers. Note that as a cannabis consumer you have the right to ask for a product's COA (certificate of analysis) which is a required lab test that lists the product's cannabinoid levels, and the results of the tests for mold, microbials, pesticides, and other contaminants per state law. It ensures that the product is safe for consumption.

How Cannabis Products Get to Market
Part of what makes an extractor and processor successful is to produce a product that is:

- in demand
- carefully dosed
- fully tested
- clearly labeled
- correctly branded

This requires market research to determine which products an extractor or processor should make. All products must be dosed and labeled in accordance with local and state regulations. Plus, consumers are becoming more sophisticated, want additional information about cannabis products, and desire the assurance that products have been fully tested. Therefore, labels should be thorough but easy to read and understand.

Then, producers should be thoughtful of their product brand. Most brands are currently being developed in-house. In some cases, producers partner with celebrity brands. Finally, a sales pipeline to dispensaries must be developed. This means that producers must forge relationships with dispensaries as soon as the product is in development. In the meanwhile, provisions need to be made to store products securely, transport them safely, and track inventory precisely.

Career Opportunities in the Extraction and Processing Sector

The primary images that may leap to mind when considering careers in cannabis extraction or processing may be a heavy machinery oil extraction technician or an edibles baker. But processing goes far beyond these careers. Extraction and processing take many of the same skills of any profitable business but with a leaning toward scientific inquiry and achievement. Some careers you may not have thought of include product research and development, salesperson or dispensary business development, lab testing (lab assistant), branding specialist or web developer, security and delivery, accounting, and compliance director or community educator. Let's take a look at some of these careers in a bit more detail.

Lab Technicians: Extraction, Processing, Testing

One of the most widely needed roles in this sector is lab technician. At any given operation, teams of lab technicians work to extract, process, and test to produce the best possible cannabis products. A technician's role is integral to ensuring the quality and safety of cannabis products through meticulous testing and analysis. Additionally, technicians must document and report test results accurately, contributing to the overall quality control process in the production of cannabis goods.

Extraction technicians utilize equipment and solvents like butane or propane to extract desired compounds from cannabis plants. Their expertise lies in understanding the intricate processes involved in separating cannabinoids, terpenes, and other valuable constituents from the plant material. By carefully controlling variables like temperature, pressure, and extraction time, they ensure the efficient extraction of target compounds while minimizing the extraction of unwanted components. This meticulous approach is essential for producing high-quality cannabis extracts that maintain the desired potency, flavor, and purity, meeting the stringent standards of the industry and ensuring consumer safety and satisfaction.

After extraction, processing technicians step in to transform these extracts into a diverse array of cannabis products. They employ their expertise to refine and formulate extracts into different forms, such as oils, concentrates, tinctures, and edibles. Using precise measurements and techniques, they carefully blend extracts with other ingredients to create products with consistent potency, flavor, and texture. Whether crafting vape cartridges, infused chocolates, or topical creams, processing technicians play a pivotal role in shaping the final products that consumers enjoy. Their attention to detail ensures that each product meets quality standards and regulatory requirements, contributing to a thriving and diverse cannabis market.

Testing technicians conduct laboratory analyses to assess potency, identify terpene profiles, and screen for contaminants like pesticides and mold. Their meticulous testing procedures and adherence to regulations play a crucial role in maintaining consumer confidence and protecting public health. These roles require attention to detail, scientific expertise, and a commitment to upholding rigorous quality standards in compliance with regulations.

While these three roles (extraction technician, processing technician, and testing technician) have much in common, there are some differences. Here is a quick overview: Extraction technicians specialize in using equipment and solvents to extract compounds from cannabis plants, focusing on separating cannabinoids and terpenes efficiently. Processing technicians refine and formulate extracts into various products, ensuring consistent potency, flavor, and texture. Testing technicians conduct analyses to assess potency, identify terpene profiles, and screen for contaminants, to ensure product safety and quality. Each role requires attention to detail, and adherence to regulations, contributing to the overall quality control process in the cannabis industry.

To become an extraction technician, one typically needs to be at least twenty-one years old and possess a degree in biology, chemistry, or physics. Candidates should have a strong foundation in laboratory sciences, including familiarity with analytical instruments and equipment.

Proficiency in interpreting test results and adherence to cannabis testing regulations are essential. Successful lab technicians demonstrate analytical thinking, meticulous attention to detail, and a dedication to ensuring product safety and quality. If you're passionate about scientific excellence and contributing to industry standards, a career as a lab technician offers stability and competitive pay.

Edibles Producer and Baker
Many edibles producers and bakers come from a cooking, catering, or food service background. An edibles producer may be an entry-level technician or a more experienced kitchen manager. As you may have guessed, an edibles employee must be able to create delicious flavors while maintaining precise cannabis dosing standards in a sanitary environment. Many states mandate that an edible single serving size be no greater than ten milligrams of THC and no more than one hundred milligrams per entire product.

Some of the most common duties that are performed include: properly using kitchen equipment, cleaning and organizing work areas, following all local and state food preparation rules, maintaining accurate records, creating accurate labels, and following SOPs. Experience in baking or cooking in a restaurant or catering company, distribution, warehouse, or product creation experience in another beverage company are all assets when joining an edibles or cannabis-infused beverage operation. Finally, another sometimes overlooked opportunity when examining the edibles market is businesses that cater to cannabis tourism and offer infused meals and cooking with cannabis demonstrations. One thing you will learn as you get into the cannabis business is that the metric system is often used. Table 5.1

Cannabis Packaging Expert
As a packager in the cannabis industry, you will play a crucial role in ensuring the safe and efficient packaging of cannabis products for distribution. Cannabis packagers often come from design studios that make packaging for diverse consumer products from toys to apparel to pharmaceuticals to food. Packaging options are dictated by local and state

Table 5.1 Measurements Table

Measurement Conversions Chart

U.S. Measurement	Metric Equivalent
1/4 ounce	7 grams
1/2 ounce	14 grams
3/4 ounce	21 grams
1 ounce	28 grams
1 pound	454 grams
Dash or pinch	About 1/8 teaspoon or less
1 teaspoon	5 milliliters (ml)
3 teaspoons	1 tablespoon
1 tablespoon	15 milliliters (ml)
2 tablespoons	1 fluid ounce
4 tablespoons	1/4 cup or 2 fluid ounces
16 tablespoons	1 cup or 8 fluid ounces
1 cup	1/4 liter
2 cups	1 pint
2 pints	1 quart
1 quart	1 scant liter
4 quarts	1 gallon

Notes:
Converting Fahrenheit to Celsius:
To convert Fahrenheit temperature into Celsius (also known as Centigrade), use the following formula: Subtract 32, multiply by 5, and then divide by 9.
For example, to convert 200 degrees Fahrenheit into Celsius:
200 − 32 = 168
168 × 5 = 840
840 ÷ 9 = 93.3 degrees Celsius
Converting Celsius to Fahrenheit:
To convert Celsius (sometimes called Centigrade) into Fahrenheit, use the following formula: Multiply by 9, divide by 5, and then add 32.
For example, to convert 150 degrees Celsius to Fahrenheit:
150 × 9 = 1350
1350 ÷ 5 = 270
270 + 32 = 302 degrees Fahrenheit

regulations and at a minimum must make clear that the product inside is cannabis, is intended for adults, is dosed at a certain percentage, and contains particular ingredients. The packager's challenge is to balance the attractiveness of the label with a clear delivery of the product contents and appropriate regulatory guidelines. Too, the packaging must balance being child- and pet-resistant while still being easily opened by adults, especially for medical patients who may have limited dexterity. Finally, the packaging shouldn't create any unnecessary waste.

Some packagers started as artists and still others specialize in graphic design. Most often these jobs are one-time, contract employees, and project-based so cannabis packagers try to get a full slate of clients across different product categories. This position requires meticulous attention to detail, as accuracy is paramount to complying with regulatory requirements and maintaining product integrity. Candidates for this role should possess strong organizational skills, precision in measuring and weighing, and the ability to follow detailed instructions consistently. Attention to detail is critical to ensure compliance with regulatory guidelines and maintain product quality. Knowledge of packaging equipment and familiarity with industry-specific regulations is a plus. Additionally, excellent communication skills and the ability to work collaboratively within a team are important.

Examining the Hemp Industry

With the excitement surrounding the rise of legal cannabis and the resulting cultivation, processing, and dispensary businesses, we shouldn't forget the many job opportunities that result from the reintroduction of hemp, one of our most valuable crops! In terms of dollars and cents, the hemp industry is primed to compete with if not eclipse the recreational cannabis industry. Given time, hemp may rise to its full potential creating more than twenty-five thousand products in nine markets: textiles, automotive, construction materials, food and beverage, agriculture, recycling (plastic and other product replacement), paper, furniture, and personal care items (think: health and beauty aids). These products are crafted from raw materials sourced from the industrial hemp plant, including fiber, hurds, and hemp seeds. It is a sustainable, naturally pest- and drought-resistant, and fast-growing crop that is ideal to replace declining crops like tobacco. While we focus our attention on the legalization of cannabis, we should not overlook what hemp will bring to our economy. Resulting hemp jobs will largely be cultivators and their support staff, extractors, processors, testers, and product developers. These positions will be paid in accordance with other similar cannabis jobs in the medical and adult-use markets.

Hemp expert Marne Coit, founder and principal, Coit Consulting LLC and adjunct law professor at Wake Forest School of Law, talks about the potential for the industrial hemp business, saying, "For seven years, I've been immersed in the evolving hemp industry, witnessing enormous growth and change. I'm hopeful that the next decade will bring the infrastructure needed to support hemp grain and fiber, leading to a variety of innovative products." As you'll see, her optimism is well-placed.

An overhead view of the hemp sector might be helpful: Starting in 2018, largely due to the 2018 Farm Bill, the US hemp market experienced rapid growth. And while that growth pace slacked in the next few years because of overproduction and the COVID-19 pandemic, the bill opened up a plethora of hemp opportunities, from farming to manufacturing and retail. In the last few years we have noted that the market is beginning to steady.

Where we stand now:

- According to the National Hemp Report released by the US Department of Agriculture on April 17, 2024, and conducted by the National Agricultural Statistics Service, here are figures from 2023 regarding hemp production. Note that "Under Protection" means that this hemp was grown indoors. "In the Open" of course refers to hemp grown outdoors.[5]
    - 2023 Industrial Hemp Value $291 Million[6]
    - 2023 Industrial Hemp in the Open Value $258 Million[7]
    - 2023 Industrial Hemp Under Protection Value $32.9 Million[8]

Of course, one of the most promising sectors within the hemp industry is farming. With steady demand for hemp-derived products, farmers across the nation are turning their attention to hemp cultivation. Jobs in cultivation include field workers and agronomists to farm managers and equipment operators. With the potential for further expansion, the demand for skilled professionals in hemp farming is only expected to grow.

Beyond farming, the hemp industry offers a myriad of job opportunities in processing and manufacturing. As the market for hemp-derived products continues to diversify, so too do the career prospects within the sector. From extraction technicians and laboratory scientists to product formulators and quality control specialists, there is a growing demand for individuals with expertise in hemp processing and manufacturing. In 2020, the hemp processing market in the United States was valued at over $800 million, and with projections indicating continued growth, the need for skilled workers in this field is poised to expand.[9]

The retail sector is another area of the hemp industry experiencing rapid growth and job creation. With hemp-derived products ranging from CBD oils and tinctures to textiles and construction materials, retailers are tapping into a booming market fueled by consumer demand for natural, sustainable alternatives. In 2022, sales of hemp-derived CBD products nearly eclipsed $2 billion, a testament to the immense potential of the retail sector within the hemp industry. This surge in demand has led to a surge in retail jobs, from sales associates and store managers to marketing specialists and e-commerce experts. As consumer awareness and acceptance of hemp products continue to grow, so too will the opportunities for employment within the retail sector.

In conclusion, the US hemp market presents a wealth of opportunities for job seekers across various sectors, from farming and processing to retail. With impressive growth numbers and a diverse range of products driving the industry forward, the potential for career advancement and job creation in the hemp industry is virtually limitless. Whether you're passionate about agriculture, science, manufacturing, or sales, there's a place for you in the rapidly expanding world of hemp.

Career Opportunities in Hemp
Hemp Grower
In previous sections, the cultivar/grower position was primarily treated as being geared toward the indoor or greenhouse growing of cannabis containing both THC and CBD. However, being a hemp grower is potentially advantageous as it can be sold for a variety of reasons, especially when produced industrially. The versatility of hemp as a crop makes it an

attractive option for farmers looking to diversify their agricultural practices and tap into emerging markets for hemp-derived products. One of the challenges that hemp farmers face is keeping the THC levels in their crops below 0.3 percent. So, a grower must start with the right seeds and must harvest before THC levels exceed the legal 0.3 percent limit.

An interesting side note is that some colleges are now offering courses in hemp cultivation that are connected to local hemp farms. In these cases, colleges collaborate with farmers to teach their students how to grow hemp. Students learn which seeds and strains to grow, which nutrients to use, how far away the plants must be planted from each other, how to deal with pests, lighting/sun requirements, growth cycles, and which parts of the plant are used for different products. Colleges often test and conduct research using hemp plants as well.

Hemp Processors

Once hemp is grown it needs to be processed to become a consumer product. Depending on the type of product that is to be created, different parts of the plants are used.

- The outside of the stems (bast fiber) is strong and stringy, so they are often used for rope, netting, canvas, and apparel.
- The inside of the stems (the hurd) is more pliable and can be used to make hempcrete, insulation, mulch, and animal bedding.
- The stalk is used to create biofuel, paper, and cardboard.
- Leaves and flower buds are valuable because they can yield CBD oil.
- Other parts of the plant that are used include seeds which are used to produce bread, milk, flour, lubricants, paint, and health and beauty aids.
- Even the roots can be brewed to make medicinal tea, and they can also be made into salves and lotions.

This all means that the processing step involves the entire plant but takes different methods and processes to secure the final product. Some experienced processors are schooled in each process, but many

CHAPTER 5

processors may have some background knowledge and then learn on the job. Compensation for hemp processors varies by experience and ranges widely. It is also a crucial step in the hemp supply chain as without industrial hemp processing many goods simply cannot be produced. Hemp processing will greatly move the whole hemp industry forward!

CBD Suppliers
According to LightSpeed, the global CBD trade hit $9.4 million in 2023.[10] This exponential growth of the CBD supplier market is emblematic of the burgeoning cannabis industry's expansion into mainstream commerce. This meteoric rise in market value underscores the widespread acceptance and adoption of CBD as a wellness remedy, fueling a robust ecosystem of suppliers catering to diverse consumer preferences and needs.

This unprecedented growth in the CBD supplier market has not only created a wealth of entrepreneurial opportunities but has also catalyzed the evolution of specialized careers within the hemp industry. From cultivation and extraction to product formulation and distribution, the demand for skilled professionals proficient in navigating the complex regulatory landscape and harnessing the therapeutic potential of CBD continues to escalate. As the industry matures, new opportunities will emerge as well.

Hemp as Fabrics
Recently Levi's announced that they were going to be making jeans out of hemp for export to China.[11] This announcement was greeted with enthusiasm by hemp farmers because it could be the start of big business in the apparel sector. Of course, jeans aren't the only item that can be made from hemp. Any article of clothing can be produced with hemp, and the plant also blends well with cotton, silk, rayon, linen, and wool. In addition to clothing, hemp can be made into rope, rugs, and more.

The expansion of the hemp industry into fabric production would create various jobs, including textile processing, fabric weaving, and garment manufacturing. Additionally, there would be roles in quality control, product design, and marketing. Jobs in logistics for transporting raw hemp and finished products, as well as retail positions for selling hemp-based clothing and goods, would also be generated. This market expansion would benefit farmers, factory workers, designers, and sales professionals, among others.

Hemp as Paper
Hemp paper is a sustainable alternative to traditional tree-based paper. Made from the fibers of the hemp plant, it is more durable and environmentally friendly. Hemp paper production uses significantly less water and energy and does not require bleaching, reducing toxic waste. Historically, hemp was a primary source for paper-making, and modern hemp paper is used for specialty items such as cigarette papers and eco-friendly packaging. Its rapid growth cycle and high cellulose content make it an ideal renewable resource for the paper industry. One of the current limitations on its market appeal, however, is that it is more expensive to produce than traditional paper. The hemp paper industry is creating numerous jobs across various sectors. According to the National Hemp Association, the industry is projected to generate thousands of jobs in the coming years, including roles in farming, processing, and manufacturing. Current estimates suggest that for every one thousand acres of hemp farmed, around fifty jobs are created.

Hemp Seed as a Superfood
Superfoods are found to have high nutritional content, and they are directly tied to healthy eating. New foods are found (or marketed) to be superfoods every day. Because hemp seeds have such attractive health advantages, they could be a lucrative business opportunity. From an international perspective, in 2023 Canada exported $55 million worth of hempseed-based products to the United States, and the United States produced roughly $4 million worth of hemp grain.[12]

Hemp production means that hemp, hemp seeds, and related products will need to be harvested, processed, packaged, and labeled like any other consumer product. Then, the products have to get to the consumer via supermarkets and direct-to-customer sales. To see evidence of the emerging popularity of varieties of hemp as a superfood just walk into a supermarket and see hemp milk, hemp hearts (the soft inside of hemp seeds used to add nutrition to cereal, yogurt, soups and more), hemp flour, and hemp cooking oil. Nutty tasting and high in protein, hemp as a foodstuff looks like it has a bright future.

Hemp in Bioplastics
Several companies are developing bioplastics made from hemp for packaging and other products. This could mark the beginning of a significant new market in the bioplastics industry. Hemp bioplastics can be used in a wide range of products, from food containers to automotive parts. Unlike traditional plastics, hemp bioplastics are biodegradable and environmentally friendly. This innovation could reduce plastic waste and promote sustainable practices.

According to industry estimates, the emerging hemp bioplastics market could generate thousands of positions in agriculture, manufacturing, research and development, and logistics. Specifically, Hemp, Inc.'s processing centers have already created over two hundred seasonal and year-round jobs. Additionally, there are hopes that the broader bioplastics market will control up to 40 percent of the plastic packaging industry by 2030, further driving job creation in various sectors such as engineering, technical support, and sales.[13]

Hemp as Building Material
Hemp can also be used as a building material. The hemp fiber (the inner woody core) is mixed with plaster or lime to create a product called Hempcrete or Hemplime. The resulting product weighs about one-eighth the weight of cement and is used as an insulating material. A fully cured block of hempcrete can float in water. It is used not only as a structural element but also as insulation between framing. Hempcrete is cheaper to produce than cement and results in less pollution.

According to the US Hemp Building Association, there are projections for substantial job creation in roles such as manufacturing, installation, and logistics, supported by both private investment and government initiatives. For instance, Oregon State University's Global Hemp Innovation Center received a $10 million grant to spur hemp-related economic development, including job creation in hemp construction across several states.[14]

Hemp as Biofuel

Hemp can be converted into biofuel through processes like cellulolysis and pyrolysis, which utilize various parts of the hemp plant, including seeds, fiber, and biomass. In cellulolysis, the plant material is shredded and chemically treated to release cellulose, which enzymes then break down into sugars. These sugars are fermented into ethanol and further processed into biofuels such as biodiesel. Pyrolysis involves heating fibrous plant matter to produce fuel-grade oils, a process economically viable due to its use of waste biomass. Hemp biofuel is renewable, potentially carbon-neutral, and can integrate with existing fuel infrastructure, offering a sustainable alternative to fossil fuels.[15]

As this sector scales up, it is expected to generate jobs in several areas, including farming, processing, research and development, and infrastructure maintenance. What's exciting is that this sector will help restore jobs in rural and agricultural regions where hemp is cultivated. These positions would span from agricultural workers and biotechnologists to engineers and logistics coordinators. However, substantial investment in infrastructure and technological advancements is necessary to realize this potential and ensure consistent fuel quality and compatibility with existing systems.

CHAPTER 6

Ancillary Cannabis Businesses

INTRODUCTION TO ANCILLARY ROLES

Consider this: how many jobs need to be done behind the scenes to facilitate that single moment of commerce—that is, the exchange of dollars for cannabis products? An ancillary cannabis job supports the plant-touching cannabis industry but does not deal directly with cannabis products. For example, a company that runs dispensaries might hire a lawyer. That lawyer would fall under the umbrella of ancillary services. Not only does the cannabis industry create the opportunity for people to work directly with the cannabis plant and cannabis products, but the industry also creates a wide-ranging set of opportunities for others to get involved in the cannabis economy.

The ancillary positions available, or rather necessary, for the hemp and cannabis industries will outpace the quantity of full-time hemp and cannabis jobs. Similar to the Gold Rush of the 1840s and 1850 when some of the most profitable businesses were, in fact, the ones that supplied and sold the picks, shovels, jeans, and other provisions to those prospecting for the gold itself, the ancillary cannabis industry will likely mirror the same dynamic.

Ancillary and support jobs are typically professional careers and their rate of pay is high. Often these companies, or individuals in the case of say, graphic designers, have multiple clients, with cannabis only being one sector they work in. For example, one might take on a career as an accountant without initially seeking to specialize as a cannabis accountant. This specialization may happen over time, but most often these professionals will continue to work with both cannabis and non-cannabis businesses alike. Depending on what state support service providers work in, cannabis may be one of the fastest-growing industries so it makes sense that some of them would become clients.

Above all, one way to think about participation in the hemp or cannabis industries is to examine your experiences and skills outside of cannabis and determine if there is a way for you to pivot your skills. Given that you are developing a baseline of cannabis knowledge by reading this book, pursuing other forms of cannabis education, and applying the guidance from chapter 4, you can be well on your way to gaining meaningful employment. The hemp and cannabis worlds need ancillary support services; perhaps this is your calling. How do your skills and interests fill in the blank: "____ and cannabis?"

BACK-OFFICE OPERATIONS

The back office is the backbone of a business. It refers to the support roles that contribute to running a business. Those in back-office positions perform roles that do not directly interact with products or customers. These roles are administrative or in support of the folks who are client-facing. While the back office may go "unnoticed" by the customer, it's essential to the daily operations of any business.

Typical back-office roles include bookkeepers, accountants, social media directors, and webmasters. Other back-office jobs often include governmental representatives, community liaisons, and compliance managers whose job is to monitor governmental cannabis regulations and to lobby on behalf of the dispensary. They develop relationships with local and state governmental officials and with other local businesses to ensure that any potential changes can be incorporated into the dispensary's business—hopefully without too much disruption and to maintain good working relationships with their neighboring businesses. Sometimes dispensaries will also hire a director of education whose job it is to write copy for the website, newsletters, informational pamphlets, and product descriptions, and to conduct educational seminars for the community and governmental officials.

Accounting, Bookkeeping, and Financial Advising

Cannabis operations want to work with knowledgeable, detail-oriented financial professionals with a keen interest in the cannabis industry. Accountants, bookkeepers, and financial advisors all play pivotal roles in a given cannabis business. Accountants and bookkeepers play a crucial part in managing financial records, ensuring compliance with the unique tax regulations of the cannabis industry, including tracking and reporting on sales, excise taxes, and deductions specific to the industry, and particularly Section 280E of the Tax Code, which "forbids businesses from deducting otherwise ordinary business expenses from gross income associated with the 'trafficking' of Schedule I or II substances, as defined by the Controlled Substances Act."[1] Responsibilities will include tracking expenses, maintaining accurate ledgers, and preparing financial reports. Bookkeepers traditionally track a business's daily transactions, bills, sales, and payroll. Accountants need the information that bookkeepers or bookkeeping systems provide. Accountants can look at a business's broad financial trends and make predictions and recommendations based on that information. As well, financial advisors can assist cannabis enterprises in finding specialized banking services or developing alternative financial solutions to manage transactions securely and compliantly.

To excel in either role, candidates need a solid understanding of accounting principles, excellent attention to detail, and the ability to juggle multiple financial tasks. Experience with industry-specific regulations and compliance is a big plus. Companies prefer candidates who have a background in accounting or finance, with specific knowledge of 280E and state regulations within the cannabis sector. A bachelor's degree in accounting, finance, or a related field is desirable, and professional certifications such as CPA (certified public accountant) or CMA (certified management accountant) or passing the Uniform Bookkeeper Certification Exam are a plus. Strong analytical skills, attention to detail, and proficiency in relevant accounting software are essential.

Stacey Udell, CPA and principal at HBK Cannabis Solutions, an accounting firm that has been specializing in cannabis services for several years, describes how "cannabis accounting" is different from traditional accounting. She explains, "Cannabis accounting differs from traditional accounting because it is more focused on gross profit than income due to the limit on deductibility of costs other than costs of goods sold and because there is limited access to financial services resulting in more cash operations than a typical business presenting challenges in terms of cash management and internal controls."

Udell goes on to tell a smile-inducing story about her first visit to a cultivation facility. When she first got started in the business she visited, "a cultivation facility in Pahrump, Nevada." She goes on to say, "After the site visit, the attorney I was with, and I had to drive an hour and a half back to Las Vegas for me to get a flight home. The attorney commented how his wife was going to be angry because her car was going to smell like pot. All of a sudden, I realized I had to go through TSA at the airport smelling like pot." While the story is somewhat tongue-in-cheek, the instance is an example of potentially unanticipated circumstances you have to deal with, including an outsider's perception of your occupational choice.

The bottom line as Stacey Udell is quick to mention is that cannabis accountants help their clients succeed. They do this by, "Educating our clients to enable them to understand their revenue, expenses, profit margins, and other key financial metrics, allowing them to make informed decisions and minimize their tax liabilities. We help clients plan with budgets and projections and provide strategic advice to our clients along the way. Our goal is to be trusted advisors, providing insights and support to help our clients achieve their financial goals and succeed in an emerging industry."

The Head of Communications

The head of communications is a critical role that will help shape a company's corporate communications strategy. The person in this role has the opportunity to put their fingerprints on the company's future. For example, they put a company's mission statement out in the world which is vital in terms of recruiting both customers and employees. They develop internal, external, and investor-facing messaging. They often write or sign off on press releases and manage incoming media requests, building ongoing relationships with media members. They must be able to court media contacts, leverage personal and professional networks, and drive interest in the company's story. Heads of communication prep colleagues and management teams for media and industry interactions, as well as lead, produce, and direct events like prospective and current investor meetings and roadshow and convention events. Then, they set social media goals across platforms, consistently analyzing corresponding data to keep senior management aware of progress toward objectives.

The ideal candidate will need to be equal parts strategist and hands-on executor with experience in the creation, management, and execution of sophisticated marketing and communications programs and campaigns including public relations, investor relations, internal employee communications, digital or social marketing, event marketing and thought leadership, and content creation, working at both the corporate level as well as with their subsidiary companies and brands.

Webmaster and Social Media Manager

Webmaster and social media manager is an essential role for any business. A company's website and online presence are often the first way a customer interacts with the business. The webmaster is responsible for the day-to-day management of a company's website and social media platforms. Webmasters ensure the smooth functioning and optimization of the company website, including regular updates, troubleshooting, and implementing search engine optimization (SEO) strategies to enhance online visibility. This role includes social media management, which involves producing engaging content, scheduling posts, and fostering community engagement across various platforms.

The ideal candidate possesses a blend of technical proficiency and creative flair. Proficiency in web development tools and content management systems, and a keen eye for design are crucial. Strong communication skills, brand knowledge, understanding of regulations, and attention to trends are a plus. The educational path for a webmaster and social media manager typically involves a combination of technical and marketing-related courses. Individuals aspiring for this role often pursue a mix of relevant courses in web development, digital marketing, social media management, writing, and graphic design. Qualifications most often include a bachelor's in computer science, web design, or a related field is required. As well, candidates must know basic programming such as CSS, HTML5, and Javascript, and SEO must be at the forefront of building out the business's online presence.

Cannabis Marketers and Content Writers
A cannabis marketer wears many hats. Depending on the type of cannabis business they are involved in they need to:

- tell the story of the business in an authentic way
- drive potential customers to the business
- interact with (or perform as) the social media manager and website designer
- get input from all other employees to get insight and help them handle problems
- provide information to customers and employees
- sometimes help train staff
- design campaigns and plan events
- create or promote thought leadership content through appearances on panels, writing articles, participating in podcasts as well as coordinating public relations or managing a separate public relations agency

People with these diverse skills often come from another industry where they handled marketing or may have a marketing degree with limited experience but with broad cannabis knowledge. Some of their experience may be in marketing, advertising, brand management, or sales. Content writing must also be in their skill set. Content writing tasks may be as diverse as describing services and hours of operation, writing blogs and articles, crafting marketing messages, and creating website content. Content writers and marketers commonly interface with other departments within a company, depending on its size. The challenge is to tell the story of the business and to help the other folks within the company do the same! Content writers also are employed to help with applications and licenses, much like grant writers in other industries. A clear communication style, simple language, and a deep understanding of cannabis issues all help to make a cannabis content writer successful. Often these jobs are paid by the hour or by the task. Of course, writers are expected to have strong editing and proofreading skills as well.

Depending on the type, size, and corporate structure of the business, there could also be a marketing manager who works in tandem with a social media manager and the head of communications. The marketing manager balances communicating stories and essential information to would-be consumers. They also create and promote thought-leadership content through appearances on panels, writing articles, participating in podcasts, as well as coordinating public relations or managing a separate public relations agency. A candidate with these diverse skills often comes from another industry where they handled marketing, or they may have a marketing degree with limited experience but with broad cannabis knowledge. Qualifications often include a bachelor's degree in business, marketing, advertising, communications, or another related field. Many employers may also require an MBA degree. You should also consider participating in a management training program or continuing education program at a business college to further improve your skills and highlight your commitment to your career development if this is the field you want to pursue.

Compliance Manager
A compliance manager ensures that company operations align with the ever-evolving laws and regulations of the cannabis sector. A compliance manager's primary responsibility is to meticulously navigate and interpret complex industry regulations, implementing and overseeing protocols to ensure a cannabis company remains in full compliance.

This unique opportunity welcomes individuals from diverse professional backgrounds, whether they are seasoned regulatory experts or someone eager to transition into a flourishing industry. Often these candidates are sourced from other sectors like casino gambling or alcoholic beverages, as these industries also face intricate legal and regulatory standards. The role demands strong attention to detail, superior organizational skills, the capacity to work across all teams, and an ability to adapt to the dynamic regulatory landscape. A compliance manager's contribution is instrumental in shaping a company's reputation for integrity and adherence to legal standards. This career is a cornerstone for success for a cannabis business. Often, a bachelor's degree in a field such as law, finance, or business administration is advantageous in pursuing a career as a compliance manager.

Cannabis Employment Recruiter
Recruiters often work as part of a third-party agency or internally in a role within a company looking to hire. Either way, these professionals handle the hiring or talent-acquisition process, finding and recruiting qualified and exciting candidates for various roles. Recruiters and recruiting agencies work in various industries, like healthcare, technology, media, and finance. The Vangst company is one of the foremost cannabis-specific recruiting agencies and works with more than 1,700 cannabis companies.[2]

As a recruiter, one must be able to explain how an employee's current skills would benefit a cannabis operation. In addition, they may have to battle a perception of stigma and prove that the cannabis industry is legitimate, regulated, safe, and an amazing opportunity. It also helps to have an outgoing personality and strong communication skills to excel in this position. Often, because there has not been a traditional path to cannabis employment, recruiters must look to comparable industries to find employees. Highly regulated industries such as pharmaceuticals and biotechnology and academic and scientific research often yield candidates who can pivot and become involved in the cannabis industry.

Human Resources
Human resource (HR) professionals in the cannabis industry deal with special requirements. HR professionals mitigate risk by interpreting compliance law and turning it into policies or actions that protect an employer or company against litigation from partners, suppliers, and employees. Some common HR responsibilities are:

- Hiring and training new employees

- Creating and maintaining policies and procedures for workers' problems, from wage questions to harassment incidents
- Relay and enforce business changes, such as disciplinary actions, contract updates, and salary adjustments
- Processing outgoing or terminated employees and contracts

HR professionals create and post appropriate, inclusive job ads, they are knowledgeable about state and local wage requirements, and they can provide guidance as to whether an employee can be considered a contract employee. Like any business, cannabis employers need to be educated in sexual harassment and discriminatory practices and the regulatory landscape. Each state has strict policies on what type of training must occur for employees and managers, and HR managers are trained to know what type of training must take place and how to document it.

One of the biggest benefits of employing a dedicated HR professional is that they effectively aid in keeping employees happy and retained. While it is a large cost to recruit, train, and replace an employee in any organization, the cost can be substantially more in an early-stage industry such as cannabis. HR personnel are imperative to ensure employees stay, helping ensure the integrity of the organization. Often HR professionals have an associate or bachelor's degree in HR management. To run a large operation, they may even have a master's in human resource management.

Legal Services

Undoubtedly, one of the largest service sectors for hemp and cannabis companies involves the employment of attorneys. Cannabis companies require a diverse range of legal services ranging from:

- helping with applications
- obtaining permits for cultivation, manufacturing, distribution, and retail operations
- fundraising
- interpreting state and national rules

- contractual matters, such as lease agreements, supplier contracts, and partnerships
- zoning advice
- representation in municipal meetings
- registering trademarks and protecting intellectual property
- general consulting

Law firms can even spearhead efforts to get cannabis legalized. One such prominent firm is Vicente LLP located in Denver with satellite offices across the country. Founding partner of Vicente LLP Brian Vicente remarked, "One of Vicente LLP's most notable achievements in the cannabis market is the pivotal role we played in shaping Colorado's cannabis landscape by drafting Amendment 64 and steering its successful campaign which laid the foundation for a thriving, regulated cannabis industry in the state. The billions in tax revenue generated since legalization have fueled essential projects like school construction and job creation, and the reduction of cannabis-related arrests has helped thousands of individuals avoid unfair sentences for recreational adult-use cannabis." Brian explains that his aha moment about entering the cannabis industry, "came as a young person when I realized the transformative potential it held from a social, legal, and economic perspective. Witnessing the tangible benefits, from tax revenues to job creation, sparked my desire to further cannabis in its capacity for positive change."

From the outright creation of legal cannabis markets, occupations providing legal services to cannabis companies encompass a variety of roles, including cannabis-focused attorneys who specialize in nearly every aspect of the business including the preparation of applications, representation at municipal meetings, zoning experts, compliance consultants, regulatory experts and more. These professionals specialize in interpreting complex legal language and applying cannabis laws and regulations, guiding companies through the intricacies of licensing processes and compliance requirements. Moreover, intellectual property lawyers play a crucial role in assisting cannabis companies with trademark and patent filings to protect their brands, innovations, and proprietary technologies.

By leveraging the expertise of these legal professionals, cannabis companies can mitigate legal risks, ensure compliance with regulations, and navigate the complexities of the legal environment in which they operate.

Insurance Services

Occupations providing insurance services to hemp and cannabis companies include insurance brokers, underwriters, and risk management consultants. These professionals work closely with companies to assess their specific insurance needs and customize policies to address their unique risks and requirements. Claims adjusters play a vital role in facilitating the claims process and ensuring timely resolution in the event of an insured loss. By collaborating with these insurance professionals, hemp and cannabis companies can safeguard their assets, mitigate liabilities, and protect against unforeseen risks, thereby supporting the sustainability and growth of their businesses.

Cannabis companies require a range of insurance services to mitigate risks inherent in their operations. They often need specialized property and casualty insurance to protect their facilities, equipment, and inventory from risks such as theft, fire, and natural disasters. Given the unique nature of cannabis cultivation and processing facilities, tailored insurance policies are essential to address the specific risks associated with these operations. Additionally, liability insurance is crucial to protect hemp and cannabis companies from potential legal claims related to product liability, bodily injury, or property damage arising from their products or services.

Zoning Specialist and Real Estate Agents

Finding a suitable location to operate a cannabis business poses a significant challenge for potential owners. Because many state markets let townships designate where cannabis businesses can and cannot function, real estate is a dear commodity. Townships often limit the number of cannabis facilities, which can spur a bidding war for compliant real estate.

Two key partners that can help navigate this tricky area are zoning specialists and real estate agents. Zoning specialists can expertly review township zoning maps to determine where cannabis businesses are allowed, and even where they should be allowed. They often interface with city officials to help businesses reach opening day.

Then, cannabis-savvy real estate agents help identify and negotiate with property owners to secure real estate. This may mean they help with an outright purchase or set up leasing agreements. In some cases, real estate may be owned by a federally regulated bank, like Bank of America, and real estate agents or attorneys will arrange to purchase the facility and then rent it back to a lessee. In some cases, it is the real estate agent who educates the property owner about the advantages and risks of getting involved with a cannabis company. Finally, in simplest terms zoning specialists, real estate agents, and even real estate attorneys take their existing knowledge and connections, which have to be informed by a baseline of cannabis knowledge, to navigate these tricky waters. They also don't need a special license to work in this area.

THE SUPPLY CHAIN

In simple terms, cannabis companies rely on a variety of supply chain services to ensure the efficient movement of products from cultivation to consumption. Warehousing plays a crucial role in the supply chain by providing storage for raw materials, intermediate products, and finished goods. These facilities are essential for maintaining product quality and inventory management, allowing companies to meet demand fluctuations while minimizing stockouts and excess inventory. Additionally, warehouses often serve as distribution centers, facilitating the movement of products to retail locations or in some cases even directly to consumers.

Efficiently and compliantly moving products is a fundamental aspect of the cannabis supply chain, involving the transportation of products between different points in the supply network. Whether it's transporting raw materials from cultivation facilities to manufacturing sites or delivering finished products to distribution centers or retail outlets, shipping ensures the timely and secure movement of goods. This may involve various modes of transportation, including ships, trucks, trains, and in the future maybe even drones, depending on the distance and urgency of delivery.

Delivery services play a crucial role in the final stage of the cannabis supply chain, ensuring that products reach consumers efficiently and safely. This may involve direct-to-consumer delivery for online orders or distribution to retail locations for purchase by consumers. Delivery services must adhere to strict regulations governing the transportation of cannabis products, including age verification and secure packaging requirements, to ensure compliance and safety. By effectively coordinating delivery logistics, cannabis companies can enhance customer satisfaction and loyalty while optimizing their supply chain operations.

Purchasing, Inventory Control, and Merchandising

Merchandising is a key role involving purchasing, managing inventory, and presenting products in their best light. This employee often has a corporate purchasing or retail buyer background. They must be up to date on product trends, know their local customers, conduct competitive research, and find reliable vendors. Sometimes this position is a promotion from a budtender position.

The main challenge for a merchandiser is to have enough product on hand without having too much product that isn't selling well. Data-driven decisions based on information from a point-of-sale system help the purchasing, inventory, and merchandising managers make more effective decisions. Finally, products must be attractively displayed and organized in an intuitive manner. Successful employees in these positions need to be team players as they work closely with all departments in the dispensary.

Wholesaling (Warehousing)

Wholesaling, also known as warehousing, serves as a crucial link between cultivators, manufacturers, and retailers. In New Jersey, for example, this class of license empowers license holders to engage in the storage, purchase, and sale of bulk cannabis flower and products, and this is a typical license in other states too. This type of business thrives in mature markets with a diverse array of products and brands. Often, cannabis wholesalers collaborate with distribution companies to efficiently bring products directly to consumers, making it a dynamic and essential aspect of the industry.

Within the realm of cannabis wholesaling, various career opportunities await individuals with diverse skill sets. Roles include warehouse managers, responsible for overseeing storage and logistics, inventory clerks managing product stock levels, salespeople connecting with retailers and negotiating deals, vehicle loaders ensuring timely and secure transportation, and back office staff like website designers, accountants, and photographers contributing to the business's overall success.

Professionals with a background in warehouse and delivery operations, gained from experiences at companies like Amazon and FedEx, may find a seamless transition into the cannabis wholesaling sector. Their expertise in managing large-scale logistics and optimizing supply chain processes can prove invaluable. As the cannabis market continues to evolve, the demand for skilled individuals in these roles is expected to grow. Finally, keep in mind that when cannabis is federally legal this segment of the market will explode as cannabis products from other states could now be sold at local dispensaries. Even international products from cannabis producers as diverse as Mexico, Colombia, and Jamaica may be sold in local dispensaries in the future.

Delivery (Direct to Consumers)

A cannabis delivery license allows the licensee to transport retail-purchased cannabis and cannabis products directly to consumers. Especially in markets where there are medical cannabis patients with limited mobility or transportation issues, this can be a useful service. In some states even though individual townships can opt out of the cannabis business they cannot prohibit delivery to their towns.

Sometimes dispensaries are also allowed to deliver, or they must subcontract with a delivery service that will pick up orders from the dispensary and deliver them directly to consumers. Often, delivery is not allowed to go to businesses, hotels, restaurants, or other public locations, so most deliveries go to private residences where deliverers check IDs. Here, payment has often already been made online. Potential careers at cannabis delivery facilities include drivers, inventory managers, general managers, website developers, security consultants, and bookkeepers or accountants. One tip about setting up a delivery operation is to try to locate your company near major roadways and in areas in which your service might be in demand, such as a locale where there's currently a lack of dispensaries.

Distribution (Business to Business)

New Jersey defines a cannabis distribution license as, "A Class 4 Cannabis Distribution license allows the holder to transport bulk cannabis and cannabis products between cannabis cultivators, manufacturers, or retailers within New Jersey." Note that this definition is fairly typical across the country and that New Jersey has six license classes. (Some states have more license categories while others have fewer.)

A helpful way to think about this kind of distribution career is to think about a truck you see rumbling down the highway emblazoned with dozens of beer, wine, and liquor logos. This truck is packed with multiple beers, wines, vodkas, tequilas, and other types of alcohol brands, destined for a liquor store. The liquor store—think dispensary!—uses this service because they can purchase multiple products from a single source to sell in their store.

Distributors are allowed to acquire and store products and must keep meticulous records. So, an inventory manager, workers to load the products, a salesperson to sign up both suppliers and dispensaries as customers, a general manager, and a driver qualified to drive a large delivery truck are all required to run this business. Usually, this type of business and career is not particularly popular until a state cannabis market starts to mature. Before this happens there are just not enough brands and products to make this business appealing.

Graphic Designer for Cannabis Packaging

As a graphic designer for cannabis packaging, you will be at the forefront of shaping the visual identity of cannabis products. Your role will involve creating visually appealing and compliant packaging designs that resonate with the target audience while adhering to regulatory guidelines. This position requires a unique blend of creativity, technical proficiency, and an understanding of the cannabis market. You will collaborate closely with cross-functional teams, including marketing and product development, to bring innovative, compliant, and eye-catching packaging designs to life.

Candidates for this role should possess strong graphic design skills, with an emphasis on packaging design. Proficiency in design software such as Adobe Illustrator or InDesign is essential. Knowledge of cannabis industry regulations related to packaging and labeling is mandatory. Successful designers are creative thinkers who can translate brand identity into delightful packaging solutions. Attention to detail, adaptability to changing trends, and the ability to meet tight deadlines are crucial skills in this dynamic and competitive field. If you are passionate about design, have a sharp eye for aesthetics, and want to contribute to the visual representation of cannabis brands, this role provides an exciting opportunity.

CONSTRUCTION

From cultivation facilities to processing plants and dispensaries, construction professionals are responsible for erecting buildings, installing specialized equipment, and ensuring compliance with stringent regulatory requirements. Some workers who are involved in hemp or cannabis construction projects include architects and engineers who design facilities optimized for the cultivation and processing of hemp and cannabis, considering factors such as climate control, security, and efficient workflow. Others, including carpenters, electricians, plumbers, and HVAC technicians, execute these designs, utilizing their expertise to create environments conducive to high-quality production while adhering to strict safety and regulatory standards. Additionally, general contractors or project managers oversee the entire construction process, coordinating various trades and ensuring projects are completed on time and within budget. Overall, construction careers are essential in facilitating the growth and success of the hemp and cannabis industries by providing the infrastructure necessary for cultivation, processing, and distribution operations.

Building or General Contractor

A building contractor is generally a project-based or one-time job, though they may be contracted on an ongoing basis for maintenance and upgrades for a facility. Before or at least during the application process, building contractors are interviewed and selected with the knowledge that if the application is granted, they will be charged with executing the plans of the dispensary designer or architect.

Dispensary Designer, Architect

This position must hire and coordinate many tradespeople including electricians, carpenters, plumbing and HVAC technicians, painters, security camera installers, communication/phone line technicians, and roofers with the goal being to bring the project in on time and on budget. In some cases, certain states will fine dispensaries if they do not open on the day they have specified in their application. Two key aspects of this job are the ability to interface with local regulators and inspectors before, during, and after construction and to have specialized knowledge of local, state, and specific cannabis building regulations.

One master cannabis builder in New Jersey, Art Hance, President of Hance Construction, Inc. explains that building in the cannabis industry is unique and challenging. He points out that, "Cannabis construction for indoor climate-controlled cultivation facilities requires an unparalleled level of environmental control requiring significant up-front cost with huge inputs of energy to operate the systems. People unfamiliar with the unique requirements of these projects are often blindsided by the required investment and limited sites that support their operation." Sometimes, too, would-be cannabis operators learn the hard way that "The money is often not there to build the project!"

HVAC Professionals, Plumbers, and Electricians

HVAC is the common abbreviation for heating, ventilation, air-conditioning, HVAC professionals are experts in exactly that! As you may imagine, one of the main challenges when cultivating cannabis is mitigating odor while maintaining consistent growing conditions. While the outside weather fluctuates from high to low temperatures

CHAPTER 6

and different levels of daily humidity, it is the job of the HVAC system to keep growing conditions the same from day to day while ensuring that local neighbors do not smell the cannabis plants. The main duties of an HVAC technician are to inspect, repair, and install HVAC systems.

Usually, HVAC technicians must have a high school diploma or GED and two years of experience as an apprentice or journeyman. They must then be certified by the EPA and pass a state-mandated exam. People who are good with their hands and like to figure out how and why things work typically excel in these fields, and these positions are in high demand.[3]

The role of a plumber or electrician can be simple or complex. Depending on the type of operation that is being constructed, plumbers and electricians may be tasked with simple construction projects such as creating a bathroom or break room for employees, or they may be involved with creating a hydroponic cultivation room from the ground up with advanced automated and electric needs. Considerations such as how to equip each grow room with water access, how to filter nutrient-rich water, whether to install solar panels, and what type of lights to use all come into play, and experienced plumbers and electricians can be invaluable when figuring out these issues.

Dispensary and Interior Designer

Part of a cannabis license application normally includes dispensary design. CAD (computer-aided design) plans are often drafted and submitted along with an application to show that the dispensary owner is ready to build if the license is granted. Workers with a background in architecture, interior design, graphic design, and construction often gravitate toward these types of jobs. Dispensary design must consider:

- lighting psychology
- customer flow and space for ID clearance
- product storage and presentation
- parking

- storefront furniture
- signage
- backroom office
- overall color scheme
- art and facility décor
- flooring materials
- security monitoring systems
- electric capacity
- access to sewer and water
- HVAC
- waste removal
- compliance with local regulations like power outlet installation

Security

From the installation of multiple video cameras both inside and outside the facility to the installation and monitoring of a large safe to store important documents, financial records, and cash, to ensure that product deliveries arrive safely to and from the facility—these are just some of the tasks that a security detail performs. Security employment opportunities are variable. Some operations employ security guards to check IDs, while some merely ask budtenders to double as ID checkers. The cannabis space's cash-only necessity has created a kind of risk as well, in terms of cannabis operators having to store and travel with large amounts of cash.

Security businesses may also be involved in employee background checks and serve as connections to local and state law enforcement. They must be conversant with state regulations and can set up systems to ensure that the facility and employees are compliant with all local and state policies. Part of the security department's responsibility is often the delivery of goods to and from the facility. Usually, vehicles will need to have special lockable storage areas for products, including a vehicle-wide alarm system and a permanently mounted GPS device to record trips. Finally, a military, law enforcement, or security background is often recommended, and applicants must be twenty-one or older.

Chapter 7

The Cannabis Industry's Expanding Horizons

There are many other potential pathways into the cannabis industry that don't necessarily fall under the categories of plant-touching or ancillary. The roles discussed in this chapter tend to be full-time careers that work with or depend on the sectors of the industry responsible for getting cannabis products to market. Yet still they allow one to be involved in the cannabis world, from education and advocacy to health and wellness, to shaping the culture and more. These careers hinge on the kaleidoscopic ecosystem that the plant-touching and ancillary sectors create in tandem.

GREEN HEALTH: CANNABIS AND THE HEALTHCARE INDUSTRY

The medicinal potential of cannabis has spurred a seismic shift in public perception, prompting an unprecedented convergence of traditional medicine and alternative therapies. As societal attitudes toward cannabis shift, health, and medical professionals find themselves at the nexus of this transformative wave. Within the cannabis industry, an array of impactful careers has emerged, each playing a distinctive role in fostering a necessary and beneficial relationship between cannabis and healthcare.

Medical Cannabis Overview

In the United States, medical marijuana became legal for the first time in late 1996 in California via Ballot Proposition 215. This momentous legal shift was in large part due to the hard work of the LGBTQ+ community's commitment to compassionately and effectively care for AIDS patients. Sympathetic activists saw HIV/AIDS patients battle pain, experience nausea (because of the cocktail of pharmaceutical drugs they were often prescribed), and fight to maintain their appetite. Often, cannabis soothed their pain, mitigated their nausea, and stimulated their appetite. It made sense that California citizens would work to legalize medical cannabis, which, again, happened in 1996.

Under this provision, if a California citizen obtained a physician's recommendation, the patient could possess and grow cannabis as long as they were receiving treatment for various conditions as recommended by their physician. Medical cannabis legalization in California was the beginning of a major shift in public attitudes, as shortly thereafter in 1998, the states of Alaska, Oregon, and Washington legalized medical marijuana as well.

Medical cannabis and recreational cannabis can be the same end product, but the purpose and way they are each used is what differs. Medical patients go to a doctor for relief from a particular medical condition. They may discuss strains, potency, and dosing for their particular condition, or their physician will simply give them a recommendation to use cannabis. It would not be unusual to find a medical and a recreational user with the same product. Both THC-dominant and CBD-dominant strains are used for medical treatment. Depending on the condition one is trying to treat, different products, different THC and/or CBD potencies, different consumption methods, and particular doses are employed.

Patients must see, or connect with via telemedicine, a qualified doctor to acquire their medical cannabis cards. They need to present their card for purchase and to carry their card for legal protection. Some states offer reciprocity when it comes to medical cannabis, which means if a patient travels to another state, they still have access to their medicine. But before you travel to another legal medical cannabis state, check their regulations as there may be some paperwork you have to complete and submit in advance. Other states will simply let you walk into a dispensary as long as you have proper ID, such as a driver's license, state ID, passport, passport card, and military ID, showing that you are twenty-one or older.

Medical patients, in consultation with their physicians, consider the rate of absorption, how much medicine will be delivered to their body, and if patients are limited to particular ingestion methods. For example, a patient may have trouble swallowing pills or capsules, so they may look to smoking, vaping, topicals, or suppositories. Each of these methods provides some benefits and challenges, but the good news is that more and more options are available and the creativity in this market shows no evidence of slowing.

In practical terms, medical patients may have access to products that are not available to recreational users. Medical cannabis products are often less expensive than recreational products and are often not taxed. Medical patients can usually buy more products in a single purchase as well. And things continue to change. For example, a few years ago, medical patients in Oregon had access to one part of a dispensary, and recreational users were led to another part of the dispensary. Recreational users could only look longingly at edibles and tinctures as their choices were limited to smokeable flower or bud.

In Washington State, where adult use is legal, many of the medical dispensaries have merged with the recreational ones, making for a one-stop shop for any cannabis user. This is generally what happens in markets that move from medical cannabis only to medical and adult-use cannabis. A good percentage of medical patients do not renew their cards plus the rate of growth in the medical cannabis patients ranks slows considerably. So, both medical and adult users end up visiting the same dispensaries, with medical patients receiving some considerations such as closer parking spots, going to the head of a line, and even reserved shopping hours.

OPPORTUNITIES IN THE CANNABIS HEALTHCARE FIELD

Because cannabis is in some ways a newly discovered and appreciated source of accepted medicine and an alternative to some pharmaceuticals, opportunities exist in both the alternative medical field and the more traditional medical fields. In the alternative medical field, which appreciates cannabis as a natural pain reliever and anti-inflammatory, there are jobs in acupuncture, massage therapy, chiropractic, kinesiology (movement therapy, physical therapy, sports medicine, certified personal trainer), nutritional consultant, and homeopathy. All these opportunities would be enhanced by your knowledge of cannabis. In the traditional Western medical field, there are jobs such as medical assistant, nurse, physician's assistant, physician, veterinarian, pharmacist, and psychiatrist.

In contemporary healthcare, it's an absolute necessity that professionals are cannabis-fluent and are aware of their patients' cannabis use. Cannabis contains compounds like THC and CBD that interact with the body's ECS, influencing mood, perception, and other physiological functions. Understanding a patient's cannabis use is crucial for assessing potential interactions with prescribed medications, as cannabinoids can affect the metabolism of certain drugs. In some states, physicians, including psychiatrists, have the authority to recommend medical cannabis for conditions like chronic pain or anxiety. Therefore, having knowledge about cannabis and its effects enables physicians to make informed recommendations, ensuring safe and effective treatment plans for their patients. Note, too, that physicians in states where it is allowed by state law can only recommend cannabis rather than prescribe it because cannabis is federally illegal.

The bottom line is that cannabis is an effective tool for a number of medical conditions. As an example, New Jersey recognizes the following conditions to be eligible for a medical cannabis card; this is a typical state list of medical qualifying conditions:

- chronic pain related to musculoskeletal disorders
- chronic pain of visceral origin
- migraines
- anxiety
- dysmenorrhea
- amyotrophic lateral sclerosis
- multiple sclerosis
- opioid use disorder as an adjunct to medication-assisted therapy
- terminal cancer

- muscular dystrophy
- inflammatory bowel disease, including Crohn's disease
- terminal illness, if the physician has determined a prognosis of less than twelve months of life
- Tourette's syndrome

The following conditions apply if the patient is resistant to, or intolerant to, conventional therapy:

- seizure disorders, including epilepsy
- intractable skeletal muscular spasticity
- glaucoma
- PTSD

The following conditions apply, if severe or chronic pain, severe nausea or vomiting, cachexia or wasting syndrome results from the condition or its treatment:

- positive status for human immunodeficiency virus (HIV)
- acquired immune deficiency syndrome (AIDS)
- cancer

Successful health and medical cannabis employees include individuals with diverse skill sets and a passion for pioneering change. Essential traits for working in the cannabis-healthcare space are:

1. Compassion and Empathy: Patient care lies at the heart of health and medical careers in the cannabis industry. Compassion and empathy are essential qualities that facilitate effective communication and foster trust between professionals and patients.
2. Ethical Decision-Making: Given the sensitive nature of healthcare, ethical decision-making is paramount. Health and medical cannabis employees must navigate legal and ethical considerations while providing the best care for their patients.

3. Passion for Education: Health and medical cannabis employees need to be enthusiastic educators. Whether guiding patients on product selection or informing colleagues about the latest research, a commitment to education is crucial.
4. Continuous Learning: The cannabis industry is in a constant state of evolution. Those who flourish in health and medical cannabis careers are committed to continuous learning, by staying abreast of the latest research, regulations, and advancements in both conventional medicine and cannabis therapy.
5. Open-Mindedness: Cannabis challenges traditional medical norms, and successful professionals in this field exhibit open-mindedness. They are willing to explore alternative therapies and integrate them into conventional practices when beneficial.
6. Collaborative Spirit: The interconnected nature of healthcare and the cannabis industry requires collaboration. Successful professionals are team players who can work seamlessly with colleagues from various disciplines to provide comprehensive care.
7. Adaptability: The cannabis industry is dynamic and subject to rapid regulatory changes. Professionals who thrive in this environment are adaptable, quick learners, and are comfortable navigating ambiguity.

In the sections that follow, we will delve deeper into each of the aforementioned health and medical careers in the cannabis industry, exploring the nuances, challenges, and rewards that come with these roles. By understanding the qualities that make individuals successful in this unique field, aspiring professionals can embark on a journey that not only aligns with their passion for health and medicine but also contributes to the ongoing transformation of healthcare on the green frontier. The following roles form the backbone of health and medical careers within the cannabis business. Each of these roles contributes uniquely to the field, offering expertise that spans the continuum of patient care, product knowledge, and therapeutic applications of cannabis.

Physician, Medical Doctor, and Psychiatrist

A physician, medical doctor, or psychiatrist is a healthcare professional who diagnoses, treats, and prevents illnesses and provides comprehensive medical care to patients. Physicians may specialize in various fields such as internal medicine, surgery, pediatrics, or psychiatry. They play a central role in the healthcare system, utilizing their knowledge and expertise to help individuals maintain good health or manage medical challenges. Medical doctors work in hospitals, clinics, or private practices, and they often collaborate with other healthcare professionals to provide well-rounded patient care.

To become a physician, one must complete an extensive education and training path. This typically involves earning a bachelor's degree, followed by completing a medical degree (MD or DO, doctor of osteopathy) from a recognized medical school. After medical school, physicians go through residency programs, which provide hands-on training in their chosen specialty. The entire process can take over a decade, and physicians must continue learning throughout their careers to stay abreast of medical advancements.

Physician's Assistant

A physician's assistant (PA) is a healthcare professional who works under the supervision of a licensed physician, providing a wide range of medical services. PAs conduct physical exams, diagnose and treat illnesses, order and interpret tests, and assist in surgeries. They play a crucial role in various medical settings, including hospitals, clinics, and primary care offices. PAs work collaboratively with physicians to deliver comprehensive and accessible healthcare services to patients. Knowledge about a client's cannabis use is crucial for physician's assistants, particularly in states where they can recommend cannabis as part of medical treatment. In states where PAs have the authority to recommend cannabis, staying up to date on the latest research and regulations is essential to ensure responsible and effective integration of cannabis into patient care.

To become a PA, individuals typically need a master's degree from an accredited PA program after completing a bachelor's degree. These programs include both classroom instruction and clinical rotations, preparing PAs with the knowledge and skills necessary for their role. After completing their education, PAs must pass the Physician Assistant National Certifying Exam (PANCE) to obtain state licensure. Individuals interested in a physician's assistant career should be detail-oriented, possess strong interpersonal and communication skills, and have a genuine desire to help others.

Nurse
There are three main steps to becoming a nurse:

1. Students must graduate from an accredited program. An associate's program generally takes two years to complete and a bachelor's degree in nursing usually takes four years.
2. Students must take and pass the NCLEX-RN test. A typical test includes over one hundred questions with a six-hour time limit for completion. About 75 percent of the students who take the test pass.
3. You have to get a state license, which is mostly an issue of completing paperwork and possibly passing a background test.

A nurse should know the effects, methods of consumption, qualifying medical conditions, how a patient can obtain a medical cannabis card, and dosing instructions. Now more than ever there are additional opportunities to take classes, both online or through colleges and universities on cannabis specifics in nursing.

Some nurses may find work in medical dispensaries. A medical dispensary nurse serves a crucial role, as some states mandate the presence of a healthcare professional for patient counseling. These specialized nurses assess patient needs, conduct consultations, and provide expert guidance on medicinal cannabis options. They educate patients about various strains, consumption methods, and dosage considerations, ensuring a comprehensive understanding of the potential benefits and risks. Dispensary nurses collaborate with patients to tailor treatment plans, considering individual health conditions, preferences, and desired outcomes.

Janna Champagne, who is a Board-Certified Master Herbalist, Diplomate Medical Cannabinoid Sciences, and professor at John Patrick University, had this to say about being a cannabis nurse, "As you witness cannabis patient outcomes, you will wonder why nursing school curricula omitted the science explaining its effectiveness. The cannabis industry may be a good fit if you're interested in contributing to our inevitable paradigm shift in medical care!"

Champagne goes on to explain why some nurses are drawn to cannabis. "In many cases, nurses are called to specialize in cannabis after witnessing its benefits in patients. Some cannabis nurses are patients themselves, who discovered its therapeutic potential firsthand. As a result, cannabis nurses are passion-driven, which helps them succeed in this industry where adhering to nursing ethics often constitutes operating in a licensure gray area."

Physical Therapist

A physical therapist is a healthcare professional who helps individuals recover from injuries, surgeries, or other physical conditions by designing and implementing exercise programs and rehabilitation plans. Physical therapists work to improve mobility, reduce pain, and enhance overall function. They assess their clients' physical abilities, create personalized treatment plans, and guide them through exercises and therapeutic activities to promote recovery and prevent further issues. These professionals play a crucial role in assisting people of all ages in regaining strength and independence after injuries or medical procedures. To become a physical therapist, one typically needs to complete a doctoral degree in physical therapy (DPT). The DPT program includes both classroom education and extensive clinical practice to prepare therapists for the diverse challenges they may encounter. After completing their education, physical therapists often need to pass licensing exams to practice in their specific region.

Understanding a client's cannabis use is essential for physical therapists as cannabis can impact pain perception and affect the body's response to exercise and rehabilitation. Cannabis contains THC and CBD that interact with the endocannabinoid system, which plays a role in pain modulation, inflammation, and overall homeostasis. By knowing about a client's cannabis use, a physical therapist can tailor treatment plans accordingly, considering factors such as potential interactions with medications, variations in pain tolerance, and the influence of cannabis on the individual's ability to engage in therapeutic activities. Open communication about cannabis use enables a more comprehensive and personalized approach to rehabilitation, fostering a collaborative and effective therapeutic relationship between the physical therapist and the client.

Pharmacist
A cannabis dispensary pharmacist holds a crucial role in states where regulations mandate the presence of a licensed pharmacist for patient counseling in dispensaries. These professionals leverage their pharmaceutical expertise to conduct patient consultations, assess medical histories, and recommend appropriate cannabis products tailored to individual needs. Dispensary pharmacists play a key role in ensuring the safe and effective use of medical cannabis, educating patients on dosages and potential interactions with other medications and providing guidance on consumption methods.

Successful cannabis dispensary pharmacists possess a combination of clinical knowledge, strong communication skills, and a commitment to patient education. They stay updated on the latest research and developments in cannabis therapeutics, applying their pharmaceutical background to offer informed recommendations. Educational requirements typically include a doctor of pharmacy (PharmD) degree, state licensure, and compliance with any additional regulations specific to cannabis dispensing. Pharmacists with certifications or training in cannabis pharmacology further enhance their ability to navigate the unique considerations of medical cannabis. By integrating their pharmaceutical expertise with a patient-centric approach, cannabis dispensary pharmacists contribute significantly to the responsible and therapeutic use of cannabis within the healthcare landscape.

Massage Therapist

A massage therapist is a professional who uses hands-on techniques to manipulate muscles and soft tissues in the body, providing relaxation and relief from tension and pain. Massage therapy can offer various benefits, such as stress reduction, improved circulation, better sleep quality, and decreased muscle and joint stiffness. Massage therapists may specialize in different modalities, such as Swedish massage, deep tissue massage, or sports massage, tailoring their approach to the specific needs and preferences of their clients.

Becoming a massage therapist typically requires completing a formal education program, which can vary in length from a few months to two years, depending on the program and the specific requirements of the region. Many states or countries may also require massage therapists to be licensed, which often involves passing a certification exam. Education in massage therapy includes learning anatomy, physiology, and various massage techniques, both through classroom instruction and hands-on practice.

Incorporating cannabis into massage therapy is a growing trend that some practitioners explore for its potential therapeutic benefits. Cannabis-infused massage oils or lotions, containing cannabinoids like CBD, can be applied during a massage session. CBD, known for its anti-inflammatory and relaxing properties, may complement the soothing effects of massage, promoting a deeper sense of relaxation and potentially assisting with pain management.

Acupuncturist

Acupuncture is a traditional Chinese medicine technique that involves inserting thin needles into specific points on the body. The goal is to stimulate energy flow, known as qi or chi, and restore balance to the body's systems. Acupuncturists often work to alleviate various health issues such as pain, stress, and digestive disorders by promoting the body's natural healing abilities.

To become an acupuncturist, one typically needs to complete a formal education program, usually a bachelor's and even a master's degree in acupuncture or a related field, like anatomy, physiology, or biology.

These programs cover both the theoretical and practical aspects of acupuncture, including anatomy, Chinese medicine theory, and hands-on training in needling techniques. After completing their education, acupuncturists may need to pass licensing exams to practice in their respective state.[1]

When integrating cannabis into their practice, some acupuncturists may explore the potential benefits of medical cannabis in conjunction with acupuncture treatments. Cannabis, as we know, has been researched for its analgesic and anti-inflammatory properties, which could complement the goals of acupuncture in managing pain and promoting comfort. Acupuncturists interested in incorporating cannabis into their practice should stay informed about local regulations, collaborate with other healthcare professionals, and consider the individual needs and preferences of their clients.

GREEN EDUCATION: EXPLORING CAREERS IN CANNABIS ED

A primary obstacle for the cannabis industry is the lack of commonsense cannabis education for would-be industry members and consumers alike. The industry is battling not only a lack of education but also miseducation and misinformation from prohibition's generational hangover. So, as the cannabis industry matures, the need for cannabis educators is clear. This means that a variety of careers await individuals with a background in education or a keen interest in fostering knowledge about cannabis. This section delves into the intricacies of educational professions within the cannabis industry, shedding light on the various roles that contribute to the integration of cannabis education into learning environments. From professors to writers, content creators to health coaches, these roles are at the forefront of a transformative journey that is reshaping traditional education. Further, each of these roles contributes uniquely to the field, offering expertise that spans the continuum of cannabis knowledge, therapeutic applications, and responsible use.

Teachers, Instructors, and Professors

Because cannabis is a new industry, the mold for cannabis educators, especially those working in higher education has not yet been created.

Some traditional academics, those having expertise in a particular field such as biology with at least a master's degree, are often tapped to enter this new field. But there is an equally strong contingent of educators who have practical hemp or cannabis experience in cultivation, processing, product creation, managing business operations, and more that have entered the classroom. This is in part because there was no standardized curriculum nor traditional cannabis degrees such as a master's in cannabis science until very recently. The most popular degree programs that are offered on college campuses focus on cultivation, lab science, or business. Occasionally, one can find a program that takes a social science approach as well. Currently, there are about thirty colleges that offer a for-credit degree program, and this number is growing.

Because much of the knowledge that the current industry was built on was developed in the legacy or traditional market by mavericks (who worked boldly outside the dominant legal and cultural framework of the prohibition era) some of them have even made it into traditional classrooms on state-run campuses. One of the authors of this book fits this description!

As a cannabis professor, not only do I get to embrace the coolest job title ever, but also I get to work with motivated, enthusiastic students. Every day of class starts with the following greeting: "Welcome Cannabis Ospreys. It is 12:45 p.m. and it is time to go to work!" This greeting sets the tone for the semester. We develop a tight-knit community, but there is no doubt that our purpose is to become cannabis professionals. I'm pleased to say that dozens of my students are just that: budtenders, shift leaders, IT professionals, compliance officers, government officials, general managers, hemp farmers, and more. They are the backbone of this new industry, and I'm proud to mentor and support them.

Here is what Koral Brady, a friend and assistant (cannabis) professor at Lake Superior State University in Michigan, had to say about the importance of cannabis education, "Cannabis and cannabis-related issues intersect so many aspects of our society and systems that it will take decades of unlearning and relearning to find true equity and understanding on this topic." Cannabis professors like Brady ensure that we focus on both business opportunities and equity—equally important issues in the cannabis world.

Also, educators should not overlook opportunities to develop cannabis curricula and teach cannabis courses for private education companies such as Oaksterdam, the Cleveland School of Cannabis, and Clover Leaf University. They offer courses to private individuals, cannabis companies, and sometimes via college continuing education departments. College continuing education departments are expanding their cannabis offerings rapidly and this can be a way to introduce yourself and your expertise to a college. We know several current cannabis professors who started their careers by developing an online, self-paced course and offering it through a local college's continuing education department.

Individuals who are attracted to these types of opportunities often feel mission-driven to work with students. They are passionate about their field of study, are experts when transferring knowledge and often have a personal connection to the plant. Other characteristics that make them successful are empathy, patience, curiosity, and the ability to stay informed in a mercurial industry.

Cannabis Internships

An internship is an active professional learning experience, designed mainly for students, completed to gain experience and skills in an industry where they are interested in forging a career. In turn, the internship lends the employer a new voice, fresh energy, and the opportunity to educate. Some internships are paid, while others are not, and they can be organized with full or part-time hours. In some internships, students will directly shadow staff members or, in other instances, interns might directly participate in work projects, gaining firsthand experience in the given field. When an internship goes well, it might result in the full-time hiring of the intern into a full-time position.

As cannabis education becomes more widespread, especially in colleges and universities, cannabis internships will become more and more common. Students studying in programs like New Jersey's Stockton University's cannabis studies minor can take an independent study project or internship for course credit with local cannabis operations, from dispensaries to cultivation facilities, getting direct, hands-on access to life in the cannabis industry. Also, for employers in the cannabis industry, it's advantageous for them to develop relationships with universities like Stockton, as it provides them with a reliably educated pool of potential employees in an industry that, because of prohibition, has very little formal training when compared to other more traditional industries.

Writers and Journalists

In the world of cannabis, writers and journalists play a crucial role in informing and engaging audiences about the latest developments, trends, and stories within the industry. As a cannabis writer, you'll find yourself crafting compelling articles and news pieces that cover a wide range of topics, from the science behind different strains to the latest regulatory changes. Your goal is to educate and entertain readers, whether they're seasoned cannabis enthusiasts or newcomers eager to learn more. Note that many cannabis publications, similar to other publications, are largely online. To put your name and work out in the industry space, you'll likely have to embrace social media platforms like X, Instagram, and TikTok. There are some print publications, but they tend to offer regional or specific state coverage as their overall mission.

It's important to note that there are no rigid standards or educational minimums when it comes to becoming a writer. A degree in English might provide a foundation, for example, but there are plenty of successful writers who have no formalized training. Then, when considering moving into cannabis writing, think about where you might have expertise or insider knowledge, or if you have a particular stance on a given issue. The best writing comes from a place of honesty, and your "voice" as a writer is strongest, most distinctive, and thus most attractive and authoritative when you're writing confidently as yourself.

So, depending on what you're bringing to the metaphorical table, your writing might dig into diverse aspects of the cannabis industry. Additionally, you may choose to interview industry experts, growers, and business professionals, providing readers with profiles of those working in the industry. Remember, your work as a cannabis writer not only contributes to the growth of the industry but also can help break down stereotypes and stigmas associated with cannabis. If you have a passion for storytelling, a keen interest in cannabis, and a commitment to accurate reporting, a career as a writer or journalist in the cannabis field can be a fulfilling and exciting journey. Realistically, it's difficult to earn large salaries or advances as a writer, in cannabis, or, say, as a novelist. Most often, writers are paid certain sums per article, interview, or book project. However, writers will often gain other financial opportunities based on the quality and notoriety of their writing, such as teaching positions or speaking engagements.

Here is what Andrew Ward, president of Andrew Ward Media which specializes in cannabis-specific copywriting and SEO, had to say about becoming a cannabis writer, "I became a journalist and copywriter in 2017 after leaving the startup tech space. After three months of not knowing where to go, I saw Dave Grohl say in an interview, 'Find someone who will pay you to do what you love.' I happened to be smoking a bowl and writing when that happened and took that as a sign."

Content Creators, Bloggers, and Social Media Influencers

Content creators, bloggers, and social media influencers play a unique and impactful role in shaping the cultural narrative. Unlike traditional writers and journalists, your focus is on creating visually appealing and engaging content that resonates with the diverse community of cannabis enthusiasts. As a content creator, you'll use various platforms like YouTube, Instagram, TikTok, and blogs to share your experiences, insights, and recommendations, bringing the cannabis culture to life in a way that's relatable and accessible.

Each platform has its requirements and regulations for what kind of content it allows to be published. For example, traditional media platforms like Facebook have specific restrictions around publicizing cannabis because it is federally illegal. Media outlets such as radio, television, and print media like magazines are subject to state and sometimes federal restrictions and regulations as well. Knowing where and how to produce content is a nuanced decision process.

These roles function as advertisers. Brands spend thousands of dollars on influencers each year. Folks with business and marketing savvy, including SEO, are primed to excel here. Your work involves not only crafting compelling written pieces but also leveraging the power of images, videos, and social media to build a community around your own brand, or the brand that pays you to advertise their products. Whether you're reviewing the latest strains, sharing cannabis lifestyle tips, or documenting your cannabis journey, your goal is to foster a connection with your audience. Being a content creator in the cannabis industry allows you to have a more personal and interactive relationship with your followers, creating a sense of community and trust that sets this career apart from traditional cannabis writing or journalism. If you have a knack for visual storytelling, a passion for cannabis, and a desire to engage with a vibrant online community, this career path offers an exciting and influential way to contribute to the evolving cannabis landscape.

Health Coach

A cannabis health coach specializes in helping individuals navigate the use of cannabis for health and wellness purposes. They work with clients to develop personalized plans that incorporate cannabis products, dosage, and consumption methods to address or augment specific health goals or concerns. Cannabis health coaches may educate clients on the potential benefits and risks associated with cannabis use, guide them in selecting suitable strains or products, and provide ongoing support to optimize their cannabis experience. These professionals often take a holistic approach, considering factors such as overall lifestyle, nutrition, sleep patterns, and mental well-being to enhance the therapeutic effects of cannabis.

To become a cannabis health coach, individuals typically need a combination of education and certification in areas such as cannabis science, health coaching, and wellness practices. Some may pursue formal education in cannabis studies, including courses on cannabinoids, terpenes, and the endocannabinoid system. Additionally, certification or training in health coaching is beneficial, as it equips professionals with the skills to support clients in setting and achieving health-related goals. Depending on the jurisdiction, there may be specific requirements or licenses related to cannabis counseling or coaching, and staying informed about the evolving legal landscape surrounding cannabis is crucial for practitioners in this field. Usually, health coaches have personal experience in successfully using cannabis to achieve optimal health.

Creating Change with Compassion: Exploring Nonprofit Careers in the Cannabis Realm

The cannabis space is highly intersectional, which means there is an opportunity to make positive change in terms of a variety of social justice issues. Issues of class, race, gender, sexuality, community policing standards, and more are cannabis issues too! As societal perceptions of cannabis transform, nonprofit professionals find themselves at the forefront of social justice issues, bridging gaps in knowledge, advocating for responsible cannabis use, and aiding communities that have been devastated by the war on drugs.

Nonprofit organizations are entities that exist to further a charitable mission or cause. These organizations are not set up to make a profit yet still need a strong financial base to be successful. Usually, nonprofits have a board of directors and an executive director who oversees and guides teams of employees and volunteers. They can vary dramatically in size and scope. Fundraising and grant writing are often the lifeblood of these entities. Individuals who are driven by a commitment to promote social impact, education, advocacy, and charitable initiatives may be attracted to nonprofit, mission-based cannabis careers. From educational initiatives that dispel myths surrounding cannabis to advocacy groups working toward policy reform, these roles contribute to the positive integration of cannabis into mainstream society. Each role plays a vital part in cultivating a compassionate relationship between cannabis and the community. Successful professionals in nonprofit cannabis careers share common characteristics that set them apart:

- Passion for Social Impact: Nonprofit cannabis professionals are driven by a strong commitment to making a positive impact on society. They are dedicated to advancing education, social justice, and community well-being through their work.

- Advocacy and Communication Skills: Effective communication and advocacy are essential in navigating the complex landscape of cannabis-related issues. Professionals in this field excel at articulating the benefits of responsible cannabis use, dispelling misconceptions, and advocating for sensible policies.
- Collaborative Approach: Nonprofit cannabis careers often involve collaboration with diverse stakeholders, including government bodies, community leaders, and other nonprofit organizations. Successful professionals exhibit a collaborative spirit, working collectively toward common goals.
- Ethical and Inclusive Practices: Nonprofit work requires a commitment to ethical practices and inclusivity. Professionals in this field navigate legal and ethical considerations while promoting fairness, equity, and inclusivity in their initiatives.
- Adaptability: The cannabis industry, even in its nonprofit sector, is subject to evolving regulations and societal attitudes. Professionals thrive in this environment by being adaptable, staying informed about changes, and adjusting their strategies accordingly.

Running or Participating in a Nonprofit or Charitable Cannabis Organization

In the cannabis realm, organizational missions are often based on issues such as health and wellness, social equity, job creation, helping the prison or post-prison population, and providing low-cost or free education. Usually, an individual has a personal interest or connection to the cause they are promoting.

One of the biggest challenges of starting or working at a nonprofit organization is sourcing and securing funding. In the cannabis nonprofit space, common sources of funding are state grants, individual donations, and sponsorships from private cannabis companies. As well, sometimes states mandate that cannabis businesses, like dispensaries or grow operations, must contribute to local nonprofits. Savvy charitable operators familiarize themselves with state cannabis regulations to find out what the "community engagement" requirements are for cannabis businesses. These requirements are often outright donations or sponsorships for experiences such as expungement clinics, educational seminars, or medical cannabis card sign-up events.

Folks working in nonprofits wear many hats and excel in areas such as sales, fundraising, event planning, marketing, and working with government officials. The pay for these positions fluctuates widely and again, is contingent on funding sources. However the satisfaction founders and employers receive in these endeavors gives many a purpose and a way to give back.

While most jobs in the nonprofit cannabis sector involve managing a nonprofit or working in advocacy or education, there are many other roles involved as well. Here's a list of some additional potential positions within nonprofit cannabis organizations:

- Grant writers seek and secure funding through grants, donations, and other fundraising efforts.
- Legal counselors provide legal expertise on cannabis-related issues, navigating complex regulations and offering guidance on advocacy strategies.
- Researchers conduct studies on the medicinal, economic, and social aspects of cannabis to support evidence-based advocacy.
- Administrative assistants provide general administrative support to ensure the smooth functioning of the organization.
- Finance managers oversee the financial health of the organization, managing budgets, and ensuring compliance with financial regulations.
- HR specialists manage personnel matters, recruitment, and employee relations within the organization.
- IT specialists handle technology needs, including website management, data security, and technology infrastructure.
- Volunteer coordinators recruit, train, and coordinate volunteer efforts that support the organization's initiatives.
- Lobbyists engage with policymakers and advocates for cannabis-friendly legislation at local, state, and federal levels.

Cannabis Education Nonprofits

A nonprofit cannabis education organization is dedicated to promoting awareness of the responsible use of cannabis and in preparing workers to excel in the cannabis business. The primary aim is to use the organization's expertise to empower individuals with accurate information about cannabis, dispelling myths and stigma and contributing to a well-informed community that values responsible consumption.

Teach for America, AdoptAClassroom, and UNESCO are three examples of education nonprofits that seek to promote various educational opportunities for communities in the United States and around the world. Education nonprofits can help schools or education programs augment their reach, scope, supplies, staffing, program offerings, and more. They can provide specialized training in their specific area of expertise. For example, the National Science Teaching Association will provide different services than the National Art Education Association. A few examples of cannabis education nonprofits are:

- The Society of Cannabis Clinicians: A nonprofit professional association of physicians and other healthcare providers. Their mission is to provide continuing education—for themselves, their patients, and their colleagues—about the medical use of cannabis and best practices in clinical care.[2]
- Cannabis Education Guild: The guild offers online learning series, webinars, and live seminars to help people learn and measure their cannabis and social impact knowledge.[3]

Cannabis Advocacy Groups

Nonprofit cannabis advocacy groups play a crucial role in research and policy reform surrounding the use and legalization of cannabis. Nonprofit cannabis advocacy groups engage in public outreach, community education, and influence policymakers to shape fair and evidence-based cannabis regulations. These groups often work to destigmatize cannabis use and challenge the existing legal frameworks through grassroots campaigns, public speaking engagements, and strategic partnerships with other advocacy organizations and universities. Some examples of cannabis advocacy groups are:

- NORML, the oldest and largest marijuana legalization organization in the country.[4]
- The Drug Policy Alliance is another leading organization in the United States working to end the drug war.[5]
- The Marijuana Policy Project (MPP) is another organization in the United States dedicated to legalizing cannabis.[6]
- The Indigenous Cannabis Industry Association (ICIA) exists to promote the exploration, development, and advancement of the cannabis industry for the benefit of all Indigenous communities. ICIA is dedicated to the advocacy and empowerment of Indigenous cannabis businesses, influencers, and aspiring entrepreneurs along with being a conduit of connection and data for Indigenous Nations as they push toward a vision of an equitable, just, and sustainable Indigenous cannabis economy.[7]

A variety of jobs are available within nonprofit cannabis advocacy groups, catering to individuals with diverse skill sets and interests. Policy analysts and researchers are crucial for evaluating existing legislation and conducting studies to support evidence-based advocacy. Communications professionals are needed to develop and execute public relations campaigns, manage social media, and engage with the media to shape an effective narrative around cannabis. Grassroots organizers play a pivotal role in mobilizing communities, organizing events, and building support at the local level. Legal experts are essential for navigating the complex legal landscape surrounding cannabis and crafting persuasive arguments for policy reform. Additionally, fundraising professionals, event coordinators, and outreach specialists contribute to the financial stability and broader impact of these organizations. Successful advocates in this field often possess strong communication skills, a passion for social justice, a deep understanding of cannabis-related issues, and the ability to collaborate with diverse stakeholders.

GOVERNMENT ROLES IN CANNABIS REGULATION: NURTURING THE GREEN INDUSTRY

A range of government positions play a pivotal role in regulating and supporting the cannabis industry. This section investigates the significance of government jobs in the cannabis business, particularly those focused on oversight, compliance, and assistance to small businesses. Commissioners, zoning officers, compliance officers, and business development administrators are instrumental in shaping the regulatory framework that governs the cannabis sector.

As the cannabis industry continues to expand, governmental entities dedicated to supporting small businesses play a crucial role in ensuring a competitive but fair environment. This involves creating and implementing regulations that foster the growth of small businesses within the cannabis space. Sometimes existing governmental agencies can help cannabis businesses, but some may be restricted due to federal regulations.

Cannabis Commissioners

Cannabis commissioners, who are often appointed by a state's governor or legislators, play a pivotal role in overseeing and regulating the cannabis industry within their state. These are powerful positions, and those appointed are often experienced leaders, legislators, or businesspeople. Given the complexity of regulations, license classes, and overarching goals across states, these commissioners serve as key liaisons between legislative bodies, other governmental agencies, the public, and cannabis business owners. Typically possessing diverse backgrounds in law, health, politics, social work, psychology, government, or business, commissioners must navigate the intricate web of state-specific cannabis laws and policies. Their primary responsibility lies in establishing and maintaining a vibrant cannabis business environment that balances compliance, safety, transparency, and social equity with entrepreneurial freedom, competition, and creativity.

Collaboration with legislators is crucial, as commissioners work toward aligning cannabis regulations with evolving legal frameworks and societal expectations. They engage with various stakeholders, including public health officials, law enforcement, business owners, and advocacy groups, to address concerns and develop comprehensive strategies. Balancing social equity efforts is a significant challenge, requiring commissioners to design policies that promote fair access to the industry for historically marginalized communities.

Furthermore, they must oversee complex licensing processes, ensure that safety standards are met, and implement rigorous compliance measures. Transparency in their operations is paramount, and commissioners must communicate effectively with the public to foster understanding and trust in the regulatory process. In essence, the role demands a delicate equilibrium between diverse interests, ensuring the cannabis industry thrives while serving the broader interests of public health and social equity.

Zoning Officers

Zoning officers play a crucial role in determining where cannabis businesses can operate. These professionals are responsible for assessing and enforcing zoning laws and regulations related to cannabis cultivation, processing, distribution, storage, and retail. They work closely with local government authorities to identify suitable locations for cannabis businesses while ensuring compliance with municipal ordinances and state regulations. Some of the issues that zoning officers will be concerned with include the availability of parking, traffic flow, lighting, security, trash removal, and signage. Often, they can help potential operators secure the proper permits, or at least point them to the correct municipal department.

A background in urban planning, land-use law, or public administration is highly beneficial for individuals aspiring to work as zoning officers in the cannabis industry. Strong knowledge of zoning regulations, land development codes, and permitting processes is essential for success in this role. Additionally, they must be familiar with the complexities of the cannabis industry in their state. Effective communication skills and the ability to collaborate with various stakeholders, including government officials, property owners, and prospective entrepreneurs, are also essential traits for individuals pursuing a career as a zoning officer in the cannabis sector.

Governmental Compliance Officers

A cannabis governmental compliance officer is tasked with ensuring that all cannabis businesses within their jurisdiction adhere to relevant laws and regulations. Their responsibilities encompass a thorough examination of various facets of cannabis operations to guarantee compliance. This includes scrutinizing SOPs, confirming adherence to training and education requirements, evaluating security protocols, assessing community engagement plans, and ensuring proper waste management procedures are all in place. Furthermore, they meticulously verify that all licenses held by cannabis establishments are current and valid.

To excel in this role, individuals typically need a background in law enforcement, regulatory compliance, or a related field with a solid understanding of legal frameworks and industry standards surrounding cannabis operations. Strong attention to detail, analytical skills, and the ability to interpret complex regulations are crucial. Given the dynamic nature of the cannabis industry and the diverse regulatory landscape across states, adaptability and a willingness to stay updated with evolving laws and policies are essential traits for success. This position is typically a government job, requiring a dedication to upholding public safety and ensuring the integrity of the cannabis market within their jurisdiction.

Business Development Administrator for Local or State Government

A cannabis governmental business development officer plays a pivotal role in supporting the growth and success of cannabis businesses within their state. These officers are responsible for spearheading initiatives aimed at fostering the development of the cannabis industry through various means such as providing grants, offering low- or no-interest loans, and delivering technical assistance. Technical assistance often encompasses education on cannabis-specific topics, ranging from "how to apply for a license" to regulatory compliance to how to operate a cannabis business. These officers may coordinate professional business mentorship programs to guide entrepreneurs through the complexities of operating within the cannabis market.

Individuals aspiring to work as cannabis governmental business development officers typically require a background in business development, economics, public administration, governmental operations, or a related field. They should possess a strong understanding of governmental processes, economic development principles, and the nuances of the cannabis industry. Effective communication skills, strategic thinking, and the ability to build relationships with stakeholders are essential for success in this role. Given the unique regulatory landscape of the cannabis industry, adaptability and a proactive approach to navigating complex legal frameworks are highly valuable traits. As this position is typically within a government agency, a commitment to upholding state regulations and fostering responsible growth within the cannabis sector is paramount. Finally, some states mandate that these services must help social equity applicants first and foremost and business development officers help create effective programs to meet this aim.

Opportunities in Cannabis Tourism, Hospitality, Marketing, and Communications

Now more than ever, consumers are seeking experiences rather than "things." Think of the rise of escape room businesses or brewpub tours. Well, it's not hard to see how cannabis experiences are joining the business throng! Because legal cannabis is rapidly expanding across the nation, consumers are looking for cannabis experiences. This has led to the development of a variety of services designed to engage the new, and returning, cannabis community. These experiences include activities as diverse as:

- grow tours or guided visits to a hemp or cannabis cultivation site
- learning to roll sushi and a joint
- going to a cannabis painting class (puff, puff, paint)
- experiencing cannabis yoga
- enjoying a cannabis-infused meal

In states with legalized adult use, these businesses can be as practical and simple as providing a limousine ride from the airport to a dispensary and providing inside information about the local cannabis market. Or it could be more broad-reaching such as setting up a cannabis-friendly hotel that includes events such as cannabis yoga, tours of growing facilities, and infused cannabis meals. There are even opportunities to conduct business overseas and set up private club tours in Spain or publish guides to the cannabis scene in Amsterdam and other popular cannabis tourism destinations. But whatever hospitality or tourism angle is pursued, know that it is a viable and expanding business. To begin with, many trends point to growing opportunities in many hospitality markets. Consider the following:

- The average cost of a wedding is over $33,000 with people getting married later in life and looking for new wedding experiences (i.e., destination weddings, themed weddings).[8]
- A total of 2.38 billion domestic trips were taken in the United States in 2023, seventy million more than recorded in 2019.[9]
- According to the National Travel and Tourism Office,[10] in 2022, international departures from the United States totaled 80.7 million. This was an increase of 65.7 percent from 2021 (48.7 million).
- Millennials are traveling in increasing numbers and spend the most on vacations compared to other groups.[11]
- Restaurant.org notes that 61 percent of adults say they would rather spend money on an experience, such as a restaurant or other activity, compared to purchasing an item from a store.[12]
- A major restaurant trend in legal adult-use cannabis states is offering cannabis-based items on the menu (mostly CBD for legal reasons) and this appeals to multigenerations.[13]

An anchor of the cannabis hospitality, tourism, and events pyramid is the need for education. Whether someone is traveling to experience cannabis or staying in a hotel that has cannabis events or touring a grow facility, they are trying to increase their knowledge, which will help them better enjoy the experience and will enable them to make more informed cannabis decisions down the road. If you pursue opportunities in the cannabis hospitality business, make sure that cannabis education is baked into your product or experience from the beginning.

CHAPTER 7

Yet another reason why cannabis events and tourism are popular is because it is one of the ways to get into the cannabis business that is not cost-prohibitive. Mark Twain made this observation when he saw the gold rush starting: "During the gold rush it's a good time to be in the pick and shovel business." And this bit of wisdom applies to the cannabis market. As cultivation operations, processing facilities, and dispensaries are opening, there is a need for supporting cannabis industries such as transportation, seminars, services to help people better enjoy their products, and more. By paying attention to trends and by listening to new and experienced users, supporting cannabis industries and opportunities should become apparent.

This leads to the need to "get the word out" about cannabis services and events largely by social media and proactive marketing. Web presence is key for these businesses! Especially for an industry that is still fighting stigma, how do you think most people find out about how to visit a dispensary, what products are available, what it's like to have a cannabis wedding, what it's like to have an infused meal, and more? They'll likely go online before they ask a friend or even a medical professional. Online, they can feel safe and anonymous. It's a little like using Yelp to find a restaurant. You scan the choices, read the reviews, and make your decision.

Choosing your Cannabis Tourism or
Hospitality Business Opportunity
Some of the considerations that influence the type of hospitality, tourism, events, or social media cannabis company you may want to develop include:

- Industry experience: It may be easier to pivot into cannabis when you have experience and connections that are already established in a parallel industry. For instance, moving from being a limousine driver to owning a cannabis transportation service or adjusting your social media skills to become an expert in cannabis content.
- Interests: It may sound cliché to say, "Choose your passion," but at a minimum, you want to do something daily that engages you. Fill

in the blank: "＿＿ and cannabis," and you'll likely have a great opportunity! If yoga is your thing, consider cannabis yoga classes.

- Initial Investment: Before starting any business, you should map out what your likely expenses are. Investing in hotels or cruise lines might be a big reach, but there are plenty of smaller, more localized opportunities that need little more than a solid plan, passion, commitment, and some elbow grease.
- Difficulty in Acquiring Licenses and Exposure to Liability: Businesses that "touch the plant" have to get special licenses and liability insurance, which can be difficult to get and are expensive. Be sure to research what specific licenses and insurance you will need for your business and plan your time to market and your costs accordingly.
- Market Research: Do your research to make sure your business is of high interest and will have repeat customers. Is what you're offering in demand? Is there local competition? For instance, a seminar and a local tour of a dispensary may be great for beginners, but how does your business expand past "first timers"?
- Number of Employees and Complexity of Business: You will need to consider the levels of experience and the kind of employees you want to hire. In the cannabis business, those with the most experience are also those who may have records or work "off the grid." Consider employing those most harmed by mass incarceration and prejudice.

Brian Applegarth, founder of the Cannabis Travel Association International and the Cannabis Trail, provides this perspective about working in cannabis hospitality and tourism, "My journey in the cannabis travel and tourism industry has been a rewarding experience. It's a fun space where play, education and entertainment all intersect, and the relationship between mindset and setting shines through. It embodies the future of travel as a vehicle for well-being and balance and is an exciting new frontier to be a part of." In terms of market segments, he goes on to explain, "The four archetypes of the cannabis travel audience are the canna-curious audience niche, the cannabis wellness traveler, the cannabis connoisseur, and the ceremonial traveler, an audience drawn to ritual and intentional cultural experiences that expand awareness and consciousness with the support of entheogenic effects."

Of course, as with any business, you'll need to write up a business plan with revenue projections and you should meet with your accountant and possibly an attorney to discuss challenges, opportunities, and any other special requirements to get your business underway.

Business Development Considerations

In comparison to some cannabis businesses, cannabis hospitality businesses can be a little less taxing to set up. However, again, as with any business you need to ask yourself the following questions:

- What will my business structure be (corporation, LLC, etc.), how do I get an EIC (tax ID number), will I need a board of directors, and do I need to register my business with the city, state, or any other regulatory entity?
- Do I need to be concerned with local politics, zoning, or permits, and do I need to interface with law enforcement prior to company launch?
- If I need to buy or lease real estate, what size building do I need, what are the construction requirements, and does my landlord need to grant approval for me to run the business?
- Are there any environmental controls to be put into place, and do I need special security equipment such as special cameras and safes?
- What is the list of equipment and inventory that I need to start and what will be ongoing equipment and inventory expenses?
- How will I finance my business? (Note that the majority of cannabis businesses are still self-financed or financed by "friends and family" in the range of $25,000 to the low six figures.)
- Can I find an accountant who knows cannabis regulations, especially tax code 280E (which only allows for certain deductions and allowable expenses for some cannabis businesses)?
- Do I need a separate payroll and HR provider (because again, payroll in the cannabis trades can be different)?

- Do I need staff and if so, how will I find them, train them, check their backgrounds, and comply with any other local and state requirements?
- What will my day-to-day operations look like? Will I have to develop SOPs? Do I need special software for point of sale, inventory control, and local or state-required compliance reports?
- What legal, banking, and insurance services do I need?
- Have I written a business plan with financial projections and expenses?
- What does my marketing plan look like? Who are my competitors, what is my pricing strategy and how will I attract customers and repeat customers?

This may look like an exhaustive list but being more thorough and thoughtful in the cannabis business upfront will save you headaches in the future and will set you up for success.

Cannabis Tourism and Hospitality Roles

Probably the three most common cannabis hospitality or tourism jobs are travel agents, tour guides, and drivers. Sometimes a driver will also function as a tour guide. Cannabis experiences can start with cannabis travel agents who are knowledgeable about experiences that are available and can offer a variety of choices. And of course, they have experience in setting up events and working with reputable hospitality providers.

Travel agents have the opportunity to work domestically or internationally. As countries around the world increasingly embrace cannabis, it has become a viable tourist attraction. Some of the most popular cannabis destinations include Amsterdam, Spain, Jamaica, Mexico, Colombia, Panama, Costa Rica, Canada, Malawi, and many US destinations including several cities in California, Las Vegas, Denver (and surrounding mountain towns such as Aspen, Telluride, and Vail), Portland, Oregon, Seattle, Washington, and Atlantic City, New Jersey. Given that some of the destinations only tacitly approve of cannabis consumption, discretion and planning are paramount.

In states where adult use is legal, drivers may pick up guests and take them to a dispensary. Along the way the driver will educate their customers about local cannabis laws, places to visit, and events to experience. Often, the tour company has made a deal with grow operations, restaurants, brewpubs, and dispensaries as those are common destinations for their guests. In most cases, there is no minimum education level or formal training required to become a limo driver or tour guide. You simply need the proper credentials for driving in your state.

It's important to note that online presence and social media are critical in this sector of the cannabis industry. Instagram, X, and TikTok are major ways in which customers seek and find cannabis experiences. Curating your business's online image is a worthwhile endeavor.

Cannabis Tourism Information
Another common cannabis hospitality and tourism job is in the information sector. These companies can publish cannabis guides, provide online reviews of cannabis events, be booking agents, or even be a branch of the state whose job it is to educate visitors on local regulations so that responsible consumption can take place. In-person seminars on any number of cannabis topics may be offered as well.

This growing sector not only caters to the increasing interest in cannabis-related activities among tourists but also fills a crucial gap in knowledge dissemination and regulatory compliance. In destinations where cannabis consumption is legal, providing accurate and up-to-date information on regulations, products, and experiences ensures a safe and enjoyable visit for tourists. As the cannabis market continues to expand globally, establishing a foothold in the hospitality and tourism sector presents a lucrative opportunity for businesses to capitalize on this emerging trend and shape the narrative surrounding cannabis tourism.

Cannabis Event Planner and Coordinator
Perhaps the best-known role in this area is the wedding planner. But event planners do similar work for all kinds of other events, like concerts, speaking engagements, and more. Sometimes they're hired by colleges or municipalities to coordinate event series on campus or in towns. This

same role is needed in the cannabis event space. Someone good with details, marketing, and envisioning events that will be popular could make a successful career out of being a cannabis events planner. A bit like a general contractor, this person has to forge strong relationships with service providers as diverse as tent companies, food service partners, sign printers, cannabis speakers, musicians, and the list goes on and on. Cannabis event planners are good networkers who enjoy interacting with the public.

We've seen cannabis combined with 5K races, three-on-three basketball tournaments, pickleball events, adult volleyball, and more. Concerts and cannabis have a long-standing tradition going back to the prohibition era, so these events are ripe with opportunity in the new legal markets. Events such as these do require more attention to legislative and compliance issues than non-cannabis events so factors such as security, liability insurance, proper venue, transparent rules (where and if attendees can consume cannabis) and an overall marketing strategy to attract participants have to be factored in with timing and event costs. For this type of work, sponsors or creators of these events can make an hourly wage, charge a per-event fee, and make significant income from ticket sales and sponsorship packages.

Cannabis Chef and Caterer

As proof of the viability of this next trend, the next time you read a cannabis publication, you will likely read an article or two about cooking with cannabis. Interest from diners in experiencing a cannabis-infused meal, whether it's infused with CBD or THC, is at an all-time high. Many people are dining with cannabis for special events such as retirement dinners, thirtieth, fortieth, fiftieth, or sixtieth birthdays, bachelorette parties, cannabis weddings, or just to experience something different in the dining scene.

This job can take many forms such as a personal caterer who goes to a client's house, a restaurant owner who hosts cannabis dinners on specified dates (such as once a month), or a chef who is hired to cook at a special event (outdoor cannabis barbeque or wedding for example). Cannabis caterers and chefs have to have a background in cooking or baking, know how to properly dose, and be cognizant of local and state regulations. It is also helpful if the chef or caterer is adept at answering customer questions about many segments of the cannabis industry.

Cannabis Lodging: Glamping and Bud and Breakfasts
Hotels and bed and breakfasts which pair the traditional experience with cannabis are becoming more and more popular. In most cases, these are run in states that allow for adult use such as Colorado, California, Washington, Oregon, and Alaska and are natural tourist destinations in their own right. Services can be as simple as providing guests with information about the local cannabis environment and allowing them to use cannabis in their rooms or outdoors on private property. But some bud and breakfast establishments offer much more, including a welcome cannabis basket, yoga sessions, tours to cultivation operations and dispensaries, and the chance to try a professionally infused meal.

Another type of cannabis lodging option that has become popular recently is outdoor camping, or glamping. These operations sometimes offer lodging in A-frame buildings or large tents. Popular add-on activities include wine and weed tours (especially in California), guided hikes, boating, paddleboarding, and other outdoor sports done during the day. These businesses seek to combine the classic camping, fireside experience with cannabis. Mostly, the advertising angle of these facilities is to offer customers a chance to more closely appreciate nature, health, and wellness activities, all while enjoying some cannabis.

Unusual Cannabis Careers

Now that we have covered many of the more "traditional" cannabis jobs, we will turn our attention to cannabis opportunities that you may not have thought of. As with any new industry, market needs arise as legal and organizational frameworks are put into practice. In many ways, it is the implementation of regulations that can create jobs and opportunities. Take security cameras for example. Because dispensaries and cultivation operations are required to document and record their activities, these operations must install many security cameras. Who, in the security camera installation business, could have guessed that the legalization of cannabis would be a boon to their industry? There are dozens of examples of job opportunities like these that arise.

Yet another intriguing career in cannabis is that of a cannabis artist. I have a student, Nick Randazzo, who just completed three mural projects for a local dispensary. He created murals showing the cannabis plant, key landmarks in the area, and a few icons from the owner's hometowns. They added these images to their portfolio while continuing to find other opportunities to create cannabis art.

Noted Canadian cannabis artist and founder of Crater Crater, Spencer Charlton had this to say about the message he is trying to deliver to the world through his cannabis sculpture-making, "I am using my cannabis art to convey the problem of excess packaging waste and single-use plastics produced by the legal cannabis industry. I plan to continue creating these works to keep the dialogue going and bring more attention to this issue until meaningful changes are made." He cleverly uses cannabis flower labels and empty plastic containers to create animal sculptures, thereby emphasizing the impact that cannabis trash has on the natural world. His sculptures will soon be seen in cannabis museums across the country.

Creating or Finding Nontraditional Cannabis Jobs

Some people are creating their own jobs by anticipating industry needs. Because each state has its own requirements, unique opportunities may be available state by state. For example, in New Jersey, the creation of "consumption lounges" looks like it will be a new opportunity for existing operators and may be a new stand-alone business for others in the future. Consumption lounges are places where people can legally smoke cannabis, similar to the way a bar is a place where folks can legally have a beer. In other words, if you are twenty-one or older, it is legal for you to purchase cannabis, but currently you cannot partake in a hotel, apartment buildings (subject to the landlord's approval), in student housing on campus, on a public sidewalk, in a car, or in a national park. This essentially leaves private residences as the only legal place to consume. And if you are a visitor or live in federal housing, you may not have access to a private residence. The way New Jersey is tackling this issue is to allow for the creation of consumption lounges, which are special buildings located next to or attached to a dispensary. The idea is that a customer could buy, say, a pre-rolled joint, and then walk into the consumption lounge and smoke it.

It's interesting to note that consumption lounges are only novel to parts of the contemporary United States. For example, San Francisco and Barcelona are two cities that have had lively cannabis club cultures for many years. Since consumption lounges are a new entity, new jobs that may be developed could be:

- consumption lounge interior designer
- host
- entertainer
- cannabis educator who hosts specific cannabis events
- transportation and "car storage" manager for guests who want to leave their cars
- odor control manager

Other opportunities arise from newly discovered needs such as the growth in the interest in cannabis experiences and international travel. As you might imagine, if you decided to pursue a business that specialized in international travel offering cannabis experiences such as tours, you would need to set up:

- a website
- a booking or payment system
- secure cannabis-friendly lodging
- secure qualified tour operators or drivers who have good relationships with growers, cannabis chefs, yoga studios that offer cannabis classes, and more
- a social media plan to support sign-ups, promote services, and collect reviews
- have a plan to keep your guests safe

- write and compile a local travel frequently asked questions about what to expect, things to see and do, local customs, a summary of how cannabis is treated, lists of resources

Yoga and Cannabis Instructor

Would it surprise you to know that cannabis and yoga go hand in hand? Yoga's popularity in recent years has blossomed, and probably because yoga practitioners are interested in health, wellness, and natural remedies, they often offer classes that discuss how to use cannabis to maximize your productivity and for recovery. Many classes offer the opportunity to partake before or after your session. Yoga instructors find that their students are more relaxed and often more open to yoga when using cannabis. This is also one of the least expensive "cannabis" businesses to get started. At a minimum it takes yoga expertise (training), a studio (or private outdoor venue), local or state business registration, insurance, minimal supplies, and clientele.

Art and Cannabis Franchisee

One of the more unusual cannabis activities you may have read or heard about is a franchise called Puff, Puff, Paint.[14] This business was started in Colorado by a twentysomething artist who decided that she could attract more customers by letting them use cannabis before and during painting instruction. Especially as adults, some of us have become more self-conscious about painting or drawing but feel freer while using cannabis, as it helps the creative process. Students are not required to use cannabis, but most do. As mentioned, the concept has become so popular that the concept is being franchised in Arizona and other states.

Cannabis Photographer

If you have spent any time looking at cannabis websites or visited a dispensary you have seen some beautiful photos. Sometimes they are merely for entertainment, but often they are educational. If a dispensary has rotating products, such as what flower is on offer, photos must be taken nearly every day. Cannabis businesses need high-quality photos: cultivators (for their "About Us" section of their website), processors (to show their extraction and production processes), dispensaries (for any number of needs including photos of the dispensary and all product photos, some of which need to be updated on a daily or near-daily basis), cannabis branding agencies who need appropriate photos of cannabis users, consumption lounges (to show what their facilities look like), cannabis travel agencies (to show the exotic locales that their visitors frequent) and really, any cannabis business that has a website or prints cannabis information. As you may have guessed, cannabis photographers are most often self-employed and must hustle to fill their time. However, once a cannabis photographer makes a name for themselves, they are in high demand. There is also the requirement to capture the right feeling with photos. For example, if your audience is educated older adults, then photos of "young stoners" are not going to cut it.

Cannabis Inventors

There are also opportunities for the creation of new products. Most often this happens organically as a cannabis user has their aha moment when they say, "Wouldn't it be nice to have a particular product that does . . ." Skip Stone is an engineer based in Colorado who wanted to keep his cannabis products away from his kids and pets. Rather than just buying a safe or trying to hide his product, he looked at the problem from a different angle and set out to solve the following issues:

- A storage container must look stylish and have subtle non-cannabis-looking branding.
- There must be a simple lock on the container.
- It must mitigate or stop any smell.
- There should be several built-in storage spaces to accommodate different-sized products.
- Several sizes and colors should be offered.

The result was the creation of a company called StashLogix.[15] Their products have a built-in rubber gasket and come with a charcoal pack to stop smell, the lock ingeniously uses the ends of the zipper for the three numbered tumbler lock, there are removable, repositionable dividers, and the overall look is stylish, fashion-forward, and subtly branded. This company continues to grow, and it all started by addressing a need in the cannabis market with an invention.

Cannabis Brand Creation, Trademarking, and Consumer Products Licensing

As with any growing industry, intellectual property is a valuable asset. One opportunity that's in its infancy in the cannabis space is the development of cannabis consumer brands. Recognizable brands are all around us. From the apparel we wear to the food we buy at the market to the car we drive, our consumer choices are often driven by brand recognition. Think for a moment of your favorite brand of jeans. Would you consider buying a different brand? Probably not, because you know that regardless of where you buy it, the size and fit, the experience, will be the same. Now apply this to cannabis. Can you list ten notable cannabis brands? Again, probably not. Eventually, once a customer finds a cannabis product and brand that works for them, they are likely to be repeat customers and brand loyal.

Right now, there are only a handful of recognizable cannabis brands that are largely celebrity driven including brands by Snoop Dogg, Willie Nelson, Bob Marley's estate, and Tommy Chong. Some dispensaries are using their company name for products as a private label play. In all cases, these companies will need someone to leverage their intellectual property into complementary categories such as apparel and to make deals across state lines. A person who does this kind of work is called a licensing agent.

Being a licensing agent has nothing to do with acquiring an operator's license or any type of cannabis permit. Rather, it is the person who specializes in and understands the development of branded cannabis consumer products. Licensing agents who secure trademarks may be attorneys who have intellectual property experience, consumer goods experts, or someone from a retail background. One unique way that licensing agents can be paid is by a percentage of the royalties on the products they license on behalf of the copyright holder. This means that as branded products sell, licensing agents receive a percentage of wholesale or retail sales.

In part because dispensaries and cannabis products are heavily regulated on the state level, the notion of national brands has yet to arrive. This means that growers, processors, and dispensaries must develop their own brands or license a brand, which means borrowing the equity of an existing brand in exchange for a royalty payment. If a person knows brand licensing or consumer product development, this area is wide open for development.

Cookies, a lifestyle cannabis brand launched in California, has become so popular that dispensaries in states like Colorado and New Jersey have made deals to use strain names, specific coloring on packaging, and the Cookies logo to offer branded products. This means that in dispensaries that carry the Cookies brand you can expect to see Cookies cannabis flower, concentrates, T-shirts, rolling papers, and more. These dispensaries are betting that their customers know the Cookies name and would trust products bearing this logo, and that down the road all Cookies products whether in Las Vegas, New York, or San Francisco will provide the same experience, regardless of where the shop is located. Conversely, a multistate dispensary known as Curaleaf is developing its name and logo hoping to capitalize on its growing brand and standardizing its experience across states. This is similar to a grocery store selling their house brand.

For your reference, here are examples of two federally trademarked brands in the cannabis industry. The first logo comes from Garden State OG, which is a nod to all of the legacy cannabis pioneers in New Jersey who helped to set up the state's cannabis industry. And the second logo is from Our Community Harvest, which is an education and events company that will be pivoting into the edibles space.

Figure 7.1. Garden State OG is a trademarked cannabis brand. Rob Mejia, OCH, LLC

Figure 7.2. Our Community Harvest is a New Jersey–based cannabis education company. Rob Mejia, OCH, LLC

Federal Legalization's Impact on Planning, Shipping, Tracking, Storage, and Distribution

Federal legalization means interstate and even international commerce would be possible. Consider Oregon's case for a second. Oregon licensed too many growers, which meant that they grew too much cannabis relative to the consumer demand in their state. Under federal legalization, growers and businesses would be able to sell products and ship their flower across state lines. The market would expand widely! This transition would involve a lot of preplanning, shipping, tracking, storage, distribution, and compliance with other states' regulations, such as potency limits and packaging requirements. Plus, once cannabis is federally legal, access to traditional banking services will open up, allowing more folks to more easily get in the business. Insurance will likely blossom too.

Eventually, it would be fair to expect some national product standardization. However, the payoff would be substantial as the United States would become the largest cannabis market in the world. It would also involve a massive number of jobs including brand managers and distributors, warehouse workers, truck drivers, tracking specialists, computer experts who would develop programs to track every gram of product, storage warehouse managers, and local drivers and salespeople to contact and work with dispensaries.

Research Opportunities

Other jobs that will experience growth when national legalization occurs are in the research and testing arenas. National legalization would mean that cannabis has been removed from Schedule 1, which would open the door for research. We have heard for years that research is needed regarding cannabis and its effectiveness as medicine, and with national legalization more studies would be initiated. And while it's true that research scope and speed have been severely hampered, it's a myth to claim that there's been no cannabis research conducted, as roughly four thousand studies were conducted in 2023 and over the past ten years over thirty-two thousand studies were published.[16]

In addition, national legalization would be a boon for cultivators who grow cannabis at home. One of their options would be to start testing their homegrown cannabis. At some point, a company will be able to scale a home test, like a home pregnancy test, so a home grower can mail a specimen to be tested or can purchase their own kits to test for potency, mold, pesticides, and heavy metals. Home testing kits are available now, but they are expensive and complicated.

Another area of innovation will be in the area of cannabis-impaired driving. Current tests do not test for active cannabis inebriation, but at some point, a national Breathalyzer-type test will be developed. This could mean big business. Several parties including police departments, city officials, cannabis lounge owners, scientists and researchers, and private employers all have a large stake in ensuring that cannabis is being used safely and does not contribute to traffic accidents. Right now, several states want to use drug recognition experts (DREs; current law enforcement or who have retired from law enforcement) to detect cannabis impairment. These DREs will have to be trained and certified, which is yet another opportunity in the cannabis industry. A related opportunity will be to train workplace impairment recognition experts (WIREs) who will be trained and certified in DRE protocol and will work at private companies.

INTERNATIONAL OPPORTUNITIES

Once national cannabis legalization occurs, we will be able to participate on the international stage as well. Major job opportunities that will arise include cannabis importer (and all of the associated logistics jobs that come along with this) and cannabis exporter (again, with all of the support occupations that will be needed to make it a successful enterprise). Certainly, attorneys, bookkeepers and accountants, insurance agents, bankers, testing labs, brand managers, logistic providers, and other support jobs will all have to be involved as well.

FINAL WORDS

If you decide to pursue a career in cannabis, you will join the ranks of pioneers and individuals making a significant difference. This is an exciting time in the cannabis industry. We are still figuring out how the business will be implemented, creating a dynamic and evolving landscape.

As you step into this field, be adaptable, flexible, and determined. These qualities will help you navigate the inevitable changes and challenges.

Starting a new career is never easy. However, with the knowledge you have gained from this book and other cannabis resources, you will be more prepared than most. Education is a powerful tool. It will give you an edge and the confidence to face the unknown. Remember, every expert was once a beginner. Your journey will be full of learning experiences that will shape your personal and professional growth.

The cannabis industry needs you! Employers are constantly searching for industry participants at all levels with cannabis education essentials. Your unique skills, passion, and commitment can drive progress and innovation. We look forward to seeing you make your mark. Whether you aim to be a cultivator, budtender, marketer, advocate, or entrepreneur, your contribution matters. Embrace the adventure ahead, and don't hesitate to seek support from the cannabis community. Good luck on your journey!

Chapter 8

Cannabis Career Resources

SAMPLE JOB DESCRIPTIONS

The following cannabis job descriptions demonstrate skills needed to join a cultivation, processing, and retail team respectively. Given that these are some of the most popular job types in cannabis, we thought it would be useful to see these examples. When you examine the job descriptions be sure to note where your skills and interests intersect. Also, make a list of the keywords that will help you get your resume noticed. For example, in the first paragraph of the cultivation job description, here are some prominent words you should use if you have these skills: outdoor cultivation, stages of cultivation, cloning, pruning, transplanting, up-potting, watering, feeding, plant deficiencies, and experience with Marijuana Enforcement Tracking Reporting Compliance (METRC). The METRC system is a comprehensive, state-mandated cannabis tracking system designed to ensure compliance in the regulated cannabis industry, and it operates as "seed-to-sale" tracking software. The following three job descriptions appear courtesy of Vangst and some of the clients they work with.

Job Description: Cultivation

Our client is looking for outdoor cultivation technicians. They will report to department supervisors and are responsible for caring for medical marijuana plants during the immature, vegetative, and flowering stages. Cultivation technicians will execute operations of plant care such as cloning, pruning, transplanting, up-potting, watering, feeding, ensuring environmental control, and inspecting plants for signs of deficiency or infestation, as well as labeling and tracking plants using METRC tags.

Essential Duties and Responsibilities:

- Implement cultivation practices as indicated by supervisors and managers in an outdoor environment.
- Maintain the health of immature, vegetative, and flowering plants through observation and adherence to established standard operating procedures (SOPs).
- Ensure accuracy of plant inventory, including strain names, plant tag numbers, and counts of plants.
- Perform plant maintenance, feedings, and irrigation events, and integrated pest management (IPM) according to a set schedule and SOP, as determined by the head of cultivation.
- Ensure the grow facility is kept free of pests, viruses, or other diseases by preventing contamination through the proper use of personal protection equipment (PPE) and biological controls established within the cultivation SOPs.
- Regularly sanitize tools, equipment, pots, and production areas used in the grow facility to ensure sanitary practices.
- Abide by high personal hygiene standards.
- Apply pesticides safely and effectively, wearing appropriate PPE, and after ample training and instruction from the head of cultivation.
- Check and record accurate data daily, including but not limited to: pesticide applications, issues found when scouting plants, and any other items required by management.
- Observe and immediately address issues with plants, equipment, or environments.
- Break down and set up plant production areas after harvest, including sweeping all work areas, sanitizing crop benches, washing down rooms, and preparing to transplant new crops.

- Demonstrate accuracy and thoroughness concerning plant health and traceability, to uphold the company's standard for quality.
- Work promptly and strive to increase productivity through coordinated workflow and efficient systems.
- Maintain organization and sanitary conditions within the grow facility.
- Assist with postharvest duties as needed.
- Other duties as assigned.

Minimum Requirements:

- High school diploma or equivalent required.
- Ability to communicate clearly and accurately.
- Must comply with state regulations and guidelines.
- The ability to pass a background check is required.
- Must be 21 years of age or older.
- 1–3 years of experience in horticulture, agriculture, and/or marijuana cultivation preferred.
- Energetic team player, willing to take direction and learn new skills.
- Basic strain and plant structure knowledge preferred.
- Knowledge of the uses and benefits of cannabinoids is preferred.
- Two years of caregiver experience is preferred.
- A combination of the above shall also be considered.

Physical Requirements:

- Long periods of prolonged standing and sitting.
- Requires normal range of hearing and manual dexterity sufficient to operate a computer.
- Ability to observe and assess the material that deviates from established company standards.
- Some crouching or holding uncomfortable positions for extended periods; repetitive motions.
- Requires bending and lifting up to 70 pounds.

CHAPTER 8

Work Environment:

- Outdoors.
- Must be able to withstand the elements.
- Occasional weekends or extended hours may be necessary during certain phases of plant production.
- Constant interaction with colleagues.

Job Description: Processing and Packaging

Our client is seeking a temporary production associate to join their packaging department. Successful hires will be responsible for the careful and efficient packaging of cannabis flower products.

This entry-level position involves applying labels, packaging products into tubes, and ensuring that all items are prepared for distribution per company guidelines and regulations.

Responsibilities:

- Apply product labels accurately and consistently.
- Package cannabis into designated containers, ensuring compliance with regulatory requirements.
- Conduct visual inspections to ensure product quality meets company standards.
- Report any discrepancies or defects in the packaging materials promptly.
- Work efficiently to meet production targets and deadlines.
- Collaborate with team members to streamline packaging processes.
- Adhere to all relevant regulations and guidelines governing the packaging of cannabis products.
- Maintain a clean and organized workspace per company policies.
- Work closely with other team members and departments to achieve common goals.
- Communicate effectively with supervisors and colleagues to ensure smooth operations.

Desired Qualifications:

- High school diploma or equivalent.
- No prior experience is required; training will be provided.
- Attention to detail and ability to perform repetitive tasks with accuracy.
- Ability to work in a fast-paced environment.
- Strong communication and teamwork skills.

Physical Requirements:

- Ability to stand for extended periods.
- Lift and carry packages weighing up to 50 lbs.
- Manual dexterity for packaging tasks.

Job Description: Budtender

Our client is seeking budtenders who possess expert knowledge of all state rules and regulations and can quickly learn about all products sold at their dispensary, and cannabis in general. They must be able to accurately process transactions, correctly recording them in the point-of-sale system while making customers feel comfortable and informed.

The budtender must consistently and professionally follow all company standard operating procedures. Budtenders can adapt the shopping experience for each customer. They provide information and insight when appropriate, in a friendly and approachable manner. Those hired on will attend training so they may confidently assist customers in their cannabis product selections.

Successful candidates will continuously expand their knowledge of cannabis and cannabis products, doing research online and visiting other facilities when possible. When customers ask, they provide insight and information into the methods of consumption, safe dosages, potential effects, and storage of products. The work environment can be fast-paced and noisy. It requires someone who enjoys the intensity and can multi-task and focus while maintaining a friendly and professional demeanor.

Responsibilities:

- Provide exceptional customer service, ensuring each customer feels valued and well-assisted.
- Educate customers on different cannabis products, including strains, methods of consumption, and effects.
- Assist customers in making informed purchasing decisions based on their preferences and needs.
- Operate the POS system efficiently, processing transactions accurately and maintaining an organized workspace.
- Maintain a thorough understanding of current inventory and product availability.
- Uphold compliance with all state regulations and company policies regarding the sale of cannabis products.
- Collaborate with team members to ensure a smooth and efficient operation.
- Maintain cleanliness and organization of the dispensary at all times.

Qualifications/Requirements:

- Prior customer service experience
- Must be at least 21 years of age and legally authorized to work in the United States
- Must be able to satisfy state requirements via background checks to work in the industry
- General knowledge of cannabis products and a willingness to advance cannabis knowledge
- Excellent verbal and written communication skills
- Must be highly energetic, positive, and enthusiastic
- Ability to interact with all personality types and work as a team
- Ability to remain calm and organized in high-volume sales scenarios
- Ability to adapt when rules or processes change
- Flexible availability to include some nights, weekends, and holidays

- Ability to work in person, non-remote
- Ability to sit or stand for long periods
- Lift to 30 lbs.
- Computer and technology savvy

THE CANNABIS CAREERS RESUME
Resume Components

A typical resume consists of several key sections, each serving a specific purpose to effectively present your qualifications, experiences, and skills to potential employers. Here are the major parts of a resume and their purposes:

1. Header and Contact Information: This section is usually positioned at the top of the resume and includes your name, contact number, email address, and possibly your physical address. Its purpose is to provide essential contact details for potential employers to reach out to you for further consideration. Be sure to include a professional email address and avoid email addresses such as StonerGuy@gmail.com.
2. Professional Summary or Objective: This section, positioned just below the header, provides a brief overview of your career goals, skills, and experiences. A professional summary is more common and highlights your professional achievements, while an objective statement focuses on your career goals and aspirations. This is a great place to customize your professional summary or objective statement to match the needs of specific employers.
3. Work or Professional Experience: This section details your relevant work history, typically in reverse chronological order, starting with your most recent position. Include the name of the company, your job title, dates of employment, and a description of your responsibilities and accomplishments in each role. Its purpose is to showcase your past experiences and demonstrate your ability to contribute effectively in a new role. Bullet points that capture your responsibilities can be useful here.

4. Education: This section lists your educational background, including degrees earned, institutions attended, graduation dates, and any relevant academic achievements or honors. Its purpose is to highlight your educational qualifications and provide context for your skill set. If you have taken any hemp or cannabis courses, list them here.
5. Skills: This section outlines your relevant skills, both technical and soft skills, that are relevant to the job you're applying for. Skills can be categorized into sections such as technical skills, computer proficiency, language proficiency, and interpersonal skills. Its purpose is to quickly demonstrate to employers that you possess the necessary skills to excel in the role.
6. Certifications or Licenses: If you have any professional certifications or licenses that are relevant to the position you're applying for, you can include them in a separate section. This adds credibility to your qualifications and demonstrates your commitment to professional development.
7. Achievements or Awards: If you've received any notable awards or recognition throughout your career, you can include them in this section. This can include accolades such as employee of the month and year, performance awards, or industry-specific recognition. Its purpose is to highlight your accomplishments and demonstrate your value as an employee.
8. Additional Sections (Optional): Depending on your specific experiences and qualifications, you may include additional sections such as volunteer work, professional affiliations, publications, clubs, or relevant projects. These sections provide further insight into your background and interests.

Preparing Your Resume

When crafting your resume, you should keep in mind the primary goal: secure an interview! Resumes are used to eliminate candidates from opportunities as much as if not more than they are used to recruit candidates. Yes, you must demonstrate your qualifications. Likewise, you must not give hirers a reason to disqualify you. Here, then, are key considerations to keep in mind:

Accuracy and spelling matter. Be sure to double-check your dates, phone number, and email address for accuracy. Then, you must proofread the entire resume to make sure there are no errors. A single spelling error or using the past tense instead of the present tense when applicable can send your resume to "the round file," better known as the trash can!

Can you work the words "cannabis" or "hemp" into your resume? Often, at larger companies, resumes are screened for certain words that will move the resume to the top of the stack. If you can sensibly work these terms into your resume, this will help. Perhaps you have taken a cannabis course, attended a seminar, or even read and studied a cannabis book. All these activities are fair game to be listed on a resume.

Be sure to customize the summary or objective section to appeal to the specific company you are applying to. To do this, you must research the company by searching online about the organization, reading its mission statement, visiting its social media sites, and talking to anyone at the company you know. When you figure out what the company values and stands for, echo this information in your summary and objective section.

Invest in a simple, effective design. The internet is full of free or low-cost resume templates. Use a template to add appropriate color and section dividers to your resume. The format should be inviting, clear, efficient, and easy to read.

Page length matters. A one-page resume is appropriate for students, recent graduates, and professionals with roughly one to ten years of experience. Professionals with more experience or unique, specialized experience and skills may want to consider creating a two-page resume which offers the benefit of being able to add more keywords. Keywords are words or phrases that are used in a job description. Again, if you can naturally echo some of these words and phrases, your resume will receive more consideration. Finally, resumes of three or more pages are useful for researchers, with many years of experience, and used in fields such as medicine or academia. As an academic, I have seen some resumes and CVs (curricula vitae) that are as long as some of the books I assign in class! But you likely don't need to go there.

Chapter 8

Choose the appropriate approach or organization for your resume. This depends on your experience level and career goals. The three resume formats you should choose from are:

1. reverse chronological order
2. functional
3. combination of the two

The reverse chronological resume is the format most employers are used to seeing. To use this format, list your employment history and education in reverse chronological order. Be sure to use the present tense when describing your current job and skills and the past tense for jobs in the past.

A functional resume is useful for job seekers with little experience or those who are trying to pivot their careers. It focuses on your skills rather than your job experience but may be a tougher sell. Be sure to highlight transferable skills that align with the job you are applying for.

Finally, a combination resume balances the two aforementioned choices. It focuses equally on experience and skills using the reverse chronological technique in the employment section. It is best for those who want to change careers, have gaps in their work history, or are veteran workers with a lot of experience.

Overall, the purpose of each part of a resume is to effectively communicate your qualifications, experiences, and skills to potential employers clearly and concisely. This should demonstrate why you are a strong candidate for the position.

Here are a few sample resumes for the cannabis industry. They demonstrate effective resumes that were created by individuals who were seeking opportunities in cultivation, processing, and dispensary operations respectively. Given that these are some of the most popular job types in cannabis, these should be useful examples. Note that if you are interested in different opportunities in hemp or cannabis, refer to resumes from reputable websites or if you are a college student don't overlook the resources that are available through your career education center. Many cities, counties, or nonprofits have employment services, including resume preparation.

CANNABIS CAREER RESOURCES

SAMPLE RESUMES
Sample Resume: Entry-Level Cultivation

Alex Monroe
123 Wayne Lane, Millbrook, IL 60612 Email: AMonroe22@gmail.com Phone: 201-867-5309

Professional Summary	Dynamic and dedicated professional with a college degree in Psychology from Bowling Green University. Experienced in various customer service and leadership roles, with a proven track record of success in team environments. Skilled in communication, problem-solving, and time management. Seeking to leverage expertise in psychology and diverse work experiences to contribute effectively in a new role in the cannabis industry.

Work Experience

Assistant Supervisor — **Plumbing Department, Home Depot**

Dates of Employment: [Month, Year]–[Month, Year]

- Demonstrated leadership skills by effectively supervising and coordinating daily operations within the plumbing department.
- Provided exceptional customer service, addressing inquiries and resolving issues promptly and efficiently.
- Trained and mentored new team members to ensure adherence to company standards and procedures.

Waiter — **ABC Diner**

Dates of Employment: [Month, Year]–[Month, Year]

- Delivered outstanding customer service in a fast-paced restaurant environment, consistently exceeding guest expectations.
- Managed multiple tasks simultaneously, including taking orders, serving meals, and processing payments.
- Collaborated with kitchen staff to ensure accurate and timely delivery of food orders.

Lifeguard — **Summer Pool Club**

Dates of Employment: [Month, Year]–[Month, Year]

- Maintained a safe swimming environment by enforcing rules and regulations and responding promptly to emergencies.
- Conducted routine inspections of pool facilities to identify and address potential hazards.
- Provided assistance and first aid to patrons as needed, promoting a positive and enjoyable experience for all.

Education

Year of Graduation: 2020   Bachelor of Arts in Psychology Bowling Green University

Skills

- Strong interpersonal and communication skills
- Excellent customer service abilities
- Leadership and team management
- Time management and multitasking
- Proficient in Microsoft Office Suite

Certifications   CPR and First Aid Certification (American Red Cross)

Achievements/Awards   Club Treasurer, Lions Club

Additional Information

- Completed horticulture course
- Avid gardener
- Proficient in cannabis cultivation techniques

CHAPTER 8

Sample Resumes: Mid-Level Cannabis Laboratory Processing Job
Dylan Rodriguez
123 Springbrook Road, Parsons, NY 21892 Email: DylanRodZ@gmail.com Phone: 301-867-5309

Professional Summary	Detail- oriented and driven professional with a college degree in Biology from the University of Michigan, with a minor in Sustainability. Experienced in laboratory environments, administrative support, and customer service roles. Strong organizational and analytical skills, with a passion for promoting sustainability initiatives. Seeking to leverage diverse experiences and skills to contribute effectively in a new role in a cannabis testing and processing lab.

Work Experience

Administrative Support and Testing Supervisor **Dr. Norman Lewis, Private Practice**

Dates of Employment: [Month, Year]–[Month, Year]

- Provide administrative support to Dr. Lewis, including scheduling appointments, managing correspondence, and maintaining records.
- Supervise and coordinate laboratory testing procedures, including blood tests and other diagnostic tests.
- Ensure compliance with regulatory standards and protocols to maintain the highest quality of patient care.

Hostess **Chop House**

Dates of Employment: [Month, Year]–[Month, Year]

- Greeted and seated guests in a timely and courteous manner, enhancing the overall dining experience.
- Managed reservations and coordinated seating arrangements to optimize restaurant efficiency.
- Assisted with various tasks to support restaurant operations, including answering phones and assisting servers.

Pfizer Intern Program **Pfizer**

Dates of Employment: [Month, Year]–[Month, Year]

- Participated in a comprehensive internship program, gaining valuable experience in pharmaceutical research and development.
- Assisted with various projects, including data analysis, laboratory experiments, and documentation.
- Collaborated with cross-functional teams to support research initiatives and achieve project objectives.

Education

Year of Graduation: 2022 Minor: Sustainability   Bachelor of Science in Biology University of Michigan

Skills

- Laboratory techniques and protocols
- Data analysis and interpretation
- Administrative support and coordination
- Customer service and interpersonal skills
- Proficient in Microsoft Office Suite

Certifications   [List any relevant certifications or licenses here]

Achievements/Awards   Member of Chemistry Club

Additional Information

- Completed several lab courses in college
- Passionate about promoting sustainability initiatives
- Interest in cannabis/hemp research and product development

Sample Resume: Entry-Level Dispensary Position with Goal to Move into Marketing
Coleman Griffin
9388 E Ash Drive, Jerome, AZ 80470 Phone: 401-867-5309 Email: colemangriffin_1@outlook.com

Objective	Motivated and dependable individual seeking a position in retail operations, media, or marketing to leverage organizational skills and cannabis knowledge. Experienced in team collaboration and independent project completion. Known for a positive attitude and delivering work on time and within budget.

Education

| Minor: Cannabis Concentration | Roanoke College |
| Foundations of Project Management Certificate: January 2021 | Dual Major: Business and Marketing |

Experience

Freebird Casino	**Table Games Assistant**
(location) July 2022–July 2024	Maintained a welcoming atmosphere and ensured adherence to company policies. Managed financial transactions and monitored patron behavior.
JCPenney	**Brand Ambassador**
(location) January 2022–June 2022	Created and maintained displays, provided customer assistance, upsold products, and prevented theft.
Sand Beach Motel	**Social Media Director**
(location) May 2021–August 2021	Promoted the hotel through online forums and social media posts, managed bookings, handled inventory, and supervised team members.
Chipotle Mexican Grill	**Hospitality Captain**
(location) January 2019–May 2021	Welcomed customers, took orders accurately, trained new employees, and managed transactions.

Skills

- Leadership: Ability to inspire and motivate team members with innovative thinking and actions.
- Marketing: Proficient in effectively promoting products and services to target customers.
- Productivity and Time Management: Prioritize tasks and delegate effectively for optimal outcomes.
- Team Management: Skilled in motivating and assigning tasks based on individuals' abilities and interests.
- Creativity and Problem Solving: Think critically and find innovative solutions by considering multiple perspectives.

Cover Letter Tips

A cover letter is a one-page document submitted alongside your resume or CV. A cover letter allows you to give more context to your application and showcase your unique qualifications, personality, and ability to follow directions. A cover letter is a personal pitch letter about your job skills and accomplishments. Think of it as persuasive writing. You are trying to convey why you would be a good fit for the company, and how you would contribute to their success. For that reason, make sure to research your targeted company before you reach out; you want to echo what is important to them. Here are some tips to keep in mind:

- Pick skills that the job requires and provide examples of how you put these skills into action.
- When possible, include data proving your accomplishments.
- If you are a recent graduate, you may not have lengthy work experience, in which case highlight transferable skills that may include volunteer experience or classroom projects.
- Include some of the keywords from the job listing when targeting your experience for the job.
- If there is an obvious gap in your work history, address it briefly and then move on.
- Research the company and hiring manager to customize the letter as much as you can.
- Address your cover letter to a specific person or use the salutation, "Dear Hiring Manager."
- Whenever you know someone at the company, ask if you can use their name. If they agree, use the name in the first paragraph or two and definitely in the subject line if sent via email.
- Use a business letter format with the date and your contact information.
- Your cover letter should not be longer than one page.
- Be sure the font is easy to read and that there are no typos.
- Follow all application instructions carefully.
- Finally, if you include an email address make sure it is professional.

Sample Cover Letters
The following cover letters are examples of the types of cover letters that could accompany a cultivation resume, a lab processing resume, and a dispensary resume respectively. Of course, be sure to write a customized

cover letter for each job, even if you are tempted to use a cover letter you submitted for another position.

Cover Letter 1: Cannabis Cultivation
[your name]
[your street address]
[city, state, zip code]
[your email address]
[your phone number]
[date]

[recipient name]
[hiring manager's title]
[company name]
[company address]
[city, state, zip code]

Dear [recipient name],
I am writing to express my enthusiasm for the cannabis cultivation position at **[company name]**, as advertised. With a deep-rooted passion for horticulture and sustainable cultivation practices, I am excited about the opportunity to contribute to your team.

In my previous role at **[previous company]**, I gained hands-on experience in cultivating high-quality cannabis strains while adhering to strict compliance and regulatory standards. I consistently implemented innovative techniques to optimize plant growth and maximize yield, resulting in **[mention any specific achievements or results—with numbers to back up your claims—if applicable]**.

Furthermore, my background in **[mention any relevant skills or experiences, such as botany, agriculture, or horticulture courses]** has equipped me with a solid foundation in plant biology and cultivation methods. I am eager to leverage my knowledge and expertise to support **[company name]**'s mission of delivering premium-quality cannabis products to consumers.

I am particularly drawn to **[company name]**'s commitment to sustainability and environmental responsibility, as demonstrated by **[mention any relevant initiatives or practices you admire about the company; also consider including language that is used in the company's mission statement without using exact wording]**. I am confident that my dedication to sustainable cultivation practices aligns well with your company values.

Thank you for considering my application. I am eager to discuss how my skills and experiences can contribute to the success of **[company name]**. I am available for an interview at your earliest convenience and can be reached at **[your phone number]** or via email at **[your email address]**.

Sincerely,
[your name]

Cover Letter 2: Mid-Level Lab Work in a Cannabis Lab
[your name]
[your address]
[city, state, zip code]
[your email address]
[your phone number]
[date]

[recipient name]
[hiring manager's title]
[company name]
[company address]
[city, state, zip code]

Dear **[recipient name]**,
I am writing to express my interest in the mid-level lab technician position at **[company name]**, as advertised. With a strong background in laboratory techniques and a passion for the cannabis industry, I am excited about the opportunity to contribute to your team.

In my previous role at **[previous company]**, I developed proficiency in various laboratory procedures, including **[mention specific techniques or methodologies relevant to the job description, along with your experience using specific lab equipment]**. I consistently maintained accurate records and ensured compliance with industry regulations, contributing to the success of **[previous company]**'s research and development projects.

Additionally, my experience in **[mention any relevant skills or experiences, such as quality control, sample analysis, or data interpretation]** has prepared me to handle the challenges of a fast-paced cannabis laboratory environment. I am confident in my ability to perform effectively and contribute to the advancement of **[company name]**'s cannabis product development initiatives.

I am particularly impressed by **[company name]**'s reputation for innovation and commitment to excellence, as evidenced by **[mention any specific projects or achievements of the company that resonate with you; and again, refer to their mission statement for hints as to what is important to them]**. I am eager to be part of a team that values continuous improvement and cutting-edge research in the cannabis industry.

Thank you for considering my application. I am enthusiastic about the opportunity to discuss how my skills and experiences align with the needs of **[company name]**. I am available for an interview at your earliest convenience and can be reached at **[your phone number]** or via email at **[your email address]**.

Sincerely,
[your name]

Cover Letter 3: Role at a Cannabis Dispensary with Future Marketing Aspirations
[your name]
[your address]

[city, state, zip code]
[your email address]
[your phone number]
[date]

[recipient name]
[hiring manager's title]
[company name]
[company address]
[city, state, zip code]

Dear **[recipient name]**,
I am excited to submit my application for the cannabis dispensary associate position at **[company name]**, as advertised. With a background in customer service and a keen interest in the cannabis industry, I am enthusiastic about the opportunity to contribute to your team and grow within the company.

In my previous role at **[previous company]**, I honed my customer service skills and developed a deep understanding of client needs and preferences. I consistently provided personalized recommendations and ensured a positive shopping experience for every customer, resulting in **[mention any specific achievements or customer feedback, if applicable, and use data, when possible, to back up your claims]**.

Furthermore, my passion for marketing and branding has inspired me to pursue a career in cannabis marketing in the future. I am eager to gain hands-on experience in the cannabis industry and learn about product offerings, consumer trends, and marketing strategies from experienced professionals at **[company name]**.

I am particularly drawn to **[company name]**'s commitment to providing education and promoting responsible cannabis consumption, as demonstrated by your mission statement **[and mention any specific initiatives or community outreach programs of the company]**. I am excited about the opportunity to be part of a team that prioritizes customer education and advocacy.

Thank you for considering my application. I am eager to discuss how my skills and experiences align with the needs of **[company name]**. I am available for an interview at your earliest convenience and can be reached at **[your phone number]** or via email at **[your email address]**.

Sincerely,
[your name]

Follow-Up Email Guidelines
A common question that arises after an interview is when and how often to follow up. It's a tricky question as you want to be engaged with your potential employer to demonstrate your interest in the position, but you don't want to check in so often that you become a nuisance. Here are some guidelines for you garnered from talking to hiring experts in the cannabis field.

To begin with, remember that each company has a hiring process, which sometimes takes a while. The person who is hiring may also be in charge of other parts of the cannabis business. Yes, it is important to hire candidates, but they have other priorities too. If you applied from a website, without knowing anyone at the company, you should follow up in five to seven business days. Even then, you may not receive a response; be prepared to be patient. But if someone referred you, check back directly with your contact, again in five to seven business days.

On the other hand, if you have been screened via phone call, you should follow up that day, or the next day at the latest. Keep this follow-up simple and short. Thank your interviewer for the conversation and their time, mention something you liked about the company, and confirm any next steps if those were discussed.

If you had an in-person interview, you should follow up that day if possible or the next day at the latest. Again, thank your interviewer for their time, reiterate something interesting or valuable that you learned about the company, express interest in the opportunity, and let them know you look forward to connecting again. When you follow up, this is also a chance to briefly clarify any responses you gave that you felt were lacking or unclear.

Since we have covered when to follow up, let's look in more depth as to the message you want to convey. First, check to make sure you submitted your application correctly. Companies often have specific procedures. The last thing you want to do is fail to follow instructions. Plus, you want to make sure that the information you submit is accurate and clear. Then, you want to personalize your follow-up and send it to the correct person who is often a hiring manager. But before you do this, make sure that the company wants to be contacted as some firms will specify that you should not check back with them. Whatever their instructions are, follow them carefully. Almost always, this information can be found in the job description document. Follow-up email guidelines summary:

- Keep your email concise, clear, and professional.
- Emphasize your enthusiasm for the position.
- Showcase your relevant skills; that is, mention your top qualifications and why they matter.
- Thank them for their time.
- "Leave the door open" by offering to answer any questions or provide additional information.
- Depending on where you are in the hiring process, diplomatically ask for an interview or next steps.
- Before pushing send, proofread your email again.

SAMPLE FOLLOW-UP EMAIL
Subject: Follow-Up on **[position]** Application

Dear **[hiring manager's name]**,
I hope this message finds you well. I am writing to follow up on my recent application for the **[position]** role at **[company name]**, which I submitted on **[date]**.

I want to reiterate my enthusiasm for this opportunity. The innovative work being done at **[company name]** greatly aligns with my professional interests and values. I am particularly excited about **[specific aspects of the company or role that speak to you]**.

With my background in **[your relevant skills or experiences]**, I am confident that I can contribute effectively to your team. I am particularly skilled in **[mention top qualifications]** and believe these would be beneficial to **[company name]**.

Thank you for considering my application. Should you need any additional information or have any questions, please do not hesitate to reach out. I am very interested in moving forward in the hiring process and would be thrilled to discuss my application in more detail.

Looking forward to hearing from you.

Best regards,
[your full name]
[your phone number]
[your email address]

Interview Tips

When it comes to landing a job, remember that resumes and applications might get your foot in the door, but it's the hiring managers who make the final decision. Your preparation and positive attitude can make all the difference in your interview. In a nutshell, interviews are a critical part of the hiring process. They give you a chance to talk more about your experience, education, and training. It's also your opportunity to learn more about the company and the job you're applying for.

It may help you to think of the job interview as a friendly, two-way conversation. The interviewer wants to find out if you have the skills and personality that fit the role. At the same time, you should be figuring out if this company and position are the right fit for you. Both sides are gathering information to make a well-informed decision.

Before the Interview
It is essential to prepare for an interview. To prepare for a cannabis interview, thoroughly research the company, including its products, culture, and any recent developments in the business. Be sure to look at their social media accounts, which reveal their culture, how they interact with customers, and what is important to them. Practice answering common interview questions, such as "What is your greatest strength?" and "Tell me about a time you solved a problem." Finally, ensure you understand key industry terms and trends, and be ready to discuss your passion for the cannabis industry. Before your interview you should also:

- Review Your Resume: Be ready to discuss your past accomplishments and experiences, both paid and unpaid, that are relevant to the job.
- Practice Interviewing: Prepare by reviewing common interview questions and practicing your responses to build confidence.
- Be Flexible and Prepared: Confirm the interview details such as time, location, and point of contact. Ask if there will be multiple interviewers so you know what to expect. If it is a remote interview, check your audio and video, ensure that you have a quiet, clean area, and in all cases, dress professionally.

During the Interview
Plan to arrive early to ensure you have enough time to navigate any security or access requirements at the site. Check with your point of contact about appropriate arrival times, check-in procedures, and other logistics. Keep in mind, your initial impression can set the tone for the entire interview.

Be ready to summarize your experience in about thirty seconds, highlighting what you bring to the position. Listen carefully to each question asked and answer as directly as possible. Focus on your achievements relevant to the job, using specific examples to show how your knowledge, skills, and abilities fit the role. Provide data if you can. If you need clarification, don't hesitate to ask the interviewer to restate a question.

Keep a positive attitude and avoid negative comments about past employers. Pay attention to your body language and tone of voice, staying engaged and giving the interviewer your full attention. Remember to put your cell phone away and on mute during the interview. You may also want to take some notes.

Be sure to ask any final questions about the organization or the position and inquire about the next steps in the selection process, including time frames. Request access to a contact person in case you have any follow-up questions. Finally, reinforce your interest in the position and thank the interviewer for the opportunity to interview. Note that questions about salary and benefits are sometimes addressed by someone other than the hiring or interviewing manager. This is why it is important to find out who the best contact person is for specific questions.

After the Interview

Once the interview is over, promptly thank the interviewer, find out what the potential next steps are, and provide any additional information requested by the interviewer. It's important to be patient as the hiring process can take time. If you haven't heard back within a reasonable time frame, it's perfectly okay to follow up with your point of contact to check on the status of your application.

Remember, the hiring manager is looking for the right person with the right skills to fill the position. Your goal during the interview is to show that you are that person. If you have a baseline of cannabis knowledge, passion to participate in the industry, and the right skills and attitude you have an excellent chance of joining the ever-intriguing, ever-growing, amazing cannabis industry. Good luck!

How and Why to Ask for a Letter of Reference

In your journey to build a successful career in the cannabis industry, a strong letter of reference can serve as a powerful tool. Whether you're applying for a job, an internship, or an academic program or scholarship, this document provides a personalized endorsement that highlights your skills, character, and achievements. Understanding how to request a letter of reference effectively—and why it's so important—can make a significant difference in your professional development.

The Importance of a Letter of Reference

A letter of reference is more than just a formality; it's a testament to your qualifications and character from someone who is well-regarded and knows you well. In a competitive field like cannabis, where employers and academic institutions are looking for candidates who stand out, a well-crafted reference letter can set you apart. It serves several key purposes:

- Validation of Skills and Experience: A letter of reference verifies the qualifications you've listed on your resume. It gives potential employers or academic committees confidence that you possess the skills and experience you claim.
- Insight into Character: Beyond your technical abilities, employers want to know about your work ethic, reliability, and interpersonal skills. A reference letter provides a glimpse into your character, often highlighting attributes that might not be immediately evident from a resume or application form.
- Networking and Relationship Building: Requesting a letter of reference can strengthen your professional network. It reinforces your relationship with the person providing the reference, which could lead to future opportunities and collaborations in the industry.

How to Request a Letter of Reference

Requesting a letter of reference is a process that requires careful thought and planning. Here's a step-by-step guide to ensure you approach it with professionalism and consideration:

1. Identify the Right Person: Choose someone who knows you well and can speak positively about your qualifications. Ideally, this person should be someone with whom you've had a professional

relationship, such as a supervisor, professor, or mentor in the cannabis industry.
2. **Make a Formal Request:** When asking for a letter of reference, reach out formally—either through email or a professional conversation. Be clear about why you're requesting the letter and what the overall purpose is. For example, you might be applying for a job at a cannabis dispensary or seeking admission to a cannabis studies program.
3. **Provide Necessary Details:** To make the process as smooth as possible, provide the reference writer with all the information they'll need:
    - Who the letter should be addressed to: If there's a specific person or organization, include their name and title.
    - The purpose of the letter: Explain the context of your application, whether it's for a job, internship, or academic program.
    - The deadline: Let them know when you need the letter by, giving them ample time to write it.
4. **Supply Supporting Materials:** To help the writer craft a strong letter, send them your current resume along with three to four bullet points you'd like them to include. These could highlight specific achievements, skills, or experiences that are particularly relevant to the position or program you're applying for.
5. **Express Gratitude:** Writing a reference letter takes time and effort, so be sure to express your appreciation. A simple thank-you can go a long way in maintaining a positive relationship.
6. **Follow-Up and Share Outcomes:** Once you've submitted your application, let the reference writer know when you hear back. Whether your application is successful or not, sharing the outcome shows respect and appreciation for their support.

A well-crafted letter of reference can open doors in the cannabis industry, helping you to stand out in a competitive field. By approaching the request with clarity and professionalism, you not only secure a valuable endorsement but also strengthen your professional relationships.

CHAPTER 8

Remember, the key to a great letter of reference is clear communication—both in what you provide to the writer and in the gratitude you show for their support.

JOB SEARCH WEBSITES AND RESOURCES

If you are looking for an entry-level position, these are often posted on the cannabis company's website or local social media. Otherwise, here are some good websites with cannabis job listings:

> Vangst, https://vangst.com/
> Ganjapreneur, https://www.ganjapreneur.com/marijuana-job-boards/
> Cannabiz, https://cannabizteam.com/
> Careers in Cannabis, https://www.careersincannabis.com/
> FlowerHire, www.flowerhire.com
> Ms. Mary Staffing, http://msmarystaffing.com/
> Work In Cannabis, https://workincannabis.com/
> The Cannabis Jobs Board, https://www.thecannabisjobboard.com/
> 420 Jobs Board, https://www.420jobsboard.com/
> Cannabis Staffing Group, https://420staffing.comTrimForce, https://trim-force.com

Other popular job sites now include cannabis job listings:

> Indeed, https://www.indeed.com/
> Glassdoor, https://www.glassdoor.com
> Zip Recruiter, https://www.ziprecruiter.com/
> Monster, https://www.monster.com/

If you are looking for an online assessment tool to determine your top skills and personality traits, here is the website for the CliftonStrengths Online Talent Assessment.
> https://www.gallup.com/cliftonstrengths/en/252137/home.aspx

Cannabis Education Resources

Backes, Michael. *Cannabis Pharmacy: The Practical Guide to Medical Marijuana*. Black Dog & Leventhal, 2017.

Barcott, Bruce. *Weed the People: The Future of Legal Marijuana in America*. Time Books, 2015.

Blesching, Uwe. *The Cannabis Health Index: Combining the Science of Medical Marijuana with Mindfulness Techniques to Treat Over 200 Chronic Diseases*. Logos Publishing, 2022.

Casarett, David. *Stoned: A Doctor's Case for Medical Marijuana*. Current, 2015.

Cervantes, Jorge. *The Cannabis Encyclopedia: The Definitive Guide to Cultivation & Consumption of Medical Marijuana*. Van Patten Publishing. 2015.

———. *Marijuana Horticulture: The Indoor/Outdoor Medical Grower's Bible*. Van Patten Publishing, 2006.

Dolce, Joe. *Brave New Weed: Adventures into the Uncharted World of Cannabis*. Harper Wave, 2016.

Dufton, Emily. *Grass Roots: The Rise and Fall and Rise of Marijuana in America*. Basic Books, 2017.

Editors of Munchies. *Bong Appetit: Mastering the Art of Cooking with Weed*. Ten Speed Press, 2018.

Goodman, David. *An American Cannabis Story*. powerHouse Books, 2023.

Graf, Nichole, Sherman, Micah, Stein, David, and Crain, Liz. *Grow Your Own: Understanding, Cultivating, and Enjoying Cannabis*. Tin House Books, 2017.

Grinspoon, Peter. *Seeing through the Smoke: A Cannabis Specialist Untangles the Truth about Marijuana*. Prometheus, 2023.

Herer, Jack. *The Emperor Wears No Clothes: A History of Cannabis/Hemp/Marijuana*. Independently Published, 1985.

Klein, Zach. *The Scientist: Are We Missing Something?* Documentary. Y. Klinik Productions, 2015.

Lee, Martin. 2012. *Smoke Signals: A Social History of Marijuana-Medical, Recreational and Scientific*. Scribner.

Mejia, Rob. 2018. *The Essential Cannabis Book: A Field Guide for the Curious*. Spring House Press. (Second edition coming soon with new publisher).

Michaels, Dan (author), and Erik Christiansen (photographer). 2023. *Higher: The Lore, Legends, and Legacy of Cannabis*. Ten Speed Press.

Picillo, Ashley, and Lauren Devine. 2017. *Breaking the Grass Ceiling*. CreateSpace Independent Publishing Platform.

Pollan, Michael. 2009. *The Botany of Desire*. Documentary. Kikim Media.

Rosenfeld, Irvin. 2011. *My Medicine: How I Convinced the U.S. Government to Provide My Marijuana and Helped Launch a National Movement*. Open Archive Press.

Rosenthal, Ed, Dr. Robert Flannery, and Angela Bacca. 2021. *Cannabis Grower's Handbook: The Complete Guide to Marijuana and Hemp Cultivation*. Quick American Archives.

Tardiff, Joseph, ed. 2008. *Marijuana: Contemporary Issues Companion*. Greenhaven Press.

Warf, Barney. 2014. High Points: An Historical Geography of Cannabis, *Geographical Review* 104:4, 414-438, DOI: 10.1111/j.1931-0846.2014.12038.x

Wolf, Laurie, and Melissa Parks. *Herb*. Inkshares, 2015.

Cannabis Podcasts

If you are a podcast fan, you may find these podcasts to be of particular interest. The number of episodes listed reflects roughly the number of episodes recorded and offered by the end of 2023.

420 Radio. Al Rapp (host). 165 episodes.

2 Be Blunt Podcast. Peezy (host). 170 episodes.

The Adam Dunn Show. Adam Dunn (host). 422 episodes.

Benzinga Cannabis Insider. Javier Haase and Elliot Lane (hosts). 255 episodes.

The Cannabis Connoisseur. Jack Stone and Islah Washington (hosts). 267 episodes.

The Cannabis Investing Podcast. Rena Sherbill (host). 320 episodes.

Casually Baked: The Podcast. Johanna Nuding (host). 270 episodes.

Deadhead Cannabis Show. Larry Mishkin and Rob Hunt (hosts). 240 episodes.

The Dr. Greenthumb Podcast. B-Real (host). Based in Los Angeles. 970 episodes.

Great Moments in Weed History. David Bienenstock (host). 120 episodes.

The Green Rush. Anne Donohoe and Lewis Goldberg (hosts). 292 episodes.

Grow Bud Yourself! Danny Danko and Mike G. (hosts). 225 episodes.

Hempresent. Vivian McPeak (host). via Cannabis Radio. 280 episodes.

Karma Koala. Sean Hocking (host) via Cannabis Law Report. 160 episodes.

Lancaster Farming Industrial Hemp Podcast. Eric Hurlock (host). 260 episodes.

The Mary Jane Society Podcast. Pam Chimiel. 155 episodes.

Still Toking With . . . Benjamin Bartlett and Jeffery Homan (hosts); 182 episodes.

Thinking Outside the Bud. Bruce Eckfedlt (host). 412 episodes.

Weed + Grub. Mary Jane Gibson and Mike Glazer (hosts). 356 episodes.

WeedMan 420 Chronicles. WeedMan (host). 230 episodes.

Wine and Weed. Steelo Brim and Chris Reinacher (hosts). 90 episodes.

Women Leading in Cannabis. Kyra Reed (host); 74 episodes.

SELECTED WEBSITE RESOURCES

Brave New Weed, Bravenewweed.com
Brave New Weed is the homeplace of cannabis expert Joe Dolce's resources and popular podcast. Now with over one hundred episodes, Dolce has created a *Brave New Weed* archive of entertaining and educational cannabis content, with interviews with experts and important people in the cannabis space.

Cannabis Benchmarks, Cannabisbenchmarks.com
Cannabis Benchmarks analyzes cannabis industry pricing, especially wholesale pricing, allowing users and customers to make scaled, longer-term market predictions.

Cannabis Now, CannabisNow.com
This publication's news section addresses cannabis current events, economics, legal topics, and politics, as well as cultivation, edibles, medical cannabis topics, and strains. Cannabis Now's website also holds resources on the history of cannabis, dispensary profiles, events, and product reviews.

Our Community Harvest, OurCommunityHarvest.com
Our Community Harvest (OCH) is a community organization for people who want to learn about and contribute cannabis knowledge.

OCH creates and offers educational information, online courses, in-person seminars, consulting services and cooking demonstrations/noteworthy information on the melding of cannabis and food. If you cook with cannabis, you will appreciate the dosing calculator that is available on this website.

Drug Policy Alliance, Drugpolicy.org
The Drug Policy Alliance is a national nonprofit organization that promotes alternatives to the war on drugs. It was founded in 2000, and the organization has been part of many landmark legislative and political moments of reform, such as the 1996 medical cannabis proposition in California, as well as other legalization bills over the last decades. There are political resources on their website that help contact one's representatives, as well as a helpful newsletter that highlights protest and mobilization opportunities across the country.

Future Cannabis Project FutureCannabisProject.com
The FutureCannabis Project website emphasizes coverage of four main marijuana topics: health, policy, business, and culture. It's a great site for a quick overview of current events.

Indigenous Cannabis Coalition, Indigenouscannabiscoalition.com
The Indigenous Cannabis Industry Association was founded by Mary Jane Oatman of the Nez Perce Tribe. The Indigenous Cannabis Industry Association is the epicenter of all things indigenous cannabis. The association produces *THC Magazine*, (Tribal Hemp and Cannabis), which covers indigenous cannabis news and culture, as well as the *Smoke Signals* podcast which features discussions with Oatman and guests.

Cannabis Law Report, https://cannabislaw.report/
The website features reporting and newsletters on cannabis legal happenings, as well as job listings, webinars, and various blog postings. The website, founded and edited by Sean Hocking, also produces *Karma Koala*, a podcast about all things law, business, cannabis culture,

and psychedelics. The show features cannabis legal discussions and interviews, as well as music selections from hosts Sean Hocking and Heather Allman. Find the podcast on Spotify and Anchor.

Laurie and MaryJane, LaurieandMaryJane.com
This is the website of accomplished cannabis chef Laurie Wolf. She runs an award-winning edibles business in Portland, Oregon. If you are fortunate enough to live in Oregon, you can purchase her precisely dosed gummies, fudge and brownie bites, cookies, and cheese crisps. Check out her recipes on her blog, DontFearTheEdible.com, as well.

Leafly, Leafly.com
Leafly is particularly useful when it comes to researching strains and dispensaries. There are plenty of lists, charts, reviews, and tips. If you are researching strains, start with peer reviews, which are often humorous, descriptive, and helpful. Leafly also modestly covers other cannabis topics.

Marijuana Moment, Marijuanamoment.net
Edited by Tom Angell, a twenty-plus-year veteran of the legalization movement, Marijuana Moment helps activists, industry professionals, consumers, policymakers, and the public understand developments and trends affecting cannabis. Topics covered include politics, business, science, and culture.

Marijuana Policy Project, Mpp.org
Marijuana Policy Project is the largest organization in the United States dedicated to ending marijuana prohibition. Their focus is on championing states' rights, as well as sensible cannabis regulation. If you want to find out or get involved in the legalization battle, visit MPP's site.

Medical Cannabis Mentor, Medicalcannabismentor.com
Medical Cannabis Mentor is an online educational provider perfect for dispensary personnel, healthcare providers, and patients. Doctor-approved courses are self-paced and interactive. Medical Cannabis

Mentor faculty include Joe Dolce, Rob Mejia, Dr. Matt Elmes, Dr. Dave Gordon, and Dr. Swathi Varanasi.

MG Magazine, Mgmagazine.com
This website provides news on the cannabis industry, focusing on business-to-business developments including corporate and retail happenings. The site also sports high-quality writing from the likes of Lance Lambert, an expert in the industry and international cannabis.

MJBizDaily, Mjbizdaily.com
MJBizDaily is a news and media website which provides a wide variety of cannabis coverage. The site has specific pieces on the daily developments of the cannabis industry, from hemp and CBD to recreational cannabis and burgeoning legal developments. MJBiz also produces thorough industry reports, such as a general industry "Factbook."

National Hemp Association, NationalHempAssociation.org
This nonprofit website advocates for the growth and development of the hemp industry. The National Hemp Association primarily serves farmers, processors, manufacturers, researchers, and investors. If you want to learn about or support the use of hemp, this is a good place to start.

NORML, Norml.org
NORML is a strong site to start with if you are just getting acquainted with cannabis, have health questions, or want to help legalize marijuana. As stated on their website, "NORML's mission is to move public opinion sufficiently to legalize the responsible use of marijuana by adults, and to serve as an advocate for consumers to assure they have access to high quality marijuana that is safe, convenient and affordable." Their information on state issues is especially helpful and specific.

Prohibition Partners, Prohibitionparters.com
Prohibition Partners provides the global cannabis industry with specialist, international information, data analytics, and digital commerce

solutions. This site takes deep-dive analyses into international cannabis developments.

Project CBD, ProjectCBD.org
This nonprofit association, which has been around since 2010, promotes and publicizes research into the medical uses of CBD and other parts of the cannabis plant. They provide education for doctors and health workers (via seminars), and educate patients, industry professionals, and the general public. Part of their mission is to help physicians and researchers collect data to determine the effectiveness or lack of effectiveness of CBD as medicine and to review CBD-rich strains and products.

SMART, Studentmmj.com
SMART (Student Marijuana Alliance for Research & Transparency) is a student-led network dedicated to learning about cannabis and its impactful role in our society. Founded at Brown University in 2017, and now with a presence on more than fifty college campuses across the United States, this student organization seeks to provide accurate cannabis education to college students in a transparent and honest fashion.

Students for Sensible Drug Policy, SSDP.org
Students for Sensible Drug Policy (SSDP) is the largest global youth-led network dedicated to influencing drug policy and ending the war on drugs. An international grassroots network, SSDP unites students who are concerned about the impact of drug misuse on our communities, but who also know that the war on drugs is failing our generation and our society.

Thinking Outside the Bud, thinkingoutsidethebud.com
Thinking Outside the Bud is a business podcast devoted to driving innovation in the cannabis space. During each episode, host Bruce Eckfeldt speaks with founders, investors, thought leaders, researchers, advocates, and policymakers who are finding new and exciting ways for cannabis to positively impact business, society, and culture.

Glossary

Adult use Adult use refers to the policy of legalized recreational cannabis, emphasizing that the market is open to responsible adults who are twenty-one and older. Sometimes the adult-use cannabis market is also called the recreational use market.

Cannabinoids Cannabinoids are the group of substances found in the cannabis plant, as well as in the human body, which compose and interact with the endocannabinoid system. THC and CBD are only two of the hundreds of cannabinoids present in cannabis, but they are generally the most common and well-known.

CBD CBD, or cannabidiol, is the now well-known component of cannabis which has been shown to have positive medical benefits for conditions such as seizures. CBD has been shown to provide pain relief, anxiety reduction, and analgesic effects without getting the user "high."

Chemovar Chemovars, also known as chemotypes, refer to the classification methods used by cultivators to reference cannabis strains, describing their chemical composition, such as a strain's ratios of THC to CBD.

Cola A cola is a flowering site on a female cannabis plant where buds cluster together. Usually, there's a large cola toward the top of the plant with other smaller ones below. A cola is also sometimes called the terminal bud.

Concentrates Concentrates, or cannabis extracts, are products made by the extraction of trichomes, the sticky resinous glands in the cannabis buds. Various methods of extraction produce concentrates, all of which create products that are generally more potent than smoking raw cannabis flower. Common names of concentrates include shatter, budder, wax, and diamonds.

Controlled Substances Act The Controlled Substances Act (CSA) was passed in 1970 and came into effect in 1971 during the Nixon administration, establishing a legal framework to regulate drugs. This act classified cannabis as a Schedule 1 drug (having a high potential for addiction and no medically approved usage); other Schedule 1 drugs include heroin, LSD, and peyote. This legal framework is also the main reason that cannabis research has been so limited.

Cultivar A cultivar is a plant that has been produced as a result of selective breeding. These are often plants that have been bred for specifically desired traits.

Decarboxylation Decarboxylation is the process by which cannabis compounds are heated and then "activated," meaning THCA is turned into THC. You must "activate" your cannabis before you make your edibles. A common method to "decarb" your cannabis is to put ground-up cannabis in the oven at 200 degrees Fahrenheit for about one hour. In the simplest sense, decarbing means slow roasting.

Dispensary Dispensary is the term for a retail business that is legally allowed to sell and distribute cannabis products. Some dispensaries are for medical cannabis patients only; others are for adult-use customers as well.

Dosing Dosing refers to the calculated amount of cannabis you administer to achieve your desired effects. It is commonly used in terms of tinctures, vapes, and edibles and when one must determine the potency of the product.

Edibles An edible is a food that is infused with cannabis, such as brownies or gummies.

Endocannabinoid system (ECS) The endocannabinoid system is a neuromodulatory body system made up of a series of receptors, known as CB1 and CB2, which help the body reach homeostasis. It's made up of endogenous cannabinoids which are cannabinoids created within the body, cannabinoid receptors, and enzymes that create and break down cannabinoids. It was only discovered in the 1990s!

Entourage effect The entourage effect refers to the theory that each component of the cannabis plant works best in conjunction with the others—cannabinoids, terpenes, flavonoids, and more—rather than in isolation. This is why it's often best to consume cannabis with certain THC to CBD ratios, and levels of terpenes and flavonoids, and not simply the strain containing the highest levels of THC.

Glossary

Flavonoids Flavonoids are chemical compounds that work in tandem with terpenes to determine the color, smell, and taste of cannabis. They're often rich in antioxidants. Flavonoids aren't unique to cannabis; they're found throughout nature, such as in fruits, vegetables, teas, and more. They also protect plants from pests and provide UV protection.

Flower Flower refers to the dried and cured buds of the female cannabis plant, rich in cannabinoids and terpenes that are commonly smoked or vaporized.

Hash Hash is compacted cannabis resin, or kief, which is a smokable substance containing a high THC content. It is made by pressing or rubbing the resin glands of a cannabis plant to form a slab or brick. The color of hash can range greatly.

Hemp Hemp is cannabis with less than 0.3 percent THC that is grown for CBD oil or fiber. Hemp is an amazingly adaptable, valuable crop that was caught up in the prohibition of cannabis. It contains negligible levels of THC, so it's not psychoactive. Hemp's fiber can be made into over twenty-five thousand products including apparel, construction material, biodiesel fuel, health and beauty aids, food, paper, and bioplastics.

Homegrow Homegrow is the term used in reference to growing cannabis at home. It is not yet legal in every state, so would-be homegrowers should check their state's regulations if homegrow is legal, and, if so, how many plants one can grow.

Hybrid The term hybrid is used to describe a cannabis strain which is a combination of indica, sativa, and/or ruderalis strains. Nearly every cannabis plant now grown is a hybrid.

Indica Indica is one of the main subtypes of cannabis plants; cannabis indica grows to be shorter and stouter than its sativa counterpart. Strains from cannabis indica plants often promote a relaxed feeling, and indica is sometimes jokingly referred to as "in-da-couch."

Infusion Infusion is the term for adding cannabis to an edible product, often by using cannabis "infused" butter or oil.

Kief Kief is the term for the resiny trichomes found in very fine cannabis shavings that are almost dust-like. This material often has higher THC content and is more potent when smoked. Kief is often collected in the bottom chamber of a cannabis grinder.

Microdosing Microdosing refers to small, controllable doses usually administered over long periods. The technique of microdosing is especially popular when a consumer is trying to figure out the lowest amount of cannabis product they can use to achieve an optimal effect.

Potency Potency refers to the levels of THC or CBD in a given strain or product. In the case of THC, generally the higher the THC percentage, the more intense the psychoactive effects can be expected, like alcohol percentage in beer.

Pre-roll A pre-roll is the term used in dispensaries to refer to a cannabis joint you can buy that is already rolled by the company or dispensary.

Ruderalis Ruderalis is a type of cannabis plant that originated in Eastern Europe and Russia. It's smaller than its cousins, but it can contain high amounts of CBD and low amounts of THC. It is used almost exclusively for breeding because ruderalis autoflowers, which means it blooms after a certain number of days instead of depending on light cycles to trigger the bloom cycle.

Sativa Sativa refers to cannabis sativa, one of the main subtypes of cannabis plant that grows taller and skinnier than its indica counterpart. Cannabis sativa yields buds that are often thought to produce a more "alert," or "energetic" high.

Strain Strain is the term referring to a genetic variant of plant species. Cannabis strains vary in ratios of THC and CBD, as well as size, shape, smell, taste, color, potency, and levels of terpenes and flavonoids.

Suppositories A suppository is a medicine inserted into the body via the rectum, vagina, or urethra, to dissolve and administer medication.

Terpenes Terpenes are the primary elements of essential oils and are responsible for the smell and taste of cannabis. They're also present in many foodstuffs. Terpenes are thought to "steer" the experience of consuming cannabis. That is, cannabis strains with high amounts of certain terpenes can be energizing, sedative, or pain relieving, partially dependent on how the terpenes interact with other elements of the cannabis plant.

THC THC (tetrahydrocannabinol) is a cannabinoid compound that is psychoactive and produces the cannabis "high." THC molecules adhere to CB1 receptors in the endocannabinoid system (ECS) which can result in pleasant and euphoric effects.

Glossary

Tincture A tincture is a cannabis-infused liquid consumed sublingually, meaning absorption under the tongue.

Topical A topical is a cannabis product applied like a lotion and is also known as a salve. Users rub topicals into the skin, often to treat joint pain or muscle aches. Topicals are almost always made up primarily of CBD.

Trichomes Most apparent on the cannabis bud, trichomes are very small appendages, almost crystalline and feel sticky. Trichomes create and hold the cannabinoids, flavonoids, and terpenes we associate with the cannabis plant.

Notes

Introduction

1. Lydia Saad, "Grassroots Support for Legalizing Marijuana Hits Record 70%," Gallup.com, November 8, 2023, https://news.gallup.com/poll/514007/grassroots-support-legalizing-marijuana-hits-record.aspx.
2. "Cannabis Industry Employs over 440,000 Full-Time Workers," April 18, 2024, NORML, https://norml.org/news/2024/04/18/report-cannabis-industry-employs-over-440000-full-time-workers/.
3. Iris Dorbian, "U.S. Cannabis Sales Could Top $72 Billion by 2030, Says Leading Researcher," *Forbes*. Accessed May 5, 2024, https://www.forbes.com/sites/irisdorbian/2022/03/24/us-cannabis-sales-could-top-72-billion-by-2030-says-top-researcher/.

Chapter 1

1. "What Is the Difference between Hemp and Marijuana?" Britannica. Accessed February 7, 2024, https://www.britannica.com/story/what-is-the-difference-between-hemp-and-marijuana.
2. Alison Mack and Janet Joy, "Can Marijuana Help?" in *Marijuana as Medicine? The Science Beyond the Controversy* (National Academies Press, 2000). https://www.ncbi.nlm.nih.gov/books/NBK224391/.
3. Lisa Manniche, *An Ancient Egyptian Herbal* (British Museum Press, 1989).
4. Martin Booth, *Cannabis: A History* (Thomas Dunne Books/St. Martin's Press, 2003).
5. "What Is the Difference between Hemp and Marijuana?"
6. Noelle Skodzinski, "Indigenous Cannabis on the Rise," *Cannabis Business Times*. 2023. Accessed February 7, 2024, https://www.cannabisbusinesstimes.com/news/indigenous-cannabis-industry-association-mary-jane-oatman-interview/.
7. Booth, *Cannabis: A History*.
8. "USP Timeline." Accessed February 7, 2024, https://www.usp.org/200-anniversary/usp-timeline.
9. "A Life of Service: Harry Jacob Anslinger," Accessed February 7, 2024. https://museum.dea.gov/exhibits/online-exhibits/anslinger.

10. "Why Is Marijuana Illegal in the U.S.?" Britannica. Accessed May 9, 2024. https://www.britannica.com/story/why-is-marijuana-illegal-in-the-us.

11. "The Controlled Substances Act." Accessed May 9, 2024, https://www.dea.gov/drug-information/csa.

12. "Drug Scheduling." Accessed May 21, 2024, https://www.dea.gov/drug-information/drug-scheduling.

13. "The Controlled Substances Act." Accessed May 9, 2024, https://www.dea.gov/drug-information/csa.

14. Richard Nixon, "202—Remarks about an Intensified Program for Drug Abuse Prevention and Control," June 17, 1971, https://prhome.defense.gov/Portals/52/Documents/RFM/Readiness/DDRP/docs/41%20Nixon%20Remarks%20Intensified%20Program%20for%20Drug%20Abuse.pdf.

15. Dan Baum, "Dan Baum Investigates Whether Gun-Control Laws Could Ever Stop the Weapon from Proliferating," *Harper's Magazine*. Accessed February 7, 2024, https://harpers.org/archive/2016/04/legalize-it-all/.

16. "The Boggs Act & Mandatory Minimums—SMART." Accessed May 21, 2024, https://studentmmj.com/learn/the-boggs-act-mandatory-minimums/.

17. "Our Work," Families Against Mandatory Minimums Foundation, October 6, 2023, https://famm.org/our-work/.

18. "The History of Mass Incarceration," Brennan Center for Justice. Accessed February 7, 2024, https://www.brennancenter.org/our-work/analysis-opinion/history-mass-incarceration.

19. Rep. Brooks, Jack B. [D-TX-9. "H.R.5269—101st Congress (1989–1990): Comprehensive Crime Control Act of 1990." Legislation, October 25, 1990. 1990-07-13. https://www.congress.gov/bill/101st-congress/house-bill/5269.

20. "Analysis: How the Media Created a 'Superpredator' Myth That Harmed a Generation of Black Youth," NBC News, November 20, 2020, https://www.nbcnews.com/news/us-news/analysis-how-media-created-superpredator-myth-harmed-generation-black-youth-n1248101.

21. Laura Arman, "Did the Du Pont Family Catalyze Cannabis Prohibition?" Emerald Media Group, n.d. file:///Users/danjohnson/Zotero/storage/4EFGIW2A/did-the-du-pont-family-catalyze-cannabis-prohibition.html.

22. "Where Marijuana Is Legal in the United States," MJBizDaily, February 7, 2024, https://mjbizdaily.com/map-of-us-marijuana-legalization-by-state/.

23. Alex Halperin, "Joint Support: Liberals and Conservatives Actually Agree on Legalized Weed," *The Guardian*, October 8, 2018, sec. Society, https://www.theguardian.com/society/2018/oct/08/marijuana-legalization-support-bipartisan.

24. "Grassroots Support for Legalizing Marijuana Hits Record 70%," Gallup.com, November 8, 2023, https://news.gallup.com/poll/514007/grassroots-support-legalizing-marijuana-hits-record.aspx.

25. Joanna Jacobus and Susan F. Tapert, "Effects of Cannabis on the Adolescent Brain." *Current Pharmaceutical Design* 20, no. 13 (2014): 2186–93.

26. You can also purchase my *The Essential Cannabis Journal: Personal Notes from the Field* on Amazon.com.

Chapter 2

1. "CREAMM Act, NJ: Personal Use Cannabis Rules." N.J.S.A., n.d. https://www.nj.gov/cannabis/documents/rules/NJAC%201730%20Personal%20Use%20Cannabis.pdf.
2. "CREAMM Act, NJ: Personal Use Cannabis Rules."
3. Jeffrey Y. Hergenrather, Joshua Aviram, Yelena Vysotski, Salvatore Campisi-Pinto, Gil M. Lewitus, and David Meiri, "Cannabinoid and Terpenoid Doses Are Associated with Adult ADHD Status of Medical Cannabis Patients," *Rambam Maimonides Medical Journal* 11, no. 1 (January 30, 2020): e0001. https://doi.org/10.5041/RMMJ.10384.
4. "Is CBG the New CBD?" *The Spokesman-Review*. Accessed May 11, 2024. https://www.spokesman.com/stories/2020/dec/28/is-cbg-the-new-cbd/.
5. Dorota Bęben, Oliwia Siwiela, Anna Szyjka, Michał Graczyk, Daniel Rzepka, Ewa Barg, and Helena Moreira, "Phytocannabinoids CBD, CBG, and Their Derivatives CBD-HQ and CBG-A Induced In Vitro Cytotoxicity in 2D and 3D Colon Cancer Cell Models," *Current Issues in Molecular Biology* 46, no. 4 (April 19, 2024): 3626–39. https://doi.org/10.3390/cimb46040227.
6. L. S. Xu, Q. L. Feng, X. P. Zhang, Y. G. Wang, and M. Yao. "[Study on analgesic effect and mechanism of cinobufagin on rats with bone cancer pain]," *Zhonghua Yi Xue Za Zhi* 99, no. 17 (May 7, 2019): 1307–11. https://doi.org/10.3760/cma.j.issn.0376-2491.2019.17.007.
7. Megan N. Huizenga, Alberto Sepulveda-Rodriguez, and Patrick A. Forcelli, "Preclinical Safety and Efficacy of Cannabidivarin for Early Life Seizures," *Neuropharmacology* 148 (April 2019): 189–98. https://doi.org/10.1016/j.neuropharm.2019.01.002.
8. A. J. Hill, M. S. Mercier, T. D. M. Hill, S. E. Glyn, N. A. Jones, Y. Yamasaki, T. Futamura, et al. "Cannabidivarin Is Anticonvulsant in Mouse and Rat." *British Journal of Pharmacology* 167, no. 8 (December 2012): 1629–42. https://doi.org/10.1111/j.1476-5381.2012.02207.x.
9. Andrea M. Tomko, Erin G. Whynot, Lee D. Ellis, and Denis J. Dupré, "Anti-Cancer Potential of Cannabinoids, Terpenes, and Flavonoids Present in Cannabis," *Cancers* 12, no. 7 (July 21, 2020): 1985. https://doi.org/10.3390/cancers12071985.
10. Ananya Mandal, "Phytocannabinoids," News-Medical, June 2, 2010. https://www.news-medical.net/health/Phytocannabinoids.aspx.
11. Guillermo Moreno-Sanz, "Can You Pass the Acid Test? Critical Review and Novel Therapeutic Perspectives of Δ9-Tetrahydrocannabinolic Acid A," *Cannabis and Cannabinoid Research* 1, no. 1 (June 1, 2016): 124–30. https://doi.org/10.1089/can.2016.0008.

12. K. Fujiwara, H. Daido, A. Yamamoto, T. Kobayashi, T. Yokoyama, H. Aoki, & H. Harada, "THC-A Inhibits Pancreatic Cancer Cell Growth via a New Mechanism of Action," *Anticancer Research* 38, no. 3 (2018): 833–37. doi: 10.21873/anticanres.12312.

13. A. Abrahamov, A. Abrahamov, and R. Mechoulam, "An Efficient New Cannabinoid Antiemetic in Pediatric Oncology," *Life Sciences* 56, no. 23–24 (1995): 2097–102. https://doi.org/10.1016/0024-3205(95)00194-b.

14. E. T. Wargent, M. S. Zaibi, C. Silvestri, D. C. Hislop, C. J. Stocker, C. G. Stott, G. W. Guy, M. Duncan, V. Di Marzo, and M. A. Cawthorne, "The Cannabinoid Δ9-Tetrahydrocannabivarin (THCV) Ameliorates Insulin Sensitivity in Two Mouse Models of Obesity," *Nutrition & Diabetes* 3, no. 5 (May 2013): e68. https://doi.org/10.1038/nutd.2013.9.

15. Khalid A. Jadoon, Stuart H. Ratcliffe, David A. Barrett, E. Louise Thomas, Colin Stott, Jimmy D. Bell, Saoirse E. O'Sullivan, and Garry D. Tan, "Efficacy and Safety of Cannabidiol and Tetrahydrocannabivarin on Glycemic and Lipid Parameters in Patients with Type 2 Diabetes: A Randomized, Double-Blind, Placebo-Controlled, Parallel Group Pilot Study," *Diabetes Care* 39, no. 10 (October 2016): 1777–86. https://doi.org/10.2337/dc16-0650.

16. Russ Hudson, *The Big Book of Terps: Understanding Terpenes, Flavonoids, and Synergy in Cannabis* (Hudson Press, 2021).

17. Hudson, *The Big Book of Terps*.

18. "What Are Flavonoids?" Live Science. Accessed May 11, 2024. https://www.livescience.com/52524-flavonoids.html.

19. Robert Clarke and Mark Merlin, *Cannabis: Evolution and Ethnobotany* (University of California Press, 2016).

20. Robert Melamede, "Endocannabinoids: Multi-Scaled, Global Homeostatic Regulators of Cells and Society," in *Unifying Themes in Complex Systems*, Ali Minai, Dan Braha, and Yaneer Bar-Yam, eds., 219–26. (Springer, 2008). https://doi.org/10.1007/978-3-540-85081-6_28.

21. Martin A. Lee, "The Discovery of the Endocannabinoid System," *Medical Cannabis Handbook*, 2019. https://doi.org/10.1891/9780826135735.0003.

22. Dustin Sulak, "Introduction to the Endocannabinoid System," NORML. Accessed May 11, 2024. https://norml.org/marijuana/library/recent-medical-marijuana-research/introduction-to-the-endocannabinoid-system/.

23. "Dr. Raphael Mechoulam: The Promise of Cannabis," *The Daily Bell*, October 19, 2014. https://www.thedailybell.com/all-articles/cannabis-marijuana/anthony-wile-dr-raphael-mechoulam-the-promise-of-cannabis/.

24. W. A. Devane, L. Hanus, A. Breuer, R. G. Pertwee, L. A. Stevenson, G. Griffin, D. Gibson, A. Mandelbaum, A. Etinger, and R. Mechoulam, "Isolation and Structure of a Brain Constituent That Binds to the Cannabinoid Receptor." *Science* 258, no. 5090 (December 18, 1992): 1946–49. https://doi.org/10.1126/science.1470919.

25. A. C. Howlett, F. Barth, T. I. Bonner, G. Cabral, P. Casellas, W. A. Devane, C. C. Felder, et al. "International Union of Pharmacology. XXVII. Classification of Cannabinoid Receptors." *Pharmacological Reviews* 54, no. 2 (June 2002): 161–202. https://doi.org/10.1124/pr.54.2.161.

26. Alicia Wallace, "Patent No. 6,630,507: Why the U.S. Government Holds a Patent on Cannabis Plant Compounds," *The Denver Post* (blog), August 28, 2016, https://www.denverpost.com/2016/08/28/what-is-marijuana-patent-6630507/.

Chapter 3

1. "How Many Acres Have Farmers Lost to Hot Hemp?" *New Frontier Data* (blog), August 5, 2021, https://newfrontierdata.com/cannabis-insights/how-many-acres-have-farmers-lost-to-hot-hemp/.

2. "Industrial Hemp." Accessed May 21, 2024. https://www.agmrc.org/commodities-products/fiber/industrial-hemp.

3. "OSU Partners with Native American Tribes to Explore Making Products and Materials with Hemp," OPB. Accessed May 13, 2024. https://www.opb.org/article/2024/03/29/think-out-loud-native-american-tribes-cannabis-hemp-farming/.

4. "OSU Partners with Native American Tribes to Explore Making Products and Materials with Hemp."

5. "Why Is Marijuana Illegal? A Look at the History of MJ in America,." Accessed February 7, 2024, https://news.medicalmarijuanainc.com/2019/07/28/the-road-to-prohibition-why-did-america-make-marijuana-illegal-in-the-first-place/.

6. "Now That Weed Is Mostly Legal, Hemp Should Be Booming. But It's Not," *Time*, April 6, 2023, https://time.com/6268420/hemp-climate-solution/.

7. "Why Is Marijuana Illegal?"

8. "Hemp: From Mythos to Monoculture," August 27, 2020. https://projectcbd.org/hemp/hemp-from-mythos-to-monoculture/.

9. Kyle Jaeger, "China Must Import More Hemp from U.S. under New Trade Deal." *Marijuana Moment* (blog), January 16, 2020. https://www.marijuanamoment.net/china-must-import-more-hemp-from-u-s-under-new-trade-deal/.

10. "Comparing Hemp Provisions in the 2014 and 2018 Farm Bills," *Congressional Research Service*, December 2, 2021. https://crsreports.congress.gov/product/pdf/IF/IF11984#:~:text=Although%20the%202018%20farm%20bill,states%20that%20allow%20for%20its.

11. Phillip M. Bailey, "3 Things to Know about Mitch McConnell and Kentucky's Hemp Industry," *The Courier-Journal*. Accessed March 6, 2024. https://www.courier-journal.com/story/news/politics/2019/07/02/u-s-senator-mitch-mcconnell-and-kentucky-hemp-business-3-things-know/1629808001/.

12. "Your Guide to CBD Legalization by State," Forbes Health, October 4, 2023. https://www.forbes.com/health/cbd/cbd-legalization-by-state/.

Notes

13. "Hemp as a Rotation Crop," Boojum Group. Accessed March 6, 2024. https://boojumgroup.com/2018/12/31/hemp-rotation-crop-2/.
14. "Weed Control," Texas Hemp Growers Association. Accessed May 13, 2024. https://txhempgrowersassociation.com/education/weed-control/.
15. Lucy Wang, "Carbon-Negative Construction," January 23, 2022, https://www.anthropocenemagazine.org/2022/01/carbon-negative-construction/.
16. Andrew Leonard, "Can Hemp Clean Up the Earth?" *Rolling Stone* (blog), June 11, 2018, https://www.rollingstone.com/politics/politics-features/can-hemp-clean-up-the-earth-629589/.
17. "Perfluoroalkyl and Polyfluoroalkyl Substances (PFAS)," National Institute of Environmental Health Sciences. Accessed May 18, 2024. https://www.niehs.nih.gov/health/topics/agents/pfc.
18. Wang, "Carbon-Negative Construction."
19. "What Is Hempcrete?" American Lime Technology Website. Accessed May 13, 2024, http://www.americanlimetechnology.com/what-is-hempcrete/.
20. "Bulk Hemp Yarn Wholesale Suppliers," Hemp Foundation. Accessed February 13, 2024. https://hempfoundation.net/hemp-plastic/.
21. "Forget Electric Cars! Henry Ford's Cannabis Car Was Made from Hemp: 10xStronger Than Steel, 100% Green!" Financialexpress, November 17, 2018, https://www.financialexpress.com/auto/car-news/forget-electric-cars-henry-fords-cannabis-car-was-made-from-hemp-10xstronger-than-steel-100-green/1384733/.
22. "Forget Electric Cars!"
23. "Hemp: From Mythos to Monoculture," Project CBD, August 27, 2020. https://projectcbd.org/hemp/hemp-from-mythos-to-monoculture/.
24. Neha Mathur, "Is Hemp the Superfood Vegetarians Have Been Waiting For?" News-Medical, September 22, 2023, https://www.news-medical.net/news/20230922/Is-hemp-the-superfood-vegetarians-have-been-waiting-for.aspx.
25. "9 Benefits of Hemp Seeds: Nutrition, Health, and Use," Medical News Today, September 11, 2018. https://www.medicalnewstoday.com/articles/323037.
26. "CBD Statistics, Data and Use (2024)," Forbes Health, October 4, 2023. https://www.forbes.com/health/cbd/cbd-statistics/.
27. "Topic: CBD Retail in the United States," Statista. Accessed March 7, 2024, https://www.statista.com/topics/6262/cbd-retail-in-the-united-states/.
28. "Ava Barry, Teenage Daughter of Medicinal Cannabis Campaigner Vera Twomey, Dies in Cork," *Irish Independent*. Accessed May 21, 2024, https://www.independent.ie/irish-news/teenage-daughter-of-medicinal-cannabis-campaigner-vera-twomey-dies/a1690076689.html.
29. "Zaki, Maggie and Jason's Stories—Realm of Caring," Charlotte's Web CBD Education Blog. Accessed May 13, 2024, https://www.charlottesweb.com/blog/story/stories-realm-of-caring.
30. "What to Know about the Types of CBD," Forbes Health, October 6, 2023, https://www.forbes.com/health/cbd/types-of-cbd/.

31. "What to Know about the Types of CBD."
32. "What to Know about the Types of CBD."

CHAPTER 4
1. "2024 Cannabis Jobs Report," Vangst Cannabis Staffing. Accessed May 13, 2024, https://www.vangst.com/2024-jobs-report.
2. Shane Lynn, "Internal Revenue Code Section 280E: Creating an Impossible Situation for Legitimate Businesses," National Cannabis Industry Association, n.d., https://legislature.vermont.gov/Documents/2016/WorkGroups/Senate%20Finance/Bills/S.241/W~Shayne%20Lynn,%20Executive%20Director,%20Champlain%20Valley%20Dispensary,%20Inc.~S.241%20280E%20White%20Paper~2-2-2016.pdf.
3. "CliftonStrengths," Gallup.com. Accessed May 21, 2024, https://www.gallup.com/cliftonstrengths/en/252137/home.aspx.
4. John Ingold, "Charlotte Figi, the Colorado Girl Who Inspired the CBD Movement, Dies Following Illness Suspected to Be Coronavirus," *The Colorado Sun*, April 8, 2020, http://coloradosun.com/2020/04/08/charlotte-figi-cbd-coronavirus/.

CHAPTER 5
1. Gary Cohen, "How Much Does It Cost to Open a Cannabis Dispensary?" Accessed May 15, 2024, https://www.covasoftware.com/blog/the-true-cost-of-opening-a-cannabis-dispensary.
2. "The Top 10 Cannabis Farms in the World 2024," Accessed May 15, 2024, https://herb.co/guides/the-herbalist/the-herbalist-the-top-10-cannabis-farms-in-the-world-2023/.
3. "Supercritical Fluids," Chemistry LibreTexts, October 2, 2013, https://chem.libretexts.org/Bookshelves/Physical_and_Theoretical_Chemistry_Textbook_Maps/Supplemental_Modules_(Physical_and_Theoretical_Chemistry)/Physical_Properties_of_Matter/States_of_Matter/Supercritical_Fluids.
4. "Critical Point," Chemistry LibreTexts, October 2, 2013, https://chem.libretexts.org/Bookshelves/Physical_and_Theoretical_Chemistry_Textbook_Maps/Supplemental_Modules_(Physical_and_Theoretical_Chemistry)/Physical_Properties_of_Matter/States_of_Matter/Supercritical_Fluids/Critical_Point.
5. "National Hemp Report." National Agricultural Statistics Service, Agricultural Statistics Board, United States Department of Agriculture, April 2024, https://downloads.usda.library.cornell.edu/usda-esmis/files/gf06h2430/3t947c84r/mg74s940n/hempan24.pdf.
6. "National Hemp Report."
7. "National Hemp Report."
8. "National Hemp Report."

NOTES

9. Kyle Jaeger, "Sales of Hemp-Derived Cannabinoids Like CBD Outpace Legal Marijuana and Are on Par with Craft Beer, Report Finds," *Marijuana Moment* (blog), November 2, 2023, https://www.marijuanamoment.net/sales-of-hemp-derived-cannabinoids-like-cbd-outpace-legal-marijuana-and-are-on-par-with-craft-beer-report-finds/.

10. Alix Fraser, "CBD Trends: 8 Vital Things to Know If You're Selling Cannabidiol Products in 2024," Lightspeed. Accessed May 18, 2024, https://www.lightspeedhq.com/blog/cbd-trends/.

11. Dario Sabaghi, "Levi's Aims to Use More Hemp for Its Fashion Collections," Forbes. Accessed May 18, 2024, https://www.forbes.com/sites/dariosabaghi/2021/10/12/levis-jeans-company-aims-to-use-more-hemp-for-its-fashion-collections/.

12. "Canadians Continue to Dominate U.S. Hemp Grain Market as 2023 Imports Total $55 Million." Accessed May 27, 2024, https://hemptoday.net/canadians-continue-to-dominate-u-s-hemp-grain-market-as-2023-imports-total-55-million/.

13. "Hemp, Inc. Welcomes USDA Approval of GMO Hemp Strain—A Step Forward in Cannabis Biotechnology," GlobeNewswire News Room, April 9, 2024, https://www.globenewswire.com/en/news-release/2024/04/09/2860309/0/en/Hemp-Inc-Welcomes-USDA-Approval-of-GMO-Hemp-Strain-A-Step-Forward-in-Cannabis-Biotechnology.html.

14. Sandra Gusinow, "OSU Receives $10M Grant to Develop Industrial Uses for Hemp," *Oregon Business* (blog), March 13, 2024, https://oregonbusiness.com/osu-receives-10m-grant-to-develop-industrial-uses-for-hemp/.

15. Tyler Gleckler, "Is Hemp the Next Great Biofuel?" GlobalSpec, April 24, 2023, https://insights.globalspec.com/article/20369/is-hemp-the-next-great-biofuel.

CHAPTER 6

1. Shayne Lynn, "Internal Revenue Code Section 280E: Creating an Impossible Situation for Legitimate Businesses." Legislature of the State of Vermont, 2016. https://legislature.vermont.gov/Documents/2016/WorkGroups/Senate%20Finance/Bills/S.241/W~Shayne%20Lynn,%20Executive%20Director,%20Champlain%20Valley%20Dispensary,%20Inc.~S.241%20280E%20White%20Paper~2-2-2016.pdf.

2. "Vangst Cannabis Staffing," Vangst, May 10, 2024, https://www.vangst.com.

3. Aaron Sweeney, "Why HVAC/R Technicians Are in High Demand," *Northeast Technical Institute* (blog), November 7, 2023, https://ntinow.edu/why-hvac-r-technicians-are-in-high-demand/.

CHAPTER 7

1. "How to Become an Acupuncturist in 5 Steps," Indeed Career Guide. Accessed May 16, 2024, https://www.indeed.com/career-advice/finding-a-job/how-to-become-acupuncturist.

Notes

2. "Society of Cannabis Clinicians," January 25, 2024, https://www.cannabisclinicians.org/.

3. "Cannabis Education Guild." Accessed May 17, 2024, https://cannabiseducationguild.com/.

4. "About NORML." Accessed May 17, 2024, https://norml.org/about-norml/.

5. "Drug Policy Alliance—No More Drug War." Accessed May 17, 2024, https://drugpolicy.org/.

6. "Marijuana Policy Project: About Us," MPP. Accessed May 17, 2024, https://www.mpp.org/about/.

7. "ICIA: Home Page," Indigenous Cannabis Industry Association. Accessed May 5, 2024, https://www.indigenouscannabis.org.

8. Kiah Treece and Taylor Medine, "Average Wedding Cost: How Much Does a Wedding Really Cost?" Forbes Advisor. Accessed May 17, 2024, https://www.forbes.com/advisor/personal-loans/average-cost-of-a-wedding/.

9. Liu Shanhong, "Infographic: US Leisure Travel Expected to Rebound Strongly Post-Pandemic," Statista Daily Data, May 19, 2023, https://www.statista.com/chart/30034/us-leisure-travel-to-rebound-strongly-post-pandemic.

10. David Huether, "National Travel and Tourism Office," n.d., https://www.trade.gov/sites/default/files/2023-05/International-Visitation-to-the-United-States.pdf.

11. Marc Truyols, "Millennials' Travel Statistics; How Do They Travel?" *Mize* (blog), September 11, 2020, https://mize.tech/blog/millennials-travel-statistics-how-do-they-travel/.

12. Allie Van Duyne, "60 Restaurant Industry Statistics and Trends for Restaurant Owners in 2024," June 7, 2019, https://pos.toasttab.com/blog/on-the-line/restaurant-management-statistics.

13. "Technomic's Take: Five Ways Legal Marijuana Impacts Restaurants," Technomic. Accessed May 28, 2024, https://www.technomic.com/technomics-take/technomics-take-five-ways-legal-marijuana-impacts-restaurants.

14. "Puff Pass and Paint Cannabis Painting Classes in Denver Colorado, Orlando, DC, NY," Puff Pass and Paint. Accessed May 17, 2024, https://puffpassandpaint.com/.

15. "StashLogix." Accessed May 17, 2024, https://stashlogix.co/.

16. Kyle Jaeger, "Scientists Published More Than 32,000 Marijuana Studies over the Past 10 Years, Including Thousands in 2023, NORML Analysis Shows," *Marijuana Moment* (blog), December 25, 2023, https://www.marijuanamoment.net/scientists-published-more-than-32000-marijuana-studies-over-the-past-10-years-including-thousands-in-2023-norml-analysis-shows/.

Bibliography

Abrahamov, A., A. Abrahamov, and R. Mechoulam. "An Efficient New Cannabinoid Antiemetic in Pediatric Oncology." *Life Sciences* 56, no. 23–24 (1995): 2097–2102. https://doi.org/10.1016/0024-3205(95)00194-b.

Arman, Laura. "Did the Du Pont Family Catalyze Cannabis Prohibition?" *Cannabis News and Culture Magazine*, September 9, 2020. https://theemeraldmagazine.com/did-the-du-pont-family-catalyze-cannabis-prohibition/.

"Ava Barry, Teenage Daughter of Medicinal Cannabis Campaigner Vera Twomey, Dies in Cork." *Irish Independent*. Accessed May 21, 2024. https://www.independent.ie/irish-news/teenage-daughter-of-medicinal-cannabis-campaigner-vera-twomey-dies/a1690076689.html.

Bailey, Phillip M. "3 Things to Know about Mitch McConnell and Kentucky's Hemp Industry." *The Courier-Journal*. Accessed March 6, 2024. https://www.courier-journal.com/story/news/politics/2019/07/02/u-s-senator-mitch-mcconnell-and-kentucky-hemp-business-3-things-know/1629808001/.

Baum, Dan. "Dan Baum Investigates Whether Gun-Control Laws Could Ever Stop the Weapon from Proliferating." *Harper's Magazine*. Accessed February 7, 2024. https://harpers.org/archive/2016/04/legalize-it-all/.

Bęben, Dorota, Oliwia Siwiela, Anna Szyjka, Michał Graczyk, Daniel Rzepka, Ewa Barg, and Helena Moreira. "Phytocannabinoids CBD, CBG, and Their Derivatives CBD-HQ and CBG-A Induced In Vitro Cytotoxicity in 2D and 3D Colon Cancer Cell Models." *Current Issues in Molecular Biology* 46, no. 4 (April 19, 2024): 3626–39. https://doi.org/10.3390/cimb46040227.

"The Boggs Act and Mandatory Minimums—SMART." Accessed May 21, 2024. https://studentmmj.com/learn/the-boggs-act-mandatory-minimums/.

Boojum Group. "Hemp as a Rotation Crop." Accessed March 6, 2024. https://boojumgroup.com/2018/12/31/hemp-rotation-crop-2/.

Booth, Martin. *Cannabis: A History*. Thomas Dunne Books/St. Martin's Press, 2003.

Bibliography

"Canadians Continue to Dominate U.S. Hemp Grain Market as 2023 Imports Total $55 Million." Accessed May 27, 2024. https://hemptoday.net/canadians-continue-to-dominate-u-s-hemp-grain-market-as-2023-imports-total-55-million/.

Cannabis Education Guild. "Cannabis Education Guild." Accessed May 17, 2024. https://cannabiseducationguild.com/.

Cannabis Regulatory Commission. "Recreational Cannabis in New Jersey." Accessed May 21, 2024. https://www.nj.gov/cannabis/adult-personal/.

Charlotte's Web CBD Education Blog. "Zaki, Maggie and Jason's Stories—Realm of Caring." Accessed May 13, 2024. https://www.charlottesweb.com/blog/story/stories-realm-of-caring.

Chemistry LibreTexts. "Critical Point." October 2, 2013. https://chem.libretexts.org/Bookshelves/Physical_and_Theoretical_Chemistry_Textbook_Maps/Supplemental_Modules_(Physical_and_Theoretical_Chemistry)/Physical_Properties_of_Matter/States_of_Matter/Supercritical_Fluids/Critical_Point.

Chemistry LibreTexts. "Supercritical Fluids." October 2, 2013. https://chem.libretexts.org/Bookshelves/Physical_and_Theoretical_Chemistry_Textbook_Maps/Supplemental_Modules_(Physical_and_Theoretical_Chemistry)/Physical_Properties_of_Matter/States_of_Matter/Supercritical_Fluids.

Clarke, Robert, and Mark Merlin. *Cannabis: Evolution and Ethnobotany*. University of California Press, 2016.

Cohen, Gary. "How Much Does It Cost to Open a Cannabis Dispensary?" Accessed May 15, 2024. https://www.covasoftware.com/blog/the-true-cost-of-opening-a-cannabis-dispensary.

"Comparing Hemp Provisions in the 2014 and 2018 Farm Bills." *Congressional Research Service*, December 2, 2021. https://crsreports.congress.gov/product/pdf/IF/IF11984#:~:text=Although%20the%202018%20farm%20bill,states%20that%20allow%20for%20its.

"The Controlled Substances Act." Accessed May 9, 2024. https://www.dea.gov/drug-information/csa.

"CREAMM Act, NJ: PERSONAL USE CANNABIS RULES." N.J.S.A., n.d. https://www.nj.gov/cannabis/documents/rules/NJAC%201730%20Personal%20Use%20Cannabis.pdf.

The Daily Bell. "Dr. Raphael Mechoulam: The Promise of Cannabis." October 19, 2014. https://www.thedailybell.com/all-articles/cannabis-marijuana/anthony-wile-dr-raphael-mechoulam-the-promise-of-cannabis/.

Devane, W. A., L. Hanus, A. Breuer, R. G. Pertwee, L. A. Stevenson, G. Griffin, D. Gibson, A. Mandelbaum, A. Etinger, and R. Mechoulam. "Isolation and

Bibliography

Structure of a Brain Constituent That Binds to the Cannabinoid Receptor." *Science (New York, N.Y.)* 258, no. 5090 (December 18, 1992): 1946–49. https://doi.org/10.1126/science.1470919.

Dorbian, Iris. "U.S. Cannabis Sales Could Top $72 Billion By 2030, Says Leading Researcher." Forbes. Accessed May 5, 2024. https://www.forbes.com/sites/irisdorbian/2022/03/24/us-cannabis-sales-could-top-72-billion-by-2030-says-top-researcher/.

Drug Policy Alliance. "Drug Policy Alliance—No More Drug War." Accessed May 17, 2024. https://drugpolicy.org/.

"Drug Scheduling." Accessed May 21, 2024. https://www.dea.gov/drug-information/drug-scheduling.

Earth Island Journal. "History Will Look at US' 77-Year Hemp Ban as More Ridiculous Than Legal DDT." Accessed May 13, 2024. https://www.earthisland.org/journal/index.php/articles/entry/history_will_view_our_77-year_hemp_ban_as_ridiculous/.

Financialexpress. "Forget Electric Cars! Henry Ford's Cannabis Car Was Made from Hemp: 10xStronger than Steel, 100% Green!" November 17, 2018. https://www.financialexpress.com/auto/car-news/forget-electric-cars-henry-fords-cannabis-car-was-made-from-hemp-10xstronger-than-steel-100-green/1384733/.

Forbes Health. "CBD Statistics, Data and Use (2024)." October 4, 2023. https://www.forbes.com/health/cbd/cbd-statistics/.

Forbes Health. "What Is Broad-Spectrum CBD? Benefits, Risks and More." November 8, 2023. https://www.forbes.com/health/cbd/broad-spectrum-cbd/.

Forbes Health. "What to Know about the Types of CBD." October 6, 2023. https://www.forbes.com/health/cbd/types-of-cbd/.

Forbes Health. "Your Guide to CBD Legalization by State." October 4, 2023. https://www.forbes.com/health/cbd/cbd-legalization-by-state/.

Fraser, Alix. "CBD Trends: 8 Vital Things to Know If You're Selling Cannabidiol Products in 2024." Lightspeed. Accessed May 18, 2024. https://www.lightspeedhq.com/blog/cbd-trends/.

Gallup. "CliftonStrengths." Accessed May 21, 2024. https://www.gallup.com/cliftonstrengths/en/252137/home.aspx.

"Genetics, Not Field Conditions, Makes Hemp 'Go Hot.'" *Cornell Chronicle*. Accessed May 21, 2024. https://news.cornell.edu/stories/2020/01/genetics-not-field-conditions-makes-hemp-go-hot.

Gusinow, Sandra. "OSU Receives $10M Grant to Develop Industrial Uses for Hemp." *Oregon Business* (blog), March 13, 2024. https://oregonbusiness.com/osu-receives-10m-grant-to-develop-industrial-uses-for-hemp/.

Bibliography

Hall, Alena, and Robby Brumberg. "CBD Statistics, Data and Use (2024)." Forbes Health, April 29, 2024. https://www.forbes.com/health/cbd/cbd-statistics/.

Halperin, Alex. "Joint Support: Liberals and Conservatives Actually Agree on Legalized Weed." *The Guardian*, October 8, 2018, sec. Society. https://www.theguardian.com/society/2018/oct/08/marijuana-legalization-support-bipartisan.

Hanus, Lumír O. "Discovery and Isolation of Anandamide and Other Endocannabinoids." *Chemistry and Biodiversity* 4, no. 8 (August 2007): 1828–41. https://doi.org/10.1002/cbdv.200790154.

Hash Marihuana and Hemp Museum. "Hemp for Victory." Accessed February 7, 2024. https://hashmuseum.com/en/collection/growing-hemp/hemp-for-victory/.

Hemp for Humanity. "Blog Hero Boxed 2 Column." Accessed February 13, 2024. https://hempforhumanity.eu/blog-hero-boxed-2-column/.

Hemp Foundation. "Bulk Hemp Yarn Wholesale Suppliers." Accessed February 13, 2024. https://hempfoundation.net/hemp-plastic/.

"Hemp: From Mythos to Monoculture." Project CBD. August 27, 2020. https://projectcbd.org/hemp/hemp-from-mythos-to-monoculture/.

Hemp Gazette. "Industrial Hemp's Energy Potential—Biofuels." Accessed February 13, 2024. https://hempgazette.com/industrial-hemp/biofuel-hemp-energy/.

"Hemp, Inc. Welcomes USDA Approval of GMO Hemp Strain—A Step Forward in Cannabis Biotechnology." GlobeNewswire News Room, April 9, 2024. https://www.globenewswire.com/en/news-release/2024/04/09/2860309/0/en/Hemp-Inc-Welcomes-USDA-Approval-of-GMO-Hemp-Strain-A-Step-Forward-in-Cannabis-Biotechnology.html.

Hergenrather, Jeffrey Y., Joshua Aviram, Yelena Vysotski, Salvatore Campisi-Pinto, Gil M. Lewitus, and David Meiri. "Cannabinoid and Terpenoid Doses Are Associated with Adult ADHD Status of Medical Cannabis Patients." *Rambam Maimonides Medical Journal* 11, no. 1 (January 30, 2020): e0001. https://doi.org/10.5041/RMMJ.10384.

Hernandez, Selden. "Hemp Industry 2024: State and Federal Changes." McGlinchey Stafford PLLC, February 21, 2024. https://www.mcglinchey.com/insights/hemp-industry-2024-state-and-federal-changes/.

Hill, A. J., M. S. Mercier, T. D. M. Hill, S. E. Glyn, N. A. Jones, Y. Yamasaki, T. Futamura, et al. "Cannabidivarin Is Anticonvulsant in Mouse and Rat." *British Journal of Pharmacology* 167, no. 8 (December 2012): 1629–42. https://doi.org/10.1111/j.1476-5381.2012.02207.x.

"The History of Mass Incarceration." Accessed February 7, 2024. https://www.brennancenter.org/our-work/analysis-opinion/history-mass-incarceration.

Howlett, A. C., F. Barth, T. I. Bonner, G. Cabral, P. Casellas, W. A. Devane, C. C. Felder, et al. "International Union of Pharmacology. XXVII. Classification of Cannabinoid Receptors." *Pharmacological Reviews* 54, no. 2 (June 2002): 161–202. https://doi.org/10.1124/pr.54.2.161.

Hudson, Russ. *The Big Book of Terps: Understanding Terpenes, and Synergy in Cannabis*. Hudson Press, 2023.

Huether, David. "National Travel and Tourism Office." n.d. https://www.trade.gov/sites/default/files/2023-05/International-Visitation-to-the-United-States.pdf.

Huizenga, Megan N., Alberto Sepulveda-Rodriguez, and Patrick A. Forcelli. "Preclinical Safety and Efficacy of Cannabidivarin for Early Life Seizures." *Neuropharmacology* 148 (April 2019): 189–98. https://doi.org/10.1016/j.neuropharm.2019.01.002.

Indeed Career Guide. "How to Become an Acupuncturist in 5 Steps." Accessed May 16, 2024. https://www.indeed.com/career-advice/finding-a-job/how-to-become-acupuncturist.

Indigenous Cannabis Industry Association. "ICIA: Home Page." Accessed May 5, 2024. https://www.indigenouscannabis.org.

"Industrial Hemp." Accessed May 21, 2024. https://www.agmrc.org/commodities-products/fiber/industrial-hemp.

Ingold, John. "Charlotte Figi, the Colorado Girl Who Inspired the CBD Movement, Dies Following Illness Suspected to Be Coronavirus." *The Colorado Sun*, April 8, 2020. http://coloradosun.com/2020/04/08/charlotte-figi-cbd-coronavirus/.

Irish Independent. "Teenage Daughter of Medicinal Cannabis Campaigner Vera Twomey Dies." May 27, 2023. https://www.independent.ie/irish-news/teenage-daughter-of-medicinal-cannabis-campaigner-vera-twomey-dies/a1690076689.html.

"Is CBG the New CBD?" *The Spokesman-Review*. Accessed May 11, 2024. https://www.spokesman.com/stories/2020/dec/28/is-cbg-the-new-cbd/.

Jacobus, Joanna, and Susan F. Tapert. "Effects of Cannabis on the Adolescent Brain." *Current Pharmaceutical Design* 20, no. 13 (2014): 2186–93.

Jadoon, Khalid A., Stuart H. Ratcliffe, David A. Barrett, E. Louise Thomas, Colin Stott, Jimmy D. Bell, Saoirse E. O'Sullivan, and Garry D. Tan. "Efficacy and Safety of Cannabidiol and Tetrahydrocannabivarin on Glycemic and Lipid Parameters in Patients with Type 2 Diabetes: A Randomized, Double-Blind, Placebo-Controlled, Parallel Group Pilot Study." *Diabetes Care* 39, no. 10 (October 2016): 1777–86. https://doi.org/10.2337/dc16-0650.

Jaeger, Kyle. "China Must Import More Hemp from U.S. under New Trade Deal." *Marijuana Moment* (blog), January 16, 2020. https://www.marijuanamoment.net/china-must-import-more-hemp-from-u-s-under-new-trade-deal/.

———. "Sales of Hemp-Derived Cannabinoids Like CBD Outpace Legal Marijuana and Are on Par with Craft Beer, Report Finds." *Marijuana Moment* (blog), November 2, 2023. https://www.marijuanamoment.net/sales-of-hemp-derived-cannabinoids-like-cbd-outpace-legal-marijuana-and-are-on-par-with-craft-beer-report-finds/.

———. "Scientists Published More Than 32,000 Marijuana Studies over the Past 10 Years, Including Thousands in 2023, NORML Analysis Shows." *Marijuana Moment* (blog), December 25, 2023. https://www.marijuanamoment.net/scientists-published-more-than-32000-marijuana-studies-over-the-past-10-years-including-thousands-in-2023-norml-analysis-shows/.

Lee, Martin A. "The Discovery of the Endocannabinoid System." *Medical Cannabis Handbook*, 2019. https://doi.org/10.1891/9780826135735.0003.

Leonard, Andrew. "Can Hemp Clean Up the Earth?" *Rolling Stone* (blog), June 11, 2018. https://www.rollingstone.com/politics/politics-features/can-hemp-clean-up-the-earth-629589/.

"A Life of Service: Harry Jacob Anslinger." Accessed February 7, 2024. https://museum.dea.gov/exhibits/online-exhibits/anslinger.

Ligresti, Alessia, Aniello Schiano Moriello, Katarzyna Starowicz, Isabel Matias, Simona Pisanti, Luciano De Petrocellis, Chiara Laezza, Giuseppe Portella, Maurizio Bifulco, and Vincenzo Di Marzo. "Antitumor Activity of Plant Cannabinoids with Emphasis on the Effect of Cannabidiol on Human Breast Carcinoma." *Journal of Pharmacology and Experimental Therapeutics* 318, no. 3 (September 2006): 1375–87. https://doi.org/10.1124/jpet.106.105247.

Lotus, Jean. "Hemp Building: Looking Ahead for 2023." HempBuild Magazine, January 3, 2023. https://www.hempbuildmag.com/home/looking-ahead-2023.

Lynn, Shayne. "Internal Revenue Code Section 280E: Creating an Impossible Situation for Legitimate Businesses." Legislature of the State of Vermont, 2016. https://legislature.vermont.gov/Documents/2016/WorkGroups/Senate%20Finance/Bills/S.241/W~Shayne%20Lynn,%20Executive%20Director,%20Champlain%20Valley%20Dispensary,%20Inc.~S.241%20280E%20White%20Paper~2-2-2016.pdf.

Mack, Alison, and Janet Joy. "Can Marijuana Help?" In *Marijuana as Medicine? The Science Beyond the Controversy*. National Academies Press, 2000. https://www.ncbi.nlm.nih.gov/books/NBK224391/.

Mandal, Ananya. "Phytocannabinoids." News-Medical, June 2, 2010. https://www.news-medical.net/health/Phytocannabinoids.aspx.

Manniche, Lisa. *An Ancient Egyptian Herbal*. British Museum Press, 1989.

Mathur, Neha. "Is Hemp the Superfood Vegetarians Have Been Waiting For?" News-Medical, September 22, 2023. https://www.news-medical.net/news/20230922/Is-hemp-the-superfood-vegetarians-have-been-waiting-for.aspx.

Melamede, Robert. "Endocannabinoids: Multi-Scaled, Global Homeostatic Regulators of Cells and Society." In *Unifying Themes in Complex Systems*, edited by Ali Minai, Dan Braha, and Yaneer Bar-Yam, 219–26. Springer, 2008. https://doi.org/10.1007/978-3-540-85081-6_28.

MJBizDaily. "Where Marijuana Is Legal in the United States." February 7, 2024. https://mjbizdaily.com/map-of-us-marijuana-legalization-by-state/.

MPP. "Marijuana Policy Project: About Us." Accessed May 17, 2024. https://www.mpp.org/about/.

Moreno-Sanz, Guillermo. "Can You Pass the Acid Test? Critical Review and Novel Therapeutic Perspectives of Δ9-Tetrahydrocannabinolic Acid A." *Cannabis and Cannabinoid Research* 1, no. 1 (June 1, 2016): 124–30. https://doi.org/10.1089/can.2016.0008.

"National Hemp Report." National Agricultural Statistics Service, Agricultural Statistics Board, United States Department of Agriculture, April 2024. https://downloads.usda.library.cornell.edu/usda-esmis/files/gf06h2430/3t947c84r/mg74s940n/hempan24.pdf.

National Institute of Environmental Health Sciences. "Perfluoroalkyl and Polyfluoroalkyl Substances (PFAS)." Accessed May 18, 2024. https://www.niehs.nih.gov/health/topics/agents/pfc.

NBC News. "Analysis: How the Media Created a 'Superpredator' Myth That Harmed a Generation of Black Youth." November 20, 2020. https://www.nbcnews.com/news/us-news/analysis-how-media-created-superpredator-myth-harmed-generation-black-youth-n1248101.

New Frontier Data. "How Many Acres Have Farmers Lost to Hot Hemp?" *New Frontier Data* (blog), August 5, 2021. https://newfrontierdata.com/cannabis-insights/how-many-acres-have-farmers-lost-to-hot-hemp/.

"9 Benefits of Hemp Seeds: Nutrition, Health, and Use." September 11, 2018. https://www.medicalnewstoday.com/articles/323037.

Nixon, Richard. "202—Remarks About an Intensified Program for Drug Abuse Prevention and Control." June 17, 1971. https://prhome.defense.gov/Portals/52/Documents/RFM/Readiness/DDRP/docs/41%20Nixon%20Remarks%20Intensified%20Program%20for%20Drug%20Abuse.pdf.

NORML. "About NORML." Accessed May 17, 2024. https://norml.org/about-norml/.

NORML. "Cannabis Industry Employs Over 440,000 Full-Time Workers." April 18, 2024. https://norml.org/news/2024/04/18/report-cannabis-industry-employs-over-440000-full-time-workers/.

Bibliography

OPB. "OSU Partners with Native American Tribes to Explore Making Products and Materials with Hemp." Accessed May 13, 2024. https://www.opb.org/article/2024/03/29/think-out-loud-native-american-tribes-cannabis-hemp-farming/.

"Our Work." Families Against Mandatory Minimums Foundation. October 6, 2023. https://famm.org/our-work/.

"Press Release Distribution and Management." Accessed May 27, 2024. https://www.globenewswire.com/en/search/organization/Hemp%CE%B4%2520Inc%C2%A7.

Puff Pass and Paint. "Puff Pass and Paint Cannabis Painting Classes in Denver Colorado, Orlando, DC, NY." Accessed May 17, 2024. https://puffpassandpaint.com/.

Rep. Brooks, Jack B. [D-TX-9. "H.R.5269—101st Congress (1989–1990): Comprehensive Crime Control Act of 1990." Legislation, October 25, 1990. 1990-07-13. https://www.congress.gov/bill/101st-congress/house-bill/5269.

Saad, Lydia. "Grassroots Support for Legalizing Marijuana Hits Record 70%." Gallup.com, November 8, 2023. https://news.gallup.com/poll/514007/grassroots-support-legalizing-marijuana-hits-record.aspx.

Sabaghi, Dario. "Levi's Aims to Use More Hemp for Its Fashion Collections." Forbes. Accessed May 18, 2024. https://www.forbes.com/sites/dariosabaghi/2021/10/12/levis-jeans-company-aims-to-use-more-hemp-for-its-fashion-collections/.

Scimed. "What Is a Supercritical Fluid?" Accessed May 16, 2024. https://www.scimed.co.uk/education/what-is-a-supercritical-fluid/.

Shanhong, Liu. "Infographic: US Leisure Travel Expected to Rebound Strongly Post-Pandemic." Statista Daily Data, May 19, 2023. https://www.statista.com/chart/30034/us-leisure-travel-to-rebound-strongly-post-pandemic.

Skodzinski, Noelle. "Indigenous Cannabis on the Rise." *Cannabis Business Times*, December 19, 2023. Accessed February 7, 2024. https://www.cannabisbusinestimes.com/news/indigenous-cannabis-industry-association-mary-jane-oatman-interview/.

Society of Cannabis Clinicians. "Society of Cannabis Clinicians." January 25, 2024. https://www.cannabisclinicians.org/.

STASHLOGIX. "STASHLOGIX." Accessed May 17, 2024. https://stashlogix.co/.

Statista. "CBD Product Dollar Sales U.S. 2022–2026." Accessed May 27, 2024. https://www.statista.com/statistics/1067467/cbd-product-dollar-sales-us/.

Statista. "Topic: CBD Retail in the United States." Accessed March 7, 2024. https://www.statista.com/topics/6262/cbd-retail-in-the-united-states/.

Bibliography

Sulak, Dustin. "Introduction to the Endocannabinoid System." NORML. Accessed May 11, 2024. https://norml.org/marijuana/library/recent-medical-marijuana-research/introduction-to-the-endocannabinoid-system/.

Sweeney, Aaron. "Why HVAC/R Technicians Are in High Demand." *Northeast Technical Institute* (blog), November 7, 2023. https://ntinow.edu/why-hvac-r-technicians-are-in-high-demand/.

Technomic. "Technomic's Take: Five Ways Legal Marijuana Impacts Restaurants." Accessed May 28, 2024. https://www.technomic.com/technomics-take/technomics-take-five-ways-legal-marijuana-impacts-restaurants.

Time. "Now That Weed Is Mostly Legal, Hemp Should Be Booming. But It's Not." April 6, 2023. https://time.com/6268420/hemp-climate-solution/.

Tomko, Andrea M., Erin G. Whynot, Lee D. Ellis, and Denis J. Dupré. "Anti-Cancer Potential of Cannabinoids, Terpenes, and Flavonoids Present in Cannabis." *Cancers* 12, no. 7 (July 21, 2020): 1985. https://doi.org/10.3390/cancers12071985.

"The Top 10 Cannabis Farms in the World 2024." Accessed May 15, 2024. https://herb.co/guides/the-herbalist/the-herbalist-the-top-10-cannabis-farms-in-the-world-2023/.

Treece, Kiah, and Taylor Medine. "Average Wedding Cost: How Much Does a Wedding Really Cost?" Forbes Advisor. Accessed May 17, 2024. https://www.forbes.com/advisor/personal-loans/average-cost-of-a-wedding/.

Truyols, Marc. "Millennials' Travel Statistics; How Do They Travel?" *Mize* (blog), September 11, 2020. https://mize.tech/blog/millennials-travel-statistics-how-do-they-travel/.

Tyler, Gleckler. "Is Hemp the Next Great Biofuel?" GlobalSpec. April 24, 2023. https://insights.globalspec.com/article/20369/is-hemp-the-next-great-biofuel.

United Nations Conference on Trade and Development. "Industrial Hemp: An Old Crop in a Modern Era." UNCTAD Policy Brief, June 20, 2023. https://unctad.org/system/files/official-document/presspb2023d4_en.pdf.

"USP Timeline." Accessed February 7, 2024. https://www.usp.org/200-anniversary/usp-timeline.

Van Duyne, Allie. "60 Restaurant Industry Statistics and Trends for Restaurant Owners in 2024." June 7, 2019. https://pos.toasttab.com/blog/on-the-line/restaurant-management-statistics.

Vangst Cannabis Staffing. "2024 Cannabis Jobs Report." Accessed May 13, 2024. https://www.vangst.com/2024-jobs-report.

Vangst Cannabis Staffing. "Vangst Cannabis Staffing." May 10, 2024. https://www.vangst.com.

Vermont Cannabis Information Portal. "How to Open a Dispensary in Vermont in 2024?" VermontStateCannabis.Org. Accessed May 15, 2024. https://vermontstatecannabis.org/business.

Wallace, Alicia. "Patent No. 6,630,507: Why the U.S. Government Holds a Patent on Cannabis Plant Compounds." *The Denver Post* (blog), August 28, 2016. https://www.denverpost.com/2016/08/28/what-is-marijuana-patent-6630507/.

Wang, Lucy. "Carbon-Negative Construction." January 23, 2022. https://www.anthropocenemagazine.org/2022/01/carbon-negative-construction/.

Wargent, E. T., M. S. Zaibi, C. Silvestri, D. C. Hislop, C. J. Stocker, C. G. Stott, G. W. Guy, M. Duncan, V. Di Marzo, and M. A. Cawthorne. "The Cannabinoid Δ9-Tetrahydrocannabivarin (THCV) Ameliorates Insulin Sensitivity in Two Mouse Models of Obesity." *Nutrition & Diabetes* 3, no. 5 (May 2013): e68. https://doi.org/10.1038/nutd.2013.9.

"Weed Control." Texas Hemp Growers Association. Accessed May 13, 2024. https://txhempgrowersassociation.com/education/weed-control/.

"What Are Flavonoids?" Live Science. Accessed May 11, 2024. https://www.livescience.com/52524-flavonoids.html.

"What Is Hempcrete?" American Lime Technology Website. Accessed May 13, 2024. http://www.americanlimetechnology.com/what-is-hempcrete/.

"What Is the Difference Between Hemp and Marijuana?" Britannica. Accessed February 7, 2024. https://www.britannica.com/story/what-is-the-difference-between-hemp-and-marijuana.

"Why Is Marijuana Illegal? A Look at the History of MJ in America." Accessed February 7, 2024. https://news.medicalmarijuanainc.com/2019/07/28/the-road-to-prohibition-why-did-america-make-marijuana-illegal-in-the-first-place/.

"Why Is Marijuana Illegal in the U.S.?" Britannica. Accessed May 9, 2024. https://www.britannica.com/story/why-is-marijuana-illegal-in-the-us.

Xu, L. S., Q. L. Feng, X. P. Zhang, Y. G. Wang, and M. Yao. "[Study on analgesic effect and mechanism of cinobufagin on rats with bone cancer pain]." *Zhonghua Yi Xue Za Zhi* 99, no. 17 (May 7, 2019): 1307–11. https://doi.org/10.3760/cma.j.issn.0376-2491.2019.17.007.

Yano, Hiroyuki, and Wei Fu. "Hemp: A Sustainable Plant with High Industrial Value in Food Processing." *Foods* 12, no. 3 (February 2, 2023): 651. https://doi.org/10.3390/foods12030651.

Zuardi, Antonio Waldo. "History of Cannabis as a Medicine: A Review." *Revista Brasileira De Psiquiatria (Sao Paulo, Brazil: 1999)* 28, no. 2 (June 2006): 153–57. https://doi.org/10.1590/s1516-44462006000200015.

Index

accounting services, 109–10, 156
acupuncturist, 137–38
ADHD. *See* attention-deficit hyperactivity disorder
adult use, defined, 16–17, 205. *See also* recreational cannabis
advocacy groups, 147–48
African Americans. *See* Black community
AIDS. *See* HIV/AIDS
Allman, Heather, 201
anandamide, 40–41
ancillary cannabis jobs: back-office operations in, 108–18; construction professionals in, 122–25; delivery services, 120–21; in distribution, 120–21; employment recruiter in, 114; Gold Rush relation to, 107, 154; head of communications in, 110–11; in human resources, 114–15; insurance services in, 117; legal services in, 115–17; legal status and, 110; marketers and content writers in, 108, 112–13; nontraditional, 160–63; overview, 107–8; plant-touching compared with, 65–66, 107; purchasing, inventory, and merchandising as, 119; security professionals as, 125, 160–61; supply chain services in, 118–22; webmaster and social media manager in, 111–12; wholesaling as, 119–20; zoning specialist and real estate agents as, 117–18. *See also* artists and graphic designers
Angell, Tom, 201
Anslinger, Harry, 7–8, 9, 12, 46
antagonists, 37
anxiety: CBD for, 38, 49; THCV for, 32
Applegarth, Brian, 155–56
architects, 123
art activities, cannabis business with, 163
artists and graphic designers, 161; brand creation role for, 122, 165–66, *167*; interior design, 124–25, 162; packaging, 121–22; photographer and, 163–64
assessment tests, 58–59, 196
attention-deficit hyperactivity disorder (ADHD), 29
Axelrod, Julius, 41

banking services, 55
bed and breakfasts, 160
beverages, cannabis, 90–91
Biden, Joe, 9, 11, 15
The Big Book of Terps (Hudson), 33, 35–36
biofuel, 48, 105
bioplastics, 48, 104
Black community, 8, 11; cannabis propaganda and, 7; "war on drugs" impact on, 9–10
blogger: edible education, 201; job as, 142–43
Bloom, Major, 71
body chemistry: cannabinoids and, 5–6; ECS and, 39–41; THC and, 4
Boggs Act of 1951, 11
bookkeeping services, 109–10
books, cannabis education, 33, 35–36, 197–98
Booth, Martin, 3
brain, ECS and, 39–41
brand creation and identity, 92, 122, 165–66, *167*
Brave New Weed (podcast), 199
Bridge City Collective, 71
budtender, 27; customer service of, 67, 73–74, 125; job description, sample, 175–77; promotion opportunities for, 75; resume sample, 181–83; wages, 74
Bush, George H. W., 11, 14
business development: experts, 76, 151–52; governmental, 151–52; tourism and hospitality, considerations, 156–57

California, 13, 84, 85–86, 127–28, 166, 200
Canada: farmgate operations in, 86; hemp seed industry in, 103; legalization in, 13
cancer, 63; CBGa for, 30; medical cannabis for, 130–31; THC-A for, 31
cannabichromene (CBC), 30
cannabidiol (CBD): broad-spectrum, 50; chemovar and chemotype classification and, 28–29; defined, 48, 205; drug tests and, 50; economic opportunities, 43–44; full-spectrum, 49–50; health and medical uses of, 5, 30, 38, 48–49, 137, 203; hemp market relation to, 49, 100, 102; isolate, 50; levels, 4; methods of extracting, 49; nonprofit supporting medical use of, 203; regulation, 51; restaurants and, 153; sales from 2014 to 2022, 49; strains with high, 38; suppliers of, 102; types of, 49–50
cannabidivarin (CBDV), 30
cannabigerolic acid (CBGa), 30
cannabinoids: in body, 5–6; defined, 209; edibles and, 90; legal status, 4; THC in, 49–50;

types and benefits of, 29–32; U.S. patent around, 41–42. *See also* endocannabinoid system
"Cannabinoids as Antioxidants and Neuroprotectants" (US patent), 41–42
cannabinol (CBN), 29
cannabis accessories, 67
Cannabis: A History (Booth), 3
Cannabis Benchmarks (organization), 199
cannabis commissioners, 149–50
Cannabis Education Guild, 147
cannabis industry: ancillary contrasted with plant-touching roles in, 65–66, 107; edibles growth in, 90; employment statistics, 53; events and networking, 59–60; getting started in, 53–62; growth by 2030, 1; lifestyle and passions fit with, 55–56, 57–58; plant-touching compared with ancillary roles in, 65–66; professionals advice for entering, 60–62; stigma, 62–64; tips for finding jobs in, 2; tourism and hospitality intersection with, 152–54. *See also specific topics*
Cannabis Law Report (website), 204–5
Cannabis Now (organization), 199
Cannabis sativa: ancient history, 3; chemistry, 4–6; CSA Schedule (categorization) of, 8–9; history in US, 6–15; reclassifying from Schedule 1 to 3, 9, 15; strains, 3–4. *See also specific topics*
career change, 2; lifestyle and passions consideration in, 55–56, 57–58, 154–55; networking in preparation for, 56–57, 59–60; professionals advice on, 60–62; steps and tips for, 53–62; stigma with, navigating, 62–64; tax consideration with, 54–55. *See also* resumes
career resources. *See* job description, samples; resources
caterer, 159–60
CBC. *See* cannabichromene
CBD. *See* cannabidiol
CBDV. *See* cannabidivarin
CBGa. *See* cannabigerolic acid
CBN. *See* cannabinol
celebrity-driven brands, 165
Certificate of Analysis (COA), 93
Champagne, Janna, 135
Chappell, Tauhid, 12–13
charitable operations, 145–46
Charlotte's Web (strain), 63
Charlton, Spencer, 161
chefs, 159–60
chemistry, body. *See* body chemistry
chemistry, *Cannabis sativa*, 4–6
chemotherapy, 31
chemotypes, 28–29
chemovars, 28–29, 205

Chinese medicine, 137–38
classification systems: chemovar and chemotype, 28–29; CSA Schedules for drug, 8–9, *10*, 14, 15, 42; Linnaeus, 37–38
CliftonStrengths Assessment, 58–59, 196
Clinton, Bill, 11, 14
COA. *See* Certificate of Analysis
cola, defined, 205
Colorado, 13, 14, 84, 116, 160, 163
commissioners, cannabis, 149–50
communications, jobs in, 110–11
community liaisons. *See* liaisons, government and community
compliance agent, 74–75
compliance officer, governmental, 151
concentrates: consumption, 21; defined, 205; time for effect, efficiency, and pros/cons of, *22*
construction: hemp used for, 47–48, 104–5; professionals in ancillary cannabis jobs, 122–25
consumption: CBD, 49; journaling about, 23, *23–25*, 25; methods of, 19–23, *22*; tips, 25
consumption lounges, 161–62
Controlled Substances Act (CSA) (1970/1971), 12, 45, 205–6; impact of, 9–11; Schedules of substances in, 8–9, *10*, 14, 15, 42
Cookies (cannabis brand), 166
cooking with cannabis: jobs and, 96; terpenes and, 33, *34*; website resource for, 201
costs. *See* financing
cover letter: samples, 185–89
COVID-19 pandemic, 55, 68, 99
crime legislation and impacts, U.S., 10–11
CSA. *See* Controlled Substances Act
cultivar, defined, 37, 206
cultivation: farmgate operation and, 85–86; growers role in, 81–82; harvesting, 80; hemp, 100–101; job description, sample, 171–74; largest US, 76–77; master grower or director of, 83–85; nursery owner or employee roles in, 85; process and operating considerations, 76–80; resume sample, 181–83; roles, overview, 65; seed breeder or genetic developer role in, 83; trimmer position in, 81
customers: budtenders interaction and skill with, 67, 73–74, 125; dispensary, getting and retaining, 70–71; dispensary experience for, 67–68

DEA. *See* Drug Enforcement Administration
decarboxylation, defined, 206
delivery, 72; licensing, 71; services, 119, 120–21

Index

Delta-8 products, 31, 50
designers: artists and graphic, 121–22, 161, 163–66, *167*; building, 123; interior, 124–25, 162
DeVane, William, 40
diabetes, 32
direct-to-consumer: delivery, 71, 72, 119, 120–21; farmgate operations and, 85–86
disease. *See* illness/disease
dispensary: building designer or architect, 123; cannabis science and, 27–28; charitable operations and, 145; competition, 70; customer experience at, 67–68; customers, getting and retaining, 70–71; defined, 210; employees, hiring, 71–72; extraction-based products at, 87; interior designer, 124–25; internships at, 140–41; licensing process, 69–70; nurses, 134; online presence, 70–71; opening a, 68–69; owner or general manager of, 72–73; regulations and financing considerations, 66–67, 68–69; resume sample for job at, 181–83; roles, overview, 65; security camera installer at, 160–61; security jobs at, 125, 160–61; vertically integrated, 66–67. *See also* budtender

distribution: ancillary cannabis jobs in, 120–22; federal legalization impacts on, 168; license, 121; roles, overview, 65. *See also* delivery
dogs, 5
dosing: defined, 206; edibles, 91
Dowling, Brian, 58
DREs (drug recognition experts), 169
driving, cannabis-impaired, 169
Drug Enforcement Administration (DEA), 7
Drug Policy Alliance, 148, 200
drug recognition experts (DREs), 169
drugs: CSA Schedule (categorization) of, 8–9, *10*, 14, 15, 42; mass incarceration and, 9–11. *See also* "war on drugs"
drug tests, CBDs and, 50
Dupej, Susan, 86

Eckfeldt, Bruce, 203
economic opportunities, 2, 62; complexity associated with, 58; entrepreneurship and, 57–58; hemp and CBD, 43–44. *See also specific fields*
ECS. *See* endocannabinoid system
edibles: blog, 201; caution with, 91; consumption, 20–21; defined, 206; fast-acting, 90–91; market for, 53; popularity of, 90; producer and baker jobs,

96; production of, 90–92, 96; regulations, 96; time for effect, efficiency, and pros/cons of, *22*
education: books for cannabis, 33, 35–36, 197–98; business and equity issues covered in, 139–40; careers in cannabis, 138–44; college-level cannabis, 12, 101, 138–41; for health coach, cannabis, 143–44; hemp cultivation, 101; as important career step, 54, 56–57, 61, 170; Leafly for, 205; medical cannabis industry and, 132; networking role in, 59–60; nonprofit cannabis, 147; OCH and, 61, 166, *167*, 203; on-going, 61, 132; online medical cannabis, 205–6; for practitioners using medical cannabis, 133–38; requirements, 173, 175, 176–77, 178; research opportunities and, 168–69; resources, 54, 201–2; sharing, with others, 62–64
electricians, 123–24
email, follow-up (in job application process), 189–91
employment. *See* cannabis industry; career change; job description, samples; retail careers; *specific topics*
employment recruiter, 114
endocannabinoid system (ECS): cannabinoids interaction with, 5–6; defined, 39, 206; patent around cannabinoid use and, 41; study and discoveries of, 39–41
entourage effect: defined, 210; of full-spectrum CBDs, 50; synergy and, 36–37
entrepreneurship, 57–58
epilepsy. *See* seizures
Erlichman, John, 9
event planner and coordinator, 158–59
extraction and processing: about, 86–87; CBD, 49; COA lab test in, 93; edibles production and, 90–92; of hash and kief, 89; hemp, 100; hemp, for biofuel, 105; hydrocarbon, caution around, 88–89; job description, sample, 174–75; lab technicians role in, 94–95; market research and, 93; networking in, 93–94; packaging expert role in, 96–98; process, 87–89; regulations, 93; resume sample, 181–83; solventless, 89; testing in, 92–93

Farm Bills: 2014, 49; 2018, 5, 46, 99; 2024, 50
farmgate operation, 85–86
farming. *See* cultivation; growers; hemp
Federal Bureau of Narcotics, 7
federal legalization, impacts of, 168

INDEX

Fiero, Valentina, 84–85
Figi, Charlotte, 63
films: cannabis education, 198; propaganda, 8, 14
financial advisors, 146; as ancillary cannabis job, 109–10; governmental business development administrators as, 151–52
financing: cannabis tourism and, 155, 156; dispensary, 66–67, 68–69
flavonoids: benefits of, 5; color and function of, 33, 35; defined, 207
flower: cola and, 205; defined, 207
Ford, Henry, 48
Fritz, Koral, 139–40
Future Cannabis Project (organization), 200

Gaoni, Yehiel, 39–40
Garden State OG (company), 166, *167*
Gateway Drug concept, 7
genetic developers, 83
glamping, 160
Global Hemp Innovation Center, Oregon State University, 104–5
glossary, 205–9
Gold Rush, 107, 154
governmental compliance officer, 151
government careers, 149–52
government liaison. *See* liaisons, government and community

graphic designer. *See* artists and graphic designers
green health. *See* health benefits; medical cannabis
Grohl, Dave, 142
growers: director of cultivation or master, 83–85; farmgate operation for, 85–86; hemp, 100–101; role and job experience, 81–82. *See also* cultivation

Hance, Art, 123
Hanus, Lumir, 40
harvesting, 80
hash: defined, 211; extraction of, 89
HBK Cannabis Solutions, 109–10
health benefits: of cannabinoids by type, 29–32; CBD, 5, 30, 38, 48–49, 137, 203; CSA impact on research and use for, 9; educating others on, 63; of hemp seeds, 48, 103–4; of medical cannabis, *18*, 18–19; suppositories and, 20; *U.S. Pharmacopeia* on, 6, 14, 63. *See also* cancer; inflammation; medical cannabis
health coach, cannabis, 143–44
heirloom strains, 38
hemp: advocacy groups, 202; as biofuel, 48, 105; for bioplastics, 48, 104; for building materials, 47–48, 104–5; CBD market

and, 49, 100, 102; defined, 44, 207; economic opportunities, 43–44; educating others about, 62–63; as fabrics, 102–3; future for, 50–51, 98; growers, 100–101; health benefits of, 48, 103–4; history, 14, 44–46; industrial, 46–48, 49, 99, 100; industry overview, 98–100; job market and opportunities, 43–44, 98, 99–105; legislation, 46, 99; market statistics, 99, 100; for Native Americans, 44–45; organic certification for, 43; as paper, 103; processor position, 101–2; seed health products, 103–4; as soil contamination remedy, 47; THC in, 4, 51; uses, 44, 98, 101–5

Hemp, Inc., 104

history, 63; ancient, 3; classification system, 37–38; hemp, 14, 44–46; precolonial and colonial, 13–14, 45; in US, 6–15; "war on drugs," 9, 11, 12, 14

HIV/AIDS: medical cannabis card and, 131; THC-A and, 31

homegrow: defined, 207; regulations, 83; specimen testing for, 169

hospitality. *See* tourism and hospitality

Howlett, Allyn, 40

Hudson, Russ, 33, 35–36

human resources professionals: as ancillary cannabis job, 114–15; nonprofit, 146

HVAC professionals, 123–24

hybrids: defined, 207; effects of, 27–28; in market, 4, 38; popular, *39*

ICANNC. *See* Indigenous Cannabis Coalition

ICIA. *See* Indigenous Cannabis Industry Association

illness/disease: diabetes, 32; medical cannabis and, *17*, 17–18; pain and, 130–31, 135–36; qualifying, for medical cannabis card, 130–31; seizures, 30, 63; synthetic cannabis for, 21–22. *See also* cancer; HIV/AIDS; medical cannabis

immigration, cannabis history and, 7

income. *See* salaries/wages

indica: defined, 211; discovery of strain, 38; effects of, 4, 27–28; popular strains of, *39*; sativa compared with, 3–4

Indigenous Cannabis Coalition (ICANNC), 200

Indigenous Cannabis Industry Association (ICIA), 6, 44–46, 148

inflammation: CBC for, 30; CBD for, 49, 137; topicals for, 20

infusion, defined, 207

instructors. *See* education; teachers
insurance services, 117
interior designer, 124–25, 162
international opportunities, 169
internship, cannabis, 140–41
interviews: follow-up protocol for, 189–90; letter of reference and, 194; tips for, 191
inventors, 164–65
inventory control, 119

Jadhav, Tanmoy "TJ," 91–92
job description, samples: budtender, 175–77; cultivation, 171–74; processing and packaging, 174–75
job search resources. *See* resources; resumes
journaling, cannabis use, 23, *23–25*, 25
journalists. *See* writers

Kabbes, Jason, 71
Karma Koala (podcast), 98, 201
kief: defined, 207; extraction of, 89

laboratory: resume sample for job in, 181–83; roles, overview, 65; seed breeders or genetic developers in, 83. *See also* extraction and processing
Lamarck, Jean-Baptiste, 38
landrace strains, 38
Laurie and MaryJane (organization), 205

law enforcement, 169
lawyers and legal services: as ancillary cannabis jobs, 115–17; nonprofit, 146
Leafly (organization), 201
legal status, 2; ancillary cannabis jobs and, 110; beginnings of modern, 14–15; in Canada and Mexico, 13; cannabis commissioners and, 149–50; Cannabis Law Report on, 200; CBD, 4; of farmgate operations, 85–86; federal, impacts of, 168; of hemp, 46; historically, 6, 8–13; lawyers helping further, 116; Marijuana Moment and, 205; medical cannabis, 13, 15, *15–16*; policy reform and, careers in, 147–48; resources regarding, 200–1, 202; as of 2024, 1, 9, 13, 15, 54; understanding specific states, 56. *See also* Farm Bills
letter of reference, 194–96
Levi's, 102
LGBTQ+, 13
liaisons, government and community, 75–76, 108
licensing: ancillary role helping with, 111–12; cannabis commissioners and, 149–50; cannabis tourism and, 155; compliance agent role for, 74; consumer products, 165–66, *167*; delivery, 71;

dispensary, 69–70; distribution, 121; farmgate operations, 85–86; governmental business development officer and, 151; legal services aiding in, 115–16; wholesaling, 119
licensing agent, 165–66
lifestyle considerations, 55–56, 154–55
Linnaeus, Carl, 37–38
lobbyists, 146
lodging. *See* tourism and hospitality

marijuana, term origins, 7
Marijuana Enforcement Tracking Reporting Compliance (METRC), 171, 172
Marijuana Moment (organization), 201
Marijuana Policy Project (MPP), 148, 201
Marijuana Tax Act of 1937, 7, 8, 14, 45
marketing: ancillary roles in, 112–13; head of communications role in, 110–11; online, ancillary roles in, 111–12; online, for dispensary, 70–71; salesperson or business development roles and, 76; writers, 70–71, 112–13, 143
massage therapist, 137
mass incarceration, 14; drug prohibition and, 9–11; statistics in US compared globally, 10

McConnell, Mitch, 46
measurement conversion chart, *97*
Mechoulam, Raphael, 37, 39–40
medical cannabis: adult use/recreational distinction from, 16–17; cannabinoids and, 29–32, 41–42; card, requirements, 130–31; career opportunities in, 129–38; CBDs as, 5, 30, 38, 48–49, 137, 203; CBN and, 29; conditions treated by, *18*, 18–19, 130–31; dispensaries and, 17; education and working in, 132; education for practitioners using, 133–38; healthcare industry and, overview, 127–29; for mental health, 130–31; online education, 201; organization supporting CBDs for, 203; pharmacist and, 136; physical therapist treating with, 135–36; physicians recommendations for, 130; process of qualifying for, 17; states with legalized, 13, 15, *15–16*; suppositories and, 20; synthetic, 21–22; traits for working in, 131–32
Medical Cannabis Mentor (online education), 201–202
mental health, 130–31. *See also* anxiety
merchandising roles, 119
METRC. *See* Marijuana Enforcement Tracking Reporting Compliance

Mexican immigrants, 7
Mexico, legalization in, 13
MG Magazine, 202
microdosing, defined, 208
minorities, 72
MJBizDaily (website), 202
MoJo Botanica, 91
MPP. *See* Marijuana Policy Project

nasal sprays, *22*
National Hemp Association, 202
Native Americans, 6, 13, 44–45, 148
nervous system, 31, 39, 41
networking, 108; career change planning and, 56–57, 59–60; in extraction and processing, 93–94
New Jersey, 28; consumption lounges, 161–62; internships in, 140–41
New York, 17, 56, 85
Nez Perce tribe, 6, 13, 44–45
Nixon, Richard, 8, 9–10, 11
nonprofits: cannabis reform, 204; careers with, 144–48; hemp industry, 202; promoting medical CBD use, 203
nontraditional cannabis jobs: creating or finding, 161–63; overview, 160–61
NORML, 148, 202
nurse, 134–35
nursery owner or employee, 85

Oatman, Mary Jane, 6, 13, 44–45, 200
Obama, Barack, 46
OCH. *See* Our Community Harvest
online marketing: ancillary roles in, 111–12; dispensary, 70–71
online resources: for cooking with cannabis, 201; for job search, 196; organization websites and, 199–203; podcasts and, 198–99, 200–201
Oregon, 17, 84, 128, 129, 160, 168, 201
Oregon State University, Global Hemp Innovation Center at, 104–5
organizations: advocacy, 147–48; websites, 199–203
Our Community Harvest (OCH), 61, 166, *167*, 199
outdoor cultivation. *See* cultivation
overdose, 40

PA. *See* physician's assistant
packaging: designer, 121–22; expert, 96–98; job description, sample, 174–75
pain, 130–31, 135–36
people of color, 7, 8, 71–72. *See also* Black community
pharmaceutical marketplace: cannabis historically in, 6; synthetics in, 21–22
pharmacist, 136

photographer, 163–64
physicians: cannabis education nonprofit, 147; in medical cannabis field, 133; recommendations from, 130
physician's assistant (PA), 133–34
Picillo, Ashley, 70
plant-touching sector, 2, 65–66, 107, 127. *See also* cultivation; dispensary; distribution; extraction and processing; laboratory
plumbers, 123–24
Pocono Organics, 43
podcasts, cannabis, 198–99, 200–1, 203
Point Seven Group, 70
policy reform, careers in, 147–48
potency: defined, 208; increase in, 25; methods of consumption and, *22*
pre-roll, defined, 208
prisons. *See* mass incarceration
processing. *See* extraction and processing
professional/expert advice: on dispensary ownership and management, 70–72; on entering cannabis industry, 60–62
professors. *See* education; teachers
prohibition, cannabis: history of, 7–13; organizations fighting, 201

Prohibition Partners (organization), 202–3
Project CBD (nonprofit), 203
propaganda, prohibition, 7–8
purchasing jobs, 119

racism: crime legislation and, 11; prohibition relation to, 7–8; "war on drugs" and, 9–10
Randazzo, Nick, 161
Reagan, Ronald, 11, 14
real estate, 156; consumption lounges and, 161–62; zoning, 117–18, 150
recreational cannabis (adult use): dispensaries and, 17; medical use distinction from, 16–17; states with legalized, 13, 15, *15–16*
reference, letter of, 194–196
regulations: CBD, 51; compliance agent understanding of, 74–75; delivery services, 119; edibles, 96; extraction, 93; farmgate operations, 85–86; government careers and, 149–52; homegrow, 83; liaison navigating, 75–76; METRC system and, 171, 172; packaging, 96–97; of synthetic cannabis, 50, 51; tourism opportunities and, 156; understanding specific states, 56, 65–66, 68–69; zoning, 117–18. *See also* legal status; licensing

research opportunities, 168–69
resources: for cannabis education, 54, 201–2; job description samples in, 171–77; job search websites and, 196; podcasts as, 198–99, 200–201. *See also* job description, samples; resumes
restaurants, 153, 154, 159–60
resumes: components, 177–78; cover letter samples, 188–95; cover letter tips for, 183–84; preparation, 178–80; samples, 181–83
retail careers: compliance agent in, 74–75; government and community liaison in, 75–76; in hemp, 100; owner or general manager in, 72–73; salesperson or business development expert in, 76. *See also* budtender; dispensary
rosin, extraction of, 89
ruderalis, 3, 4, 37–38, 208

safety: with edibles, 91; extraction and processing, 88–89; storage, 164–65
salaries/wages: budtender, 74; for director of cultivation or master grower, 84; growers, 82; hemp processor, 101–2; for lab technicians, 96; for owner or general manager, 72–73; trimmers, 81

salesperson, 76. *See also* budtender; marketing
sativa: *Cannabis sativa* difference from, 3; defined, 208; discovery of strain, 37–38; effects of, 3, 27; indica compared with, 3–4; popular strains of, *39*
Schedules, drug. *See* Controlled Substances Act
science, cannabis: consumer market and, 27–28; director of cultivation understanding of, 84; ECS and, 39–41; extraction and processing, 86–87; seed breeders or genetic developers and, 83
security professionals, 125, 160–61
seed breeders, 83
seizures: CBDV for, 30; strain for, 63
skills: adapting current, 2; assessment tests for, 58–59, 196; customer service, 67, 73–74, 125; evaluation of, 57. *See also specific positions*
sleep, indica for, 27–28
SMART. *See* Student Marijuana Alliance for Research & Transparency
smoking, consumption by: about, 19; time for effect, efficiency, and pros/cons of, *22*
social justice, careers in, 144–45
social media: dispensary operation and, 70–71; manager as

243

ancillary cannabis job, 111–12; writers and content creators on, 141–43
Society of Cannabis Clinicians, 147
SOPs. *See* standard operating procedures
SSDP. *See* Students for Sensible Drug Policy
standard operating procedures (SOPs), 74, 84, 96, 151, 157, 172
StashLogix, 164–65
states: business development administrator for, 151–52; cannabis tourism, 157–58; with legalized medical cannabis, 13, 15, *15–16*
stigma and stereotypes: early cannabis, 7–8; educating others to fight, 62–64; liaisons and, 75–76
Stockton University, New Jersey, 140–41
Stone, Skip, 164
storage: federal legalization impacts on, 168; invention of device, 164–65
strains, 3–4; classification by, 37–38, *39*; defined, 37; popular, *39*; for seizures, 63
student-led organizations, 203
Student Marijuana Alliance for Research & Transparency (SMART), 203

Students for Sensible Drug Policy (SSDP), 203
supply chain roles, 118. *See also* distribution
suppositories: benefits of, 20; defined, 208; time for effect, efficiency, and pros/cons of, *22*
synergy: entourage effect and, 36–37; flavonoids and, 33, 35; terpenes and, 32–33
synthetic cannabis: conditions treated with, 21–22; regulation of, 50, 51

taxes/tax codes: cannabis business, 54–55; Marijuana Tax Act of 1937 and, 7, 8, 14, 45; professional roles dealing with, 109–10, 156
teachers, 138–40, 147, 163. *See also* education
terms and definitions, 2, 205–9
terpenes: *The Big Book of Terps* on, 33, 35–36; characteristics of common, 33, *34*; defined, 212; extraction process and, 88, 92–93; impact of, 5, 32–33; smell and taste with, 32, 35–36
tetrahydrocannabinol (THC): in CBDs, 49–50; chemovar and chemotype classification and, 28–29; decarboxylation of, 210; defined, 208; in edibles, 91; in hemp, 4, 51; levels of, 4–5

tetrahydrocannabivarin (THCV), 32
THC. *See* tetrahydrocannabinol
THC-A, 31
THC Magazine, 200
THCV. *See* tetrahydrocannabivarin
Thinking Outside the Bud (podcast), 203
tincture: consumption by, 20; defined, 209; time for effect, efficiency, and pros/cons of, *22*
topicals: consumption by, 20; defined, 209; time for effect, efficiency, and pros/cons of, *22*
tourism and hospitality: business development considerations, 156–57; business opportunities, choosing, 154–56; cannabis intersection with, 152–54; careers in cannabis, 156–60; event planner and coordinator role in, 158–59; information sector job in, 158; market research and, 155–56; nontraditional jobs in, 162–63; popular destinations in cannabis, 157; statistics, 153; writers, 162–63
trademarking, 116, 165–66, *167*
transdermal patches, 20, *22*
trichomes, defined, 209
trimmers, 81
Twain, Mark, 154
2-Arachidonoylglycerol (2-AG), 40

unions, 74
United States (U.S.): cannabinoid patent in, 41–42; cannabis history in, 6–15; hemp legislation in, 46, 99; hemp market statistics in, 99, 100; incarceration statistics compared globally, 10; largest cannabis cultivation in, 76–77; "tough of crime" legislation and impacts in, 10–11; tourism statistics in, 153
unusual cannabis careers, 160–66
urban planning, 117–18, 150
U.S. *See* United States
U.S. Pharmacopeia (publication), 6, 14, 63

Vangst, 53, 171
vaping, consumption by: about, 19; time for effect, efficiency, and pros/cons of, *22*
Vicente, Brian, 116

wages. *See* salaries/wages
Walsh, Ashley, 43–44
Ward, Andrew, 142
warehousing jobs. *See* wholesaling jobs
"war on drugs": alternative organizations/approaches to, 204, 207; history, 9, 11, 12, 14; impacts of, 12–13
Washington (state), 17, 129

websites. *See* online marketing; online resources
weddings, 153
weight loss, 32
wholesaling (warehousing) jobs, 119–20
WIREs. *See* workplace impairment recognition experts
Wolf, Laurie, 205
workplace impairment recognition experts (WIREs), 169

writers, 108; cannabis, 141–43; grant, 146; marketing and content, 70–71, 112–13, 143; tourism and hospitality, 162–63

yoga instructor, 163
Youngblood, Ulysses, 71–72

Zaytsev, Michael, 61–62
zoning: officers, 150; specialist, 117–18

About the Authors

Rob Mejia is an award-winning adjunct cannabis professor at Stockton University, where he teaches the courses Introduction to Medical Cannabis, Cannabis and Social Justice, and Cannabis Internship Preparation. He also helped launch the Cannabis & Hemp Research Initiative at Stockton (CHRIS), as a hemp and nonmedical research hub and cannabis education center.

In addition, Rob is president of Our Community Harvest: A Cannabis Education Company, which creates cannabis educational materials including online courses. He is one of New Jersey's most sought-after cannabis and hemp speakers and presenters. His cannabis authorship includes *The Essential Cannabis Book: A Field Guide for the Curious*, *The Essential Cannabis Journal: Personal Notes from the Field*, and *Cannabis Careers: An Insider's Guide to a Budding Industry*.

Daniel Johnson is a writer and teacher living in Winooski, Vermont. He teaches English and creative writing classes at Saint Michael's College and Community College of Vermont. Dan holds a master's in creative writing from University College Cork, and he publishes prose, poetry, and literary criticism in a variety of journals and magazines.